THE
FUTURE
OF
LAND
WARFARE

For a quarter century since the fall of the Berlin Wall, the world has enjoyed an era of deepening global interdependence, characterized by the absence of the threat of great power war, spreading democracy, and declining levels of conflict and poverty. Now, much of that is at risk as the regional order in the Middle East unravels, the security architecture in Europe is again under threat, and great power tensions loom in Asia.

The Geopolitics in the 21st Century series, published under the auspices of the Order from Chaos project at Brookings, will analyze the major dynamics at play and offer ideas and strategies to guide critical countries and key leaders on how they should act to preserve and renovate the established international order to secure peace and prosperity for another generation.

THE

FUTURE

OF

LAND
WARFARE

MICHAEL E. O'HANLON

Brookings Institution Press
Washington, D.C.

The Brookings Institution is a private nonprofit organization devoted to research, education, and publication on important issues of domestic and foreign policy. Its principal purpose is to bring the highest quality independent research and analysis to bear on current and emerging policy problems. Interpretations or conclusions in Brookings publications should be understood to be solely those of the authors.

Library of Congress Cataloging-in-Publication data is available.
978-0-8157-2689-0 (cloth : alk. paper)
978-0-8157-2742-2 (pbk. : alk. paper)
978-0-8157-2690-6 (epub)
978-0-8157-2691-3 (pdf)

9 8 7 6 5 4 3 2 1

Typeset in Sabon and Scala Sans

Composition by Cindy Stock

In memory of my father
EDWARD PETER O'HANLON
and my father-in-law
PAUL GRIFFITH GARLAND

Contents

MAPS

BOX

FIGURES

TABLES

Preface

IN THIS BOOK, I have the pleasure and honor of helping initiate a new Brookings book series linked to the upcoming 2016 presidential race as part of the Foreign Policy program's Order from Chaos project of 2015–16.

The nation's next president and Congress, when they begin to govern in2017, will confront issues addressed here, especially defense planning in a time of austerity. The 2011 Budget Control Act remains in effect and, as of this writing, continues to hang like the sword of Damocles, threatening a return to sequestration for all programs funded through federal discretionary spending—the military budget, foreign aid and diplomacy accounts, homeland security funding, and domestic investment in matters ranging from education to infrastructure to scientific research to food and highway and air safety. National security funding will decrease as much as one-third from its annual peak of more than $750 billion (expressed in 2016 dollars) in the late Bush and early Obama years. Of course, that will hardly result in an austere military budget by most perspectives—$500 billion for the Pentagon would still roughly equal the cold war average adjusted for inflation and would exceed China's budget by roughly a factor of three, while accounting for nearly 40 percent of global military spending. But the projected pace and steepness of funding declines will nonetheless be severe compared to 2010 (indeed, they will be severe even if sequestration-level cuts are averted).

In this context, some, such as Gary Roughead, former admiral and chief of naval operations, have called for very deep cuts in the U.S. Army—roughly 50 percent, in his case. My analysis can be read as a counter to his proposal and, more generally, to those who would attempt to handle declines in defense spending largely by cutting the nation's ground forces. My solution is a more measured one, combining various defense reforms with modest real increases in the nation's annual spending for the base defense budget going forward (anticipating that war costs will continue to decline somewhat).

Viewed in the context of the Order from Chaos project, spearheaded by my friends and colleagues Martin Indyk and Bruce Jones, the book has a slightly different additional purpose. With parts of the world showing signs of anarchy in 2014 and beyond, the questions for the United States become, how do we reduce the chaos in ways compatible with American interests and at a reasonable cost?

The world writ large, however, is not necessarily chaotic at this juncture of history. Crises from Ukraine, to Iraq and Syria and Yemen and Libya, to Liberia and Sierra Leone and Nigeria have created a sense of deep unease in recent times. Many of the problems will surely endure through the 2016 presidential campaign and beyond. But at the same time, the prospects for stability in Asia look reasonable (Jim Steinberg and I wrote about how to make them more promising in our 2014 book, *Strategic Reassurance and Resolve*). And while the crisis in Ukraine is surely serious, it is at present confined to a relatively modest swath of that single country in Central Europe.

As such, a book focused on the future of the U.S. Army, and to a somewhat lesser but still important extent on the U.S. Marine Corps as well, should in my eyes take a balanced perspective. The goal is not to undertake a number of imminent large-scale missions; we have learned from Iraq and Afghanistan about the limits, challenges, and costs of such operations. But at the same time, the goals of maintaining deterrence of other great powers as well as smaller powers such as North Korea, and of being able to help stabilize key trouble spots that may be afflicted with various forms of civil warfare, terrorism, natural disaster, or other maladies, require substantial American ground forces. Drones, cyberwarfare, and special forces cannot do it all; pretending that we can turn our backs on insurgency simply because Iraq and Afghanistan proved so hard is not viable either. In that sense, the book is at least a partial challenge to some of the logic of the Obama administration's 2012 Defense Strategic Guidance and 2014 Quadrennial Defense Review, which deemphasized stabilization missions in American military planning.

Mine is not a radical book, relative to where the consensus in U.S. defense policymaking has been for most of the quarter century since the cold war ended. But it does sharply disagree with some of the ideas percolating through the American strategic debate today, ideas that would change the course of defense policy in a more pointed direction.

I am indebted to a wide range of colleagues, especially at the Brookings Institution but also beyond, in writing this book. Working at a defense center embedded in one of the best foreign policy programs of any think tank or university in the country has been an extraordinary privilege. It has helped me greatly with the *tour d'horizon* of the world's countries and likely future hot spots that was integral to the methodology of this book project.

Bruce and Martin have been a joy to work with, and Strobe Talbott has been a collegial and brilliant leader of the institution for more than a dozen years. I am indebted greatly to Ian Livingston, as well as to Miranda Melcher, Jennifer Lawrence, and Brendan Orino, for research and other assistance at Brookings. Others in the Brookings defense center—John Allen, Bruce Riedel, Steve Pifer, Bob Einhorn, Vanda Felbab-Brown, Brad Porter, James Tyson—as well as visiting fellows from the military services, including John Evans and Chandler Seagraves, have been wonderfully helpful colleagues. So have Tanvi Madan, Steve Cohen, Cliff Gaddy, Harold Trinkunas, Richard Bush, Jeff Bader, Ken Lieberthal, David Dollar, Jonathan Pollack, Kenneth Pollack, Kathy Moon, Mireya Solis, Dan Byman, Tamara Wittes, Shadi Hamid, Salman Shaikh, Ye Qi, Jeremy Shapiro, Tom Wright, Bob Kagan, Fiona Hill, Beth Ferris, Suzanne Maloney, Charley Ebinger, Charlotte Baldwin, Julia Cates, Nicki Sullivan, David Wessel, Alice Rivlin, Ron Haskins, Bill Gale, Bill Galston, Phil Gordon, Amy Liu, Mark Muro, Bruce Katz, William Antholis, Steven Bennett, Gail Chalef, Elisa Glazer, Emily Perkins, Peter Toto, Sadie Jonath, Maggie Humenay, Ben Cahen, Doug Elmendorf, Karen Dynan, Lois Rice, Susan Rice, Roberta Cohen, Ted Piccone, E. J. Dionne, Tom Mann, Steve Hess, Marvin Kalb, Barry Bosworth, Henry Aaron, and many others.

Beyond Brookings, my debts extend to many more, starting with Jim Steinberg and including Michael Doran, Peter Singer, Aaron Friedberg, John Ikenberry, Hal Feiveson, Frank von Hippel, Kim and Fred Kagan, Mackenzie Eaglen, Tom Donnelly, Michele Flournoy and Jim Miller and Kurt Campbell, Eric Edelman, Steve Solarz, Eliot Cohen, Vali Nasr, Steve Biddle, Max Boot, Michael Levi, Tom Christensen, Janine Davidson, Janne Nolan, Dick Betts, Ari Roth, Bruce Klingner, Bud Cole, Kathleen Hicks, Tony Cordesman, John Hamre, Eliot Cohen, Juan Carlos Pinzon, Diana Quintera, John Sattler, Ron Neumann, John Nagl, Duncan Brown, Larry Korb, David Gordon, Todd Harrison, Andrew Krepinevich, Frank Hoffman, Josh Epstein, Paul Stares, Tom McNaugher, Mike Mochizuki, Nick Lardy, David Shambaugh, Ashley Tellis, Michael Swaine, Karim Sadjapour, Ben Lambeth, Sean Zeigler, Andy Hoehn, Jim Dobbins, Mike Armacost, Bruce MacLaury, John Steinbruner, Carlos Pascual, Richard Haass, Jim Lindsay, Ivo Daalder, Barry Posen, Dave Petraeus, Stan McChrystal, Mike Meese, Barry McCaffrey, Maya MacGuineas, Woody Turner, Rebecca Grant, Bob Haffa, Richard Fontaine, Dan Benjamin, Kori Schake, Steve Hadley, Paul Wolfowitz, Robert Reischauer, Robert Hale, Jack Mayer, Wayne Glass, Neil Singer, Dave Mosher, Fran Lussier, Lane Pierrot, Michael Berger, Ellen Breslin Davidson, my many students over the years, and many members of Congress and the executive branch, who have inspired and taught me as well. Finally, I am deeply grateful to the members of Brookings's national security industrial base project and to Herb and Herbert Allen, as well as to many other members and supporters within the Brookings family.

CHAPTER ONE

Introduction: Historical, Strategic, and Technological Context

WHAT IS THE FUTURE of land warfare, and of the world's ground forces more generally? What can we realistically expect and project about the implications of interstate combat, civil conflict, and major humanitarian catastrophes for the world's armies in the decades to come?

In recent years the U.S. national security debate has been turning away from these questions. Fatigued by Iraq and Afghanistan, rightly impressed by the capabilities of U.S. special forces, transfixed by the arrival of new technologies such as drones, and increasingly preoccupied with a rising China and its military progress in domains ranging from space to missile forces to maritime operations, the American strategic community has largely turned away from thinking about ground combat.[1] This is actually nothing new. Something similar happened after the world wars, the Korean War and Vietnam War, and Operation Desert Storm in 1991, as well. That last time, the debate shifted to a supposed revolution in military affairs. Many called for a major transformation in U.S. military forces to respond to that presumed revolution, until the 9/11 attacks returned military analysis to more practical and immediate issues. But now the strategic debate seems to be picking up about where it left off at the turn of the century—except that in the intervening fifteen years, remarkable progress in technologies such as unmanned aerial systems has provided even more grist for those favoring a radical transition in how militaries prepare for and fight wars.

Much of this debate is welcome. Even if futurists understandably tend to get more wrong than right in their specific recommendations, a debate in which they challenge existing Pentagon rice bowls is preferable to complacency. As long as the burden of proof is on those who would dismantle proven concepts and capabilities when proposing a whole new approach to military operations and warfare, a world of too many ideas is preferable to a staid, unimaginative one of too few. The history of military revolutions suggests that established superpowers are more likely to be caught unprepared for, even unaware of, new ways of warfare than to change their own armed forces too much or too fast.

That said, pushback against transformative ideas will often be necessary. We have seen many unrealistic military ideas proposed for the post–World War II U.S. armed forces, from the Pentomic division of the 1950s, which relied on nuclear weapons for indirect fire, to the flawed counterinsurgency strategies of the 1960s, to the surreal nuclear counterforce strategies from Curtis Lemay onward in the cold war, to the dreamy Strategic Defense Initiative goals of the 1980s, to the proposals for "rods from God" and other unrealistic technologies in the revolution in military affairs debate of the 1990s. As such, wariness about new ideas is in order. Even in a great nation like the United States, groupthink can happen, and bad ideas can gain a following they do not deserve.

One hears much discussion today about the supposed obsolescence of large-scale ground combat. Official U.S. policy now leans in that direction too, as codified in the 2012 Defense Strategic Guidance and 2014 Quadrennial Defense Review, largely as a result of frustrations with the wars in Iraq and Afghanistan. Accordingly, the 2012 Defense Strategic Guidance, released under the signature of then Secretary of Defense Leon Panetta, with a preface signed by President Obama, states flatly that "U.S. forces will no longer be sized to conduct large-scale, prolonged stability operations."[2] The next year the Pentagon carried out a so-called Strategic Capabilities and Management Review that examined the option of reducing the Army to just 380,000 active duty soldiers.[3] Subsequently the Ryan-Murray budget compromise of late 2013 and other considerations led to a less stark goal of 440,000 to 450,000 active duty soldiers. But the 2014 Quadrennial Defense Review again dismissed the plausibility of large-scale stabilization missions, though somewhat more gently, stating that "although our forces will no longer be sized to conduct large-scale prolonged stability operations, we will preserve the experience gained during the past ten years of counterinsurgency and stability operations in Iraq and Afghanistan."[4] The emphasis changed somewhat, but the fundamental point was the same. Ground warfare, or at least certain forms of it, was not only to be avoided when possible—certainly, that is sound advice—but not even truly prepared for. That may be less sound advice.

There are lots of reasons to believe that, whether we like it or not, ground warfare does have a future, and a very significant one at that. Nearly three-fourths of the world's full-time military personnel, almost 15 million out of some 20 million, are in their nations' respective armies.[5] Most wars today are civil wars, fought within states by ground forces. Interstate wars are rare, but when they do happen, they generally involve neighboring states and generally involve a heavy concentration of ground combat. The United States may be far away from most potential conflict zones, putting a greater premium on U.S. long-range strike capabilities, including those of air and naval forces, than is the case for most countries. Yet the United States works with more than sixty allies and security partners, which tend to emphasize their own armies in force planning and tend to worry about land warfare scenarios within or just beyond their own borders. Iraq and Afghanistan revealed the limitations of standoff warfare and the problems that can ensue when the United States places severe constraints on its use of ground power (especially in the first few years of each conflict).

To paraphrase the old Bolshevik saying, we may not have an interest in messy ground combat operations in the future, but they may have an interest in us. Put differently, in contemplating the character and scale of future warfare, the enemy gets a vote, too.

As such, this book addresses two central questions. First, what is the future of land warfare, and of other possible forms of large-scale violence on land, in the coming decades? Second, what are the implications for the U.S. military, but particularly the U.S. Army and its three main components—the active duty Army, the Army National Guard, and the Army Reserve?

The U.S. Marine Corps falls partially within the scope of my analysis, but only partially. It has important capacities for substantial ground operations, to be sure. Yet it is also a naval force, being part of the Department of the Navy, as well as an expeditionary force, with an emphasis on rapid responsiveness for multiple smaller contingencies around the world. As with the special forces, therefore, its mission is somewhat different from that of the main elements of the U.S. Army—and its future size and structure seem less in doubt as well. Nonetheless, it is certainly relevant to the general subject of this book and is frequently discussed in the pages that follow.

Since the cold war ended, the U.S. Army, like much of the nation's armed forces, has been built around the prospect of fighting up to two major regional wars at a time. That thinking has evolved, especially in the years when the United States was actually fighting two wars at once, in Iraq and Afghanistan (and in the process eliminating one of the threats on which the two-war scenarios had been premised, the government of Saddam Hussein). Former Secretary of Defense Donald Rumsfeld's 2006 Quadrennial Defense Review began to shift the paradigm somewhat. The Pentagon's 2012 Defense Strategic Guidance and 2014 Quadrennial Defense Review moved further away from a two-war construct without jettisoning it altogether. Now, in the second of the two overlapping wars, it is deemed adequate to "inflict unacceptable costs" on an adversary.[6] But the vagueness of the latter standard, deterrence by the threat of punishment, and changes in the international security order suggest that perhaps it is time to think afresh about the future of the U.S. Army and the other services. Planning for regional conflict will have to be a component of future force sizing, but with less specificity about likely foes than in the past and with a fuller range of considerations to complement the contingency analysis.

In this book, I begin with a blank sheet of paper about the future of land warfare and its implications for U.S. ground forces. The time frame is envisioned to go well beyond the current decade, into the 2020s and beyond. Where are future large-scale conflicts or other catastrophes on the world's land masses most plausible? Which of these could be important enough to necessitate the option of a U.S. military response? And which of these could in turn require significant numbers of American ground forces in their resolution?

Put differently, one frequently hears the adage that the United States does not have a good track record in predicting its future wars. Some even turn the saying on its head, saying that yes, we do have a good track record—a perfect one, in fact—of getting the future wrong. Afghanistan, Iraq, Vietnam, Korea, and indeed the world wars (not to mention the American Civil War) were not accurately foreseen by most strategists or planners.

Yet it is still important to examine how the configuration of worldwide threats, resources, centers of economic power, overseas political dynamics, and American strategic interests could produce conflict in the future. Strategists may not know when or where. But having a sense of the character and likely magnitude of any future conflict is essential. To paraphrase Eisenhower, moreover, the planning process is essential, even if any plans themselves that we manage to develop may not be precisely relevant. The alternative to analysis is to have future forces and Pentagon priorities determined by guesswork, bureaucratic and political inertia, and faddishness about new technologies, as well as by apparent new trends in conflict. We cannot predict the future. But for purposes of understanding the necessary size and shape of the future American military, including its ground forces, it is important to try to delimit it as much as possible. Historically, the United States has had several periods of coherent grand strategy—the Monroe Doctrine in the nineteenth century, victory in Europe first and in the Pacific later in World War II, containment in the cold war—and the nation as well as its allies should aspire to some coherence and cogency in the future as well.[7]

Some would counsel against preparedness for plausible military missions on the grounds that by being prepared, we might stray into conflicts that would have been best avoided. The 2003 Iraq War may be a recent case in point—a "war of choice," in Richard Haass's pithy depiction, that surely would not have been undertaken without a ready and fairly large standing military.[8] But for every such case in U.S. history, there are probably several—including the two world wars and the Korean War—in which lack of preparedness proved an even greater problem. Moreover, in Iraq and Afghanistan, improper preparation for a certain type of fighting arguably made the initial years in both these wars far less successful than they might have been. Nor is it so clear that the United States is really spoiling for military action abroad. Americans may not be as restrained in the use of force as they often like to believe themselves to be. Yet at the same time, casualty aversion—and, more recently, a national souring on the kind of ground operations conducted in Iraq and Afghanistan—impose important constraints on action as well. Deliberately staying militarily unprepared for plausible missions as a way of avoiding unsuccessful military operations abroad thus seems an unwise and highly risky strategy for the nation.

The time frame of the analysis is roughly 2020 through 2040—beyond the immediate budgeting challenges of the next appropriations cycle and five-year defense plan but not so far off as to be disconnected from current policy decisionmaking. Of course, there will be surprises between now and 2020, but some of the main drivers of international conflict can probably be identified.

Several countries loom large in the pages that follow. They include the world's largest, most industrialized, most militarized, and most populous nations. These states have the wherewithal to cause or experience security challenges that could pose systemic and large-scale disruptions to the global order and to American interests. Prominent examples include Russia, China, India, Pakistan, Iran, Egypt, Saudi Arabia, Nigeria, and Mexico. What are the prospects that some of these countries could attack their neighbors, turn on themselves in large-scale civil warfare, suffer massive tragedies of some type, lose track of nuclear materials or other highly dangerous agents, or otherwise create a major international crisis that could not be easily ignored?

The analysis is not confined to traditional war scenarios. It also looks at complex humanitarian or relief activities of various types, some of which could involve an element of violence but others of which may not. It considers, for example, the chances that large, populous parts of certain countries or regions could suffer enormous tragedy that would dwarf the world's worst disasters to date and necessitate massive and sustained relief efforts. Such contingencies could have significant implications for the global order and thus should be factored into American strategic thinking and military force planning.

The policy implications of these kinds of analyses are very important. They go beyond predictable, if major, decisions about matters such as when to replace the Abrams tank, or how many brigade combat teams to retain in the U.S. Army Active and Guard force structure, or how to reshape and reconfigure such combat units. Even broader and more fundamental questions arise. Should the United States retain a large active duty army, as it has since World War II, or revert to an earlier model of a citizens' army, with greater reliance on the National Guard? Does the U.S. Army, along with the Marine Corps, need to retain a large-scale expeditionary capability of dominating maneuver warfare virtually anywhere on Earth? How great should America's reliance on allies be in the future?

This book concludes with such questions. I ultimately argue for an army not unlike that described in the Obama administration's current plan—roughly a million soldiers, with about 450,000 on active duty. However, the mathematics behind this force-sizing construct are different from those of the Pentagon today. As noted, today's Department of Defense retains some elements of a two-war capability. My framework would not. Instead, it would plan for a single decisive war, combined with a possibly prolonged U.S. role in two simultaneous, multilateral missions, which could involve counterinsurgency, stabilization, deterrence, or a major disaster response. It might be described as a "1+2" paradigm, for one war, together with two smaller and more multilateral but potentially long and complex operations.

The book does not begin with that issue, however. Instead, after a brief review of the history of U.S. ground forces in this chapter and observations about U.S. grand strategy, I attempt to determine where large-scale violence or mayhem on land is most plausible and where it would be most consequential strategically. I then ask which contingencies could require a large-scale U.S. response with ground forces, rather than some other mix of military tools. In many cases the U.S. preference would surely be—and should surely be—to avoid direct involvement in any operation with U.S. forces if at all possible. However, in light of trends in military burden sharing worldwide and the irreplaceability of American leadership for many difficult military operations, it is quite plausible that in some cases, direct U.S. intervention as part of a coalition could prove necessary. The book concludes with implications for the force postures and budgets of the U.S. ground forces.

A HISTORICAL SKETCH OF AMERICAN GROUND POWER

Throughout its history, the United States has been influenced by dueling paradigms in sizing and shaping its ground forces. On the one hand, it has retained a somewhat romanticized image of the gentleman soldier, or the farmer-soldier, who takes up arms only when his country's security demands it and returns to civilian life once the shooting stops. This narrative, grounded in part in America's geographic luxury of being protected from potential foes by two oceans and in its history as a land of

Figure 1-1. Size of the U.S. Army throughout History, 1860–2014

Number of personnel (million)

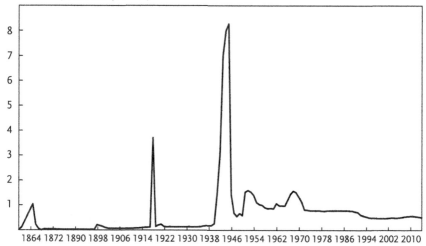

Sources: U.S. Army Center of Military History, "American Military History," vols. 1 and 2 (www.history. army.mil/books); National WWII Museum, "By the Numbers: U.S. Military" (www.nationalww2museum. org/learn/education/for-students/ww2-history/ww2-by-the-numbers/us-military.html); and U.S. Census Bureau, "Statistical Abstract of the United States," Department of Defense Personnel (www.census.gov/ compendia/statab/).

immigrants trying to escape the conflicts of the Old World, idealizes the local militia as much as the huge institutional army. It fit fairly well with reality in the United States, with a couple of very notable exceptions, for most of the country's first 140 years (see figure 1-1 on the size of the U.S. Army over the course of most American history).

This image of the reluctant warrior, and the demilitarized nation, accords with the life of the nation's first commander in chief and president, George Washington. General Washington was more than happy to resign his military commission after the Revolutionary War and resume the kinds of economic pursuits that had always been his main preoccupation. This preference for the plow over the sword earned Washington the nickname of the American Cincinnatus, after the Roman farmer-soldier who returned to his fields whenever military circumstances allowed.[9] More broadly, Washington's example helped foster and reinforce the historical theme of a United States uninterested in Europe's wars of the eighteenth and nineteenth centuries and preferring to avoid them altogether, as typified in John Quincy Adams's admonition to Congress in

1821 about championing freedom abroad without actively seeking to impose it.[10] Washington's Farewell Address had voiced similar views. It contained the following counsel to the union's states:

> Hence, likewise, they will avoid the necessity of those overgrown military establishments which, under any form of government, are inauspicious to liberty, and which are to be regarded as particularly hostile to republican liberty. In this sense it is that your union ought to be considered as a main prop of your liberty, and that the love of the one ought to endear to you the preservation of the other.[11]

This attitude was reflected as well in the rapid demobilizations of the nation's armed forces after the Revolutionary War. One result was the poor preparedness of the nation for the War of 1812, when the army had fewer than 10,000 soldiers at the outbreak of hostilities.[12] The army roughly tripled in size in the course of that war but then declined back to a paltry 11,000 or so by 1830.[13] Small standing forces were the norm in the Republic's early decades in general. Even the Mexican War in the mid-to-late 1840s typically involved only 5,000 to 10,000 U.S. troops out of a total ground force not much larger.[14] At the outbreak of the Civil War, the U.S. Army numbered just 17,000 in all.[15] After the Civil War, when some 3 million Americans served, mass demobilization occurred again.[16] From the 1870s until the Spanish-American War, the full-time army numbered fewer than 30,000 soldiers. At century's end, the U.S. Army was less than a tenth the size of any major European power's ground forces.[17]

Despite occasional colonial ambitions from Mexico to Cuba and the Philippines, most of early U.S. history fostered the image of a nation that was not militarized in the way of European powers of the day. It is striking that by the late 1800s, the United States had become easily the second most populous major power after Russia, with an 1890 population of more than 60 million (Russia's was about 115 million; Germany's was about 50 million, with other major European states and Japan each in the range of roughly 30 million to 40 million). Yet the United States had only some 35,000 military personnel (including its Navy and Marine Corps), at a time when European powers typically had 200,000 to 750,000 men at arms.[18]

Subsequently, as the United States began to focus on building up stronger armed forces, much of the effort went into building a strong battleship-oriented Navy rather than a more capable army. This dynamic, which began in the 1890s, was motivated by the writings of Alfred Thayer Mahan, the global ambitions awakened by the Spanish-American War, and the political leadership of Theodore Roosevelt, among others.[19]

These realities changed in the twentieth century, of course, but only fitfully. At the outbreak of World War I, the U.S. Army was only about 100,000 strong. After the war it was scaled back again, to less than 140,000. In the early 1930s the U.S. Army ranked seventeenth in the world in size, behind the armies of Portugal and Belgium. It was generally strapped for funds for equipment and training as well. Indeed, while its school systems and certain other characteristics were becoming more professional and serious, the army of the 1920s and 1930s was in some ways the most disengaged from combat of any army in the nation's history since there were no longer battles against Native Americans (or Mexicans or Spanish) to wage.[20] Even as the decade of the 1930s unfolded and Europe lurched toward general war, in 1938 the U.S. Army was only 165,000 strong, nineteenth largest in the world.[21] Much of the intellectual energy directed to America's armed forces was trained on new possibilities in naval and air combat, sparked by thinkers such as Billy Mitchell, rather than on ground armies.[22]

Through the end of the nineteenth century, state militias were often a very real rival to the regular army for political support and resources. They had been important in the Revolutionary War and remained so thereafter. Indeed, in its Articles I and II, as well as in the Second Amendment, the Constitution not only made militias permanent but explicitly recognized and codified their independent standing separate from the army.[23] At the onset of the Spanish-American War, the sum total of all militias exceeded 100,000 personnel, or about four times the total number of soldiers in the Active Army.

Still, even as the concept of a National Guard began to develop, this force remained essentially a conglomeration of individual state-run units, poorly trained and poorly equipped. As the historian Graham Cosmas put it, "Guardsmen in the northeastern states spent much time and money on parties, picnics, drill competitions, and elaborate dress uniforms ornamented with plumes and gold braid." Realistic training was all but unheard of; even preparation for living in difficult field conditions was minimal.[24] These circumstances contributed to the Elihu Root reforms and the Militia Act of 1903, which supplanted the 1792 Militia

Figure 1-2. Size of the U.S. Marines throughout History, 1860–2014

Number of personnel (thousand)

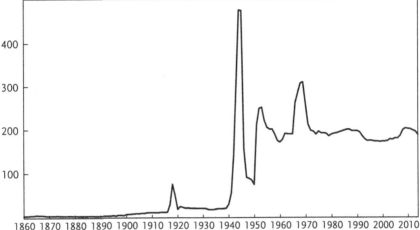

Sources: National WWII Museum, "By the Numbers: U.S. Military" (www.nationalww2museum.org/learn/education/for-students/ww2-history/ww2-by-the-numbers/us-military.html); U.S. Census, Statistical Abstract, National Security & Veterans Affairs (www.census.gov/compendia/statab/cats/national_security_veterans_affairs.html); Department of the Navy, "A Chronology of the United States Marine Corps," vol. I (and subsequent reports) (https://archive.org/stream/AChronologyOfTheUnitedStatesMarineCorps1775-1934#page/n66/mode/1up/search/strength).

Act, formalized the link of state militias to the War Department, and provided direct federal financing for these National Guard units. But even thereafter, improvement was gradual.[25]

The evolution of the U.S. Marine Corps followed a broadly similar path to that of the active duty U.S. Army. It was a tiny force throughout the nineteenth century, generally in the range of 1,000 to 3,000 Marines in total at any time, not even exceeding 4,000 during the Civil War. Then it began its upward trajectory early in the twentieth century, reaching about 10,000 uniformed personnel by 1910, temporarily growing to about 75,000 during World War I, and then averaging in the 50,000 range in the 1920s before its rapid growth in World War II to nearly half a million Marines.[26] Since 1952, its force structure has been mandated by law to include three divisions and three air wings (though the definition of divisions and wings was not formalized legally).[27] In recent decades its strength has varied from 170,000 to 200,000 active duty uniformed personnel (see figure 1-2 on the U.S. Marine Corps).

Since World War II, the United States has maintained a degree of constant military vigilance and investment previously unknown in its history. Military spending has averaged more than $400 billion annually since then, generally exceeding 5 percent of GDP during the cold war and sometimes approaching 10 percent.[28] But even through this period, the United States avoided becoming what Princeton professor Aaron Friedberg calls a garrison state.[29] Its investments went largely toward technology, including nuclear arms; its standing forces from all services combined generally numbered in the vicinity of 2 million, and even in the Vietnam period they barely exceeded 3 million.[30] These were significant numbers, to be sure. But when measured against a population base of more than 200 million citizens during most of this period, and in comparison with the forces of the Soviet Union and indeed many other states, America's military was not particularly large.

This, then, is the story of the reluctant superpower, the United States that prefers to focus on its own affairs and stay out of the world's problems whenever possible. But of course, the world wars provided important exceptions to this rule, as did the Civil War and a few other conflicts. Often even in the pre-superpower years, America's philosophy of nonintervention and neo-isolationism was observed more in the breach than in reality.

Indeed, over the last century in particular, there has been a competing image to the Cincinnatus/Washington ideal. The United States has been a committed power, bent on victory in its wars and ambitious in trying to forge an international order to its own liking, even in peacetime. The United States has hardly been reluctant to field whatever military capability seemed necessary to get the job done.

This other American military narrative comports with the industrial-scale army of World War II, which reflected a near-complete mobilization of the country's human and technological resources. In that conflict, the U.S. Army peaked at more than 8 million soldiers in total size.[31] Even without huge standing armies, the modern American way of war has continued since that time. Although it has numerous variants, in general, it has emphasized mass, maneuver, and firepower, as Russell Weigley and others have described.[32]

Indeed, this American tendency to field a strong and active military has deeper antecedents than many remember. Naturally, Civil War forces were huge. As noted, the total number of men-at-arms who served in the war may have approached 3 million.[33] But even the Continental Army and related militia forces during the Revolutionary War were fairly large by certain measures. Although they typically numbered no more than 30,000 to 50,000 soldiers at a time in aggregate, that was out of a population base of only some 3 million. Since the effort lasted seven years, the total forces involved were significant in size by the standards of the day. Indeed, when one considers all types of militia fighters and short-timers from that conflict, some estimates have concluded that nearly half of all military-age eligible men actually fought against the British in the War of American Independence.[34]

These competing tendencies in American defense planning reflected competing elements in American strategic thought as well. The nation really did avoid excessive overseas entanglements in its early decades, with the realist thinking of Washington, Adams, and Hamilton triumphing over the more activist outlooks of the likes of Jefferson in terms of how to deal with Britain, France, and the rest of the Old World.

Yet it would go too far to view the country as inherently pacifist or even isolationist in these early decades. Robert Kagan argues persuasively that historically the United States has been a "dangerous nation"—expansionist within North America in its early history, hegemonic in its view of its own role there, as reflected in the 1823 Monroe Doctrine (even if that doctrine was couched in antihegemonic terms, as a warning to European powers to stay away from the hemisphere), assertive throughout the Americas and parts of the Pacific thereafter.[35]

In George Kennan's metaphor, in the twentieth century, the United States was a sluggish giant, slow to awaken to challenges abroad, though resolute and fierce once finally shaken from its slumber.[36] Germany's reoccupation of its Rhineland in violation of the Versailles Treaty in 1936 and its subsequent annexations and invasions of Austria, Czechoslovakia, and Poland did not provoke significant American responses.[37] Even thereafter, as World War II intensified, the United States limited support for Britain, the Soviet Union, and other allies to the provision of weapons and supplies. It was not until December 1941 that it went meaningfully beyond the Lend-Lease program in its wartime role.[38] Yet once it did awaken, it knew no limits. And the expectation of victory in the nation's wars has been axiomatic in U.S. military planning ever since.

Avoiding appeasement and avoiding military unpreparedness were the two central lessons learned in World War II, at the cost of hundreds of thousands of American lives and tens of millions of others'. Since then, the collective wisdom of the nation has been to avoid any replay of this tragic past. It is probably safe to say that in the modern American mind, the dangers of appeasement against an extremist foe are seen as greater than those of spiraling into war as a result of great-power competition.[39] Put differently, for most Americans, World War II instructs more powerfully than World War I, and not simply because it was the more recent and deadlier of the two conflicts. For a brief period, the weary nation seemed to make an effort to unlearn the lesson about the importance of U.S. engagement and deterrence as soon as World War II was over. Initially, it largely dismantled and demobilized its huge military. But the growing Soviet domination of Europe, the Chinese revolution, and the North Korean invasion of South Korea put an end to any real expectation that America could disengage or return to the days of a minimalist standing military.[40] Ultimately, the lessons of World War II were therefore reinforced by the cold war experience, which again seemed to underscore the importance of resoluteness in American foreign policy. During this time, the United States built up a large alliance system, deployed forces forward in Europe and Asia in particular, used military forces frequently for signaling and crisis response, and, with its allies, developed various additional approaches for containing the Soviet Union.[41] These types of assertive practices continued after the cold war, even before the attacks of September 11, 2001, in military actions from the Balkans to Iraq to the Taiwan Strait and in the expansion of the NATO alliance, as well as in the deepening of commitments to many strategic partners in the broader Middle East.[42]

Thus there are powerful, conflictual strands of thought and practice in U.S. national security policy. The notion of the citizen soldier, available to defend the nation when duty calls but otherwise inclined to focus on civilian activities, and its complementary view of the nation's army as a modest force in peacetime, has deep and powerful historical roots, especially through the outbreak of World War II. But the need for a large and powerful military was widely accepted when the nation went to war in revolutionary times and the Civil War, in World War I, and then again in World War II. Aspects of that thinking have influenced military policy ever since, for three-fourths of a century (see figure 1-3 on the size of the modern U.S. Army since 1960).

As such, it is difficult to argue that there is a clear natural state to which U.S. land forces should return if and when global conditions permit. Was there a halcyon period in the nineteenth century that should be

Figure 1-3. U.S. Army Annual Active Duty Personnel End Strength, 1960–2014

Number of personnel (million)

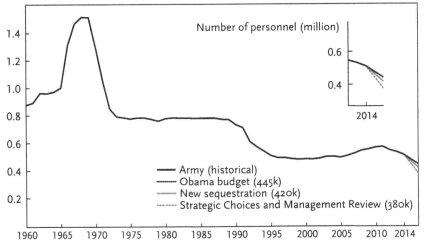

Source: DOD Personnel, *Workforce Reports & Publications* (www.dmdc.osd.mil/appj/dwp/dwp _reports.jsp).

seen as the norm to which the country will revert someday? Or was this nineteenth-century image of a generally demilitarized America something that the nation can never wisely relive in a world that now needs its leadership? Since there is no prospect of a future power to play the hegemonic role that Britain arguably played for some of the nineteenth century, does that mean that the United States has no choice but to continue the role itself, even if perhaps in an evolving form? And if so, which types of scenarios must the U.S. Army, and the nation's armed forces more generally, be prepared to handle? It is to these questions that we ultimately turn.

THE SO-CALLED REVOLUTION IN MILITARY AFFAIRS, REVISITED

Central to the question of the future of land warfare is the way in which technology is changing, and with it the ways in which military force will be built, deployed, and used. Might robotics, high-technology standoff weapons, and new technologies in space and cyber realms change ground warfare radically? The U.S. Army's budget is already headed toward

Table 1-1. Army Annual Budget as Portion of All Department of Defense Spending[a]

Billions of current U.S. dollars

Year	Army	DOD	Army (percent)
1960	103,746	397,952	26.1
1970	161,596	509,096	31.7
1980	108,049	417,269	25.9
1990	148,362	537,801	27.6
2000	104,437	416,437	25.1
2010	263,650	752,678	35.0
2014	170,484	596,206	28.6
2019[b]	122,446	520,672	23.5

Source: U.S. Department of Defense, *National Defense Budget Estimates for FY 2015* (Washington, April 2014), pp. 90–96.

a. Based on the president's budget request for 2015 and not including Department of Energy national security spending. Totals include all enacted supplemental funding.

b. Does not include any supplemental funding estimate or projection.

constituting its smallest share of the Department of Defense (DOD) total in the modern era, as shown in the accompanying table 1-1—but in light of these changes, some would argue that the trend can go even further.

Of course, there have been many ongoing improvements in the weaponry utilized for ground warfare over the ages, from the steel and muskets of the Spanish conquistadores, to the cannons of Napoleon, to the railroads and bored rifles and machine guns of the later nineteenth century and World War I, to the combined-arms tank-heavy warfare of World War II and the Arab-Israeli wars.[43] Since then, advanced reconnaissance and precision-strike technologies have changed warfare dramatically as well, including the ways in which ground armies operate.[44] Along the way, weapons became far more lethal and longer range in character; armies spread out and became better at maneuver as equipment improved. Typically, in ancient times, a force of 100,000 fighters was densely concentrated for battle within a single square kilometer, according to the military historian Trevor Dupuy, but by Napoleon's day a force of that size occupied 20 square kilometers, by World War I some 250 square kilometers, and toward the end of the twentieth century as much as 3,500 square kilometers in some conflicts.[45] These processes of rapid innovation are impressive, and are ongoing.

Still, in regard to the revolution in military affairs (RMA) debate of modern times, the hypothesis of many advocates goes much further. They often promise a form of warfare that fundamentally alters the mix of forces that will be needed in future U.S. combat operations.

We have been here before. Most recently, in the 1990s, as the United States reflected back on the new ways of precision strike exemplified in Operation Desert Storm in 1991 and took stock as well of the ongoing dot-com revolution in computers, a thesis emerged that warfare was experiencing a period of profound revolution. Harking back to previous periods of similar discontinuous change, as with the advent of the blitzkrieg, amphibious assault, strategic bombing, and nuclear weapons in World War II, proponents argued that the United States needed to fundamentally revamp its approach to war and the way in which it allocated resources within the DOD to avoid being caught unprepared in future combat.[46] The arguments varied from strategist to strategist.[47] But they tended to emphasize that the nation needed to invest less in some areas—most notably land forces, along with associated activities such as peacekeeping and maintaining a forward military presence abroad—to ensure it had resources for more pathbreaking approaches to military operations.[48]

Much of this debate was healthy. Certainly, a superpower sitting atop the global distribution of military and economic power had at least as much to fear from complacency and inertia as from an overly enthusiastic desire for change. And the debate is also well grounded in history. Thinkers like Sun Tzu have for centuries reminded strategists to pursue clever new ways of fighting, even as other thinkers, such as Carl von Clausewitz, have pointed to the timeless qualities of combat and to the fog of war, which tends to disrupt most grand new plans and efforts to achieve quick and easy victories through the use of new tactics and new technologies. These debates have surfaced numerous times in American military history over the decades as well.[49]

But the recent debate has also had its dangers. Modern America has had a fascination with technology that has sometimes led it astray in its thinking about what military force can and cannot accomplish. From the early proponents of aerial warfare as a supposedly decisive form of combat, to nuclear weapons theorists who believed in a possible strategy of preemption, to advocates of the Army's Pentomic divisions of the 1950s, which treated nuclear weapons simply as a more powerful version of artillery, to the emphasis on firepower that reinforced flawed political assumptions about how to fight the Vietnam War, to overconfidence in how high technology might permit low-casualty and highly effective operations in Somalia, Afghanistan, and Kosovo in the 1990s, America's proclivity to trust technology has produced myriad mistakes. And much of the enthusiasm of the RMA community of the 1990s was clearly breathless and excessive itself. One heard numerous predictions. Ground combat vehicles were to routinely attain speeds of 200 kilometers per hour by 2010 while relying more on situational awareness than on armor for protection. All major areas of defense technology were to advance at a pace similar to those of computers, as reflected in Moore's law. Oceans were to become effectively transparent to advanced sensors. Space launch would become 90 percent less expensive. All these beliefs were later proven badly incorrect—and should have been seen to be wrong at the time they were initially offered.[50] One hears echoes of the 1990s RMA debate in the present strategic dialogue in the United States.

In my 2000 book on the subject, I broke down key areas of enabling military technology into some twenty-nine categories. Beginning with a literature review, and then subjecting my initial estimates to scrutiny by scientists at some of the nation's best weapons laboratories, I argued that of the twenty-nine, perhaps two were experiencing or likely to experience truly revolutionary breakthroughs.[51] Those were computer hardware and software. The remaining categories of technology seemed likely to progress at modest rates. A subsequent section of the book, armed with these working premises, then examined a multitude of scenarios to reach provisional judgments about how many of them might become markedly easier (or harder) to handle in the future as a result of technological change and associated changes in military tactics and operations that the United States, its allies, and its adversaries might adopt.

The overall result of this analysis predicted, perhaps fairly unremarkably, that the kinds of wars the nation wound up preoccupied with in the 2000s—Iraq and Afghanistan, and other irregular conflicts—would remain difficult. Whatever technology offered, be it revolutionary or evolutionary, it would make the United States better at activities at which it already excelled, such as long-range precision strikes, and would help less in the kinds of urban and infantry combat that later typified its experiences in Mesopotamia and the Hindu Kush.[52] To be sure, battlefield commanders and their troops did remarkable things in these conflicts. They developed major innovations in areas such as drone technology and the creation of more responsive intelligence networks.[53] But they did not render the battlefield transparent or otherwise make it feasible for U.S. forces to dominate it through technology. The laws of physics continued to limit what sensors could accomplish in the complex terrain of the insurgent battlefield. Realities of engineering continued to make it necessary to produce large gas-guzzling vehicles for protection and mobility. The basic human need to walk the battlefield and to get to know the population in order to conduct proper counterinsurgency operations proved as timeless as ever. Not only the United States and its allies in Iraq and Afghanistan but also other countries with excellent militaries—perhaps most notably Israel—experienced similar challenges in this time period when confronting similar problems. Israel started to look for strategies emphasizing punishment and deterrence over decisive military victory, given the dilemmas involved in trying to defeat enemies equipped with even relatively modest technology, by the standards of the day.[54]

There is little reason to revise these basic assessments today. A rethinking of my graphic from the 2000 book suggests the need for only modest change. In the area of drone technology, progress appears faster than I had forecasted, making for a grand total of three of twenty-nine categories that I would now label as progressing at a revolutionary pace. All other categories, to a first approximation, would seem essentially as predicted then.

Others have cautioned against predictions of radical change in the character of warfare as well. Barry Posen has referred to America's military dominance in the modern era as "command of the commons," suggesting that military operations in the open oceans and associated regions of air and space would play to U.S. strengths much more than other forms of combat might.[55] Stephen Biddle has argued that trends in technology are gradually placing a higher premium on excellence in everything from basic infantry skills to high-level integration of theater-wide operations. Modern war is becoming increasingly lethal and thus unforgiving to the unprepared, but it is not making ground combat irrelevant or obsolete.[56]

There could be other reasons why the United States can or should focus fewer resources and plans on land forces and ground combat than it has done to this point. That question is taken up below, and in subsequent chapters. Certain specific innovations in military technology, discussed in chapter 5, will likely make a significant difference in ground operations in the coming decades. That is not, however, the same thing as making a revolution.

PURPOSES OF LAND POWER IN THE TWENTY-FIRST CENTURY

What are the core purposes of U.S. military power in general, and of U.S. land forces in particular? Many suggestions have been offered in recent decades, from creating a new world order free of interstate conflict to sustaining American primacy to preventing genocide to preempting proliferators. My analysis in this book is not, however, motivated by any such single organizing principle. Most have their utility; all have their limitations.

For example, some might argue that the United States and its allies might decide to put into effect what the first President Bush called the new world order, punishing any country that attacked another or sought to annex part or all of its territory. But not every interstate conflict is a serious threat to core U.S. national security objectives. Preserving and strengthening the international norm against cross-border aggression is a very desirable goal for American foreign policy in the future as well.[57] But conflict between Eritrea and Ethiopia, or Armenia and Azerbaijan, or the two Sudans was never serious enough to raise the strategic stakes to a high level for the United States. As such, Washington was generally correct to stay out of these conflicts militarily and seek to affect and restrain them in other ways. The same basic conclusion has been true in Ukraine in 2014 and 2015, though there the stakes were higher, in light of the location in Central Europe, the involvement of a nuclear-armed superpower in the conflict, and Washington's role in the 1994 Budapest declaration, which promised that the United States would have an interest in Ukraine's future security as an inducement for Kiev to give up its share of the post-Soviet nuclear arsenal.

Civil wars have been the most common, and deadly, of major armed conflicts in the modern world. (See figures 1-4, 1-5, and 1-6 on armed conflict by region, type, and intensity in the modern era.) They remain quite prevalent. Still, these kinds of wars can be very messy, and quite intractable, for any outside parties. The weight of historical evidence would seem to counsel against undertaking large-scale nation-building or state-building missions in most cases because of the high costs and uncertain prospects. It is also worth noting that the costs of UN or regional peacekeeping operations *after* peace accords are struck do seem more commensurate with the strategic stakes and risks associated with such armed struggles—and the overall track record of such operations, as seen

Figure 1-4. Armed Conflict by Region, 1946–2013

Number of conflicts

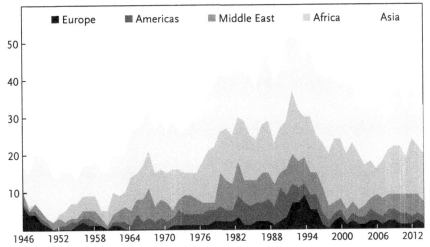

Source: Lotta Themnér and Peter Wallensteen, "Armed Conflict, 1946–2013," *Journal of Peace Research* 51, no. 4 (2014) (www.pcr.uu.se/research/ucdp/datasets/ucdp_prio_armed_conflict_dataset/).

Figure 1-5. Armed Conflict by Type, 1946–2013

Number of conflicts

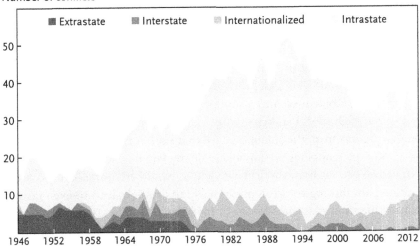

Source: Themnér and Wallensteen, "Armed Conflict, 1946–2013."

Figure 1-6. Armed Conflict by Intensity, 1946–2013

Number of conflicts

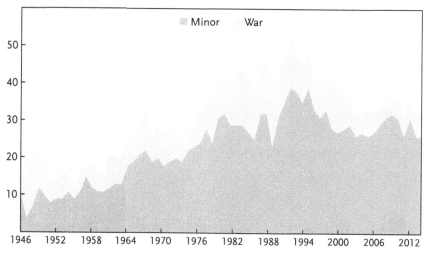

Source: Themnér and Wallensteen, "Armed Conflict, 1946–2013."

from Mozambique to Cambodia to El Salvador, is passably good, if far from unblemished.[58]

What of stopping genocide? Again, this is a mission that could be important. In theory, under the 1948 UN Genocide Convention and the more recent Responsibility to Protect doctrine of the UN, and in light of its own historical lessons and moral scruples, the United States would seem to have a strong predisposition to intervene quickly to stop genocide. President Clinton's lament about not having taken action to stop the 1994 Rwanda genocide, the world's collective shame at not having stopped the Holocaust, and a number of other cases are salient reminders of the high moral stakes involved in watching the mass slaughter of human beings from the sidelines.[59] All that said, it is important to be realistic. Not all genocides are anywhere nearly equal in scope to each other. Moreover, some hypothetical genocides would be unrealistic to stop, because attempting to do so might well fail or might lead to even greater loss of life than the genocide itself. Invading a nuclear-armed country to protect one of its oppressed minorities is a case in point.

The proliferation of nuclear weapons or fissile materials is another potentially grave threat. A half century ago, John Kennedy famously predicted that the world could see twenty nuclear weapons states within a few years. That claim, happily, has not been borne out, but enough proliferation has occurred to have increased the dangers and reminded one of the risks of a greater spread of the bomb.[60] But can the United States really prevent it? The post–cold war era has provided conflicting evidence and arguments about the inevitability of proliferation—and the international community's willingness to take forcible action to stop it. After Operation Desert Storm in 1991, the United States discovered Iraqi nuclear weapons programs that had been developed after the Israeli 1981 Osirak preemptive attack, and spent much of the next dozen years trying to ensure Iraq could not reconstitute such programs, an effort that culminated in the invasion of 2003. But that very year, as the prevention of nuclear proliferation helped justify a major military operation in the Middle East, North Korea's withdrawal from the Nuclear Non-Proliferation Treaty and its subsequent presumed acquisition of a small nuclear arsenal elicited no comparable response—just nine years after then Secretary of Defense William Perry had warned Pyongyang about the potential military consequences of a nuclear breakout attempt.[61] Pakistan and India tested the bomb in 1998, and while no military response was plausible or appropriate, they were at least significantly sanctioned at the time. But by the early years of the twenty-first century, those sanctions had been trumped by more pressing geostrategic concerns of a different nature, and were dropped. Sanctions were lifted on Qaddafi and Libya when Qaddafi gave up his nuclear technologies and aspirations, but then the message was somewhat muddled in 2011 when he was overthrown for other reasons. The United States and other countries have worked hard to find a diplomatic deal with modern Iran partly because of the mediocre prospects of a military strike intended to eliminate the nuclear program through force rather than negotiations.[62] On balance, preventive wars to stop proliferation seem rather unlikely in most cases.

Relatedly, American military power might in theory be used to punish any state that used nuclear weapons in a future conflict. The tradition against nuclear weapons usage could be seen as very important to uphold. But again, there are counterarguments. If, for example, the country that had used nuclear weapons had many more of them than initially employed, the higher priority might well be to deter further use rather than to punish the perpetrator of the initial attack. Thus, any punishment might well be exacted in economic or other nonmilitary terms.

What about the threat of terrorism? Generally, after the experiences in Iraq and Afghanistan, it seems likely that the United States will confine itself to the use of limited tools of military force, such as drones and special forces, in addressing this danger. However, there could be scenarios in which a major use of American power might seem the lesser of two dangers. The possibility of a terrorist group someday obtaining weapons of mass destruction is a chilling thought that could make the conflicts of 2001 to 2015 seem relatively modest in the threat they actually posed to Western society. Indeed, for a time in the fall of 2001, there was a credible if low-probability concern that a nuclear weapon might be smuggled into Manhattan and detonated, and officials involved in that experience recount to this day the deep anxiety it caused them.[63]

Thus, thinking through a taxonomy of possible military missions should leave us agnostic. There are many categories of hypothetical operations about which American planners, politicians, and citizens should remain wary, and should try to avoid. Yet at the same time it would be difficult and unwise to dismiss most types of operations outright and categorically.

THE UNITED STATES, U.S. GRAND STRATEGY, AND THE COURSE OF HISTORY

Beyond such specific considerations based on types of military missions, it is helpful to ask, what broad goals should U.S. power be seeking to advance on behalf of the nation? Only with such a perspective can land power be directed to serve the most important national security interests of the United States.

Over the years, a number of possible theses have been advanced to help policymakers make sense of the confusing and multiheaded course of world history. They include the following:

—Democracy is spreading quickly, and with it, the prospects for peace, since established democracies do not tend to fight each other.

—Nuclear deterrence will largely guarantee great-power peace.

—Economic interdependence will make great-power conflict such a nonsensical notion as to render the chances of interstate warfare even lower than in the recent past.

—Nuclear proliferation will make the world more dangerous, and other trends in technology in areas such as microbiology and robotics and additive manufacturing (3-D printing) could do the same.

—Burgeoning populations, combined with the effects of global climate change, will lead to new types of conflicts over water, resources, and territory.

—Strong American leadership can, as it has since World War II, help preclude the prospects of great-power competition and thereby help keep the peace, especially in areas of the global commons crucial to commerce and trade.

—Fraying American strength and leadership, and the rise of China, as well as of other powers, will make the world more anarchic and thus more dangerous.

All of these theories are serious. All have very thoughtful proponents; all capture at least a kernel of truth about international politics and war. But they have their limitations as well.

The theories that would seem to promise less conflict, while hardly lacking in merit, and supported by the general trends of reduced violence in recent decades, particularly at the interstate level, do not guarantee a peaceful planet in the future.[64] For example, it is true that the overall frequency of interstate violence has declined greatly and that casualties from all types of war (particularly when adjusted for the size of the Earth's population) are down substantially. But deterrence can still fail owing to misperception about commitments, the ascent to power of risk-prone leaders in key nations, enduring historical grievances that resurface at a future date after a period of quiet, and disputes over resources of one type or another.[65] Here we should think of Vladimir Putin and his recent behavior, or the leadership of Iran, or the ongoing rivalries between the Koreas and between India and Pakistan.

Moreover, there have been more than thirty civil wars in the years since the turn of the twenty-first century. This remains a higher figure than in much of the twentieth century.[66] Estimated fatalities from those wars, typically 20,000 to 40,000 annually in recent years, according to the Peace Research Institute Oslo at Uppsala University in Sweden, are substantially less than from the civil wars of the late 1970s, 1980s, and early 1990s but not appreciably less than those of the 1950s and certain other periods. In other words, there may be a generally hopeful trend toward decreased global violence, but it is hardly so pronounced or so definitive as to foretell an obsolescence of armed conflict.[67] Moreover, civil wars are very difficult to resolve definitively, and often recur even after peace accords are in place.[68]

There were still some seventeen UN peace operations globally as of 2014, involving more than 100,000 personnel in total. Additional non-UN missions continue in other countries. Total numbers of peacekeepers, under UN auspices and otherwise, have consistently grown in this century even without counting the Afghanistan operation.[69] In places such as Syria and Iraq, serious violence continues. Largely as a result, world totals for refugees and internally displaced persons (IDPs) remain high. More than 10 million refugees are under the care of the UN High Commissioner for Refugees (down from an early 1990s peak of 18 million but much greater than 1960s and 1970s totals), with the largest numbers from Afghanistan, Syria, Somalia, Sudan, and the Democratic Republic of Congo. These same countries, along with Colombia, have large numbers of IDPs as well. Indeed, global totals for IDPs are at historic highs, with more than 25 million under UN supervision and care and a grand total of more than 30 million worldwide. Pakistan, Iran, Lebanon, Jordan, and Turkey host the largest number of refugees from other countries. All told, forced displacement in 2013 topped 50 million globally for the first time since World War II.[70]

Terrorism broadly defined has increased dramatically in this century by comparison with the latter decades of the twentieth century.[71] And technology, as well as their tools of mobilization and organization, make terrorists more dangerous too. As Philip Bobbitt argues, for the first time since the creation of the state, nonstate entities can truly threaten the core security of societies.[72] Some extremist movements are now able to hide away within the world's great and growing megalopolises to a greater extent than many previous insurgent or rebellious movements in history. In so doing, they can gain access to information, communications, transportation systems, funding, and recruits.[73] President Obama frequently talked about al Qaeda being on the run or on the path to defeat in 2012 and 2013, but that optimism was premature at best, and could really only be said to apply to the traditional core of the organization that attacked the United States in 2001.[74] Al Qaeda affiliates remain active in dozens of countries, and the success of the self-styled Islamic State in Iraq and the Levant throughout much of Syria and then in northern and western Iraq in recent years has been stunning.[75]

When all these points are taken together, it seems clear that theories about the supposed obsolescence of land warfare need to be viewed warily.[76] It is also important to note that most countries do not seem to consider land warfare obsolete. They concentrate many of their military resources on land forces. As noted, out of the 20 million or so active duty military personnel under arms worldwide today, nearly three-fourths are in ground forces.

In regard to the so-called democratic peace, it is true that established, functioning constitutional democracies fight each other much less often, statistically speaking.[77] It is also true that such countries are becoming more common, with about 120 countries, or nearly two-thirds of the nations of the planet, electoral democracies by the turn of the twenty-first century. However, even such countries are not impervious to the possibility of civil war (as the American Civil War showed), or to a possible coup or hijacking by a strongman, who then misrules the state (as Hitler's hijacking of the Weimar Republic demonstrates), or to other aberrations. The extraordinary popularity of Vladimir Putin in Russia since 2014, even if partly fabricated and engineered by the Kremlin, should alone throw some cold water on any excessive optimism about the hypothesis that empowering the average man and woman will produce naturally peaceful nations. Egypt's extremely turbulent steps toward what may or may not prove a more democratic future provide another timely reminder. Moreover, the world has many prominent nondemocracies or partial democracies—North Korea, as an extreme case, but also Iran and China, and in total about 35 percent of the world's population. Democratic peace theory may work well for established, inclusive, constitutional democracies based on the liberal principle of the rights and worth of the individual. However, such states are rarer than are electoral democracies in general.[78]

The notion that nuclear deterrence has created a world in which major powers are less likely to engage in all-out war against each other is probably true. Such a war would make it highly credible that an attacked or invaded state, its very survival on the line, would be prepared to use nuclear weapons in self-defense. However, nuclear deterrence would seem less dependable in cases where states consider or engage in limited war (which may or may not remain limited once they start) or in situations in which one of them has a disproportionately greater interest than the other in regard to the issue that precipitated the crisis at hand and is therefore willing to risk brinkmanship, in the belief the other side will blink first. In other cases, conflict could erupt in which renegade local commanders may have their own agendas, or in which command and control systems for nuclear weapons are less than fully dependable.[79] Moreover, the history of nuclear deterrence has not been as easy or as happy as some nostalgically remember it being. There were near misses during the cold war, with the Berlin and Cuban missile crises. The spread of nuclear capabilities in places such as South Asia and the Middle East increases the odds that the tradition of nonuse may not survive indefinitely.[80]

Then there is the hope that economic interdependence and globalization will make the idea of warfare so irrational and unappealing as to ensure no major conflict among the great economies of the world. There is indeed some basis for this observation. But of course, international investment and trade were strong at the turn of the twentieth century as well, yet did not suffice to prevent the outbreak of World War I. Also, nations historically have proven able to convince themselves that future wars will be short (and victorious), allowing for the creation of narratives about how conflict would not preclude prosperity. To be sure, in today's world of global supply chains, and with the memories of the world wars now informing policymaking, it may be hard to make that case. Yet it is worth remembering that joint economic interests among nations have existed for centuries, even as war has continued.[81] And some economic factors may increase the chances of conflict at times, such as by providing resources with which extremist regimes could undertake aggression or by setting the stage for conflict over valuable contested assets.[82]

Certain elements of modern warfare—the sophistication of some militaries and thus the speed with which they can maneuver and conquer, the availability of standoff weapons and robotics—may encourage countries to again think war can be quick and relatively painless.[83] They have often mistakenly concluded as much as a result of technological advances in the past. In other words, even if, as argued above, the so-called RMA is typically overrated, some leaders may believe the hype enough to think they have found a magic bullet for future warfare—leading them to undertake aggression.

On balance, it is probably true that war has become at least somewhat less likely as a result of the sum total of nuclear deterrence, the spread of democracies, globalization, and other factors, including the destructiveness of modern conventional weaponry.[84] But that provides no grounds for complacency. The overall chances of war could be lower than before and the duration of time between catastrophic wars longer, yet the potential damage from conflict could be so great that war might remain just as much a threat to humankind in the future as it has been in the past. For example, even a small-scale nuclear war in a heavily populated part of the planet could wreak untold havoc and decimate infrastructure that might take years to repair, with huge second-order effects on human well-being for tens of millions of individuals. This is especially true in a densely populated world highly dependent on complex economic interrelationships not only for its prosperity but for the provision of its more immediate human needs, such as food and medicine. Nuclear accidents could themselves be severe, whether caused by war or not. Biological pathogens far more destructive than the generally noncontagious varieties that have been known to date could be invented. And the effects of climate change on a very densely populated globe could have enormous implications for the physical safety and security of tens of millions as well. The case for hope about the future course of the world is fairly strong—but it is a case for hope, not a guarantee.[85]

And that hope for a better future is almost surely more credible with a strong United States. To be sure, there are differences of opinion over how U.S. strategic leadership should be exercised. Some do express concern that specific mistakes in U.S. foreign policy could lead to war.[86] There is also disagreement over whether the concepts of American primacy and exceptionalism are good guides to future U.S. foreign policy.[87] But there is little advocacy of the notion that a multipolar world would be safer than, or inherently preferable to, today's system, or that a different leader besides the United States would do a better job organizing international cooperative behavior among nations, or that anarchy would be preferable to a more structured and organized international system.

Today, the United States leads a coalition or loose alliance system of some sixty states that together account for some 70 percent of world military spending (and a similar fraction of total world GDP). This is extraordinary in the history of nations, especially by comparison with most of European history of the last several centuries, when variable power balances and shifting alliances were the norm. Even in the absence of a single, clear threat, the NATO alliance, major bilateral East Asian alliances, major Middle Eastern and Persian Gulf security partnerships, and the Rio Pact have endured.

To be sure, this Western-led system is under stress and challenge. U.S. debt as a fraction of GDP is quite high relative to levels economists consider healthy (publicly held debt exceeds 70 percent of GDP) and is expected to rise substantially as entitlement spending growth likely accelerates in coming years. Middle-class income levels have stagnated as manufacturing jobs have declined dramatically in recent decades owing to automation and globalization. More recently, sequestration and related budgetary cuts have curbed key investments in infrastructure, research, and education. Many of America's allies in Western Europe as well as Japan are in even worse shape, with declining populations auguring badly for GDP growth in the decades ahead. Meanwhile, a number of emerging economies, China in particular, have advanced in leaps and bounds. Finally, for all the spread of democracy and the death of communism as a meaningful ideological competitor, the very model of the Western state, with its free-market capitalism and individual, secular liberties, may have lost a certain appeal in large swaths of the world.[88]

But it is still worth taking stock of the fact that this Western community of nations exists, and remains impressive, with income levels far superior to those of China or Russia and with far more collective investment in new ideas and new technologies than any other group of nations. It also has survived as a community, if a loose one—even after the disputes over the Iraq War during the George W. Bush administration. The form of leadership provided by the United States, while sometimes contentious and sometimes costly, seems to appeal to U.S. allies and partners around the world. Most seem to believe that America has their back, so to speak, at least on core matters of national security and survival. This is reflected in the facts that most U.S. allies do not pursue their own nuclear weapons programs or engage in arms races or preemptive attacks against potential adversaries. To be sure, there is sometimes a high price to pay for maintaining U.S. credibility, and it is probably not always worth paying in each and every conflict the nation has engaged in. There is a danger too, in that failed signaling about commitments can produce deterrence failure, and then bring in the United States, widening or even globalizing a conflict that might otherwise have stayed local, at least temporarily, as in Korea or Vietnam. (More generally, in history, big wars have often begun as small, localized wars that metastasized.)[89]

But taking a broad perspective, the overall trajectory of the international community since World War II has been highly unusual by historical standards and highly beneficial to the planet. Robust American backstopping of the liberal order, and particularly its security and stability, has produced considerable dividends—even if other factors, such as nuclear deterrence and the spread of democracies, have likely contributed to the general peace among major powers as well. The survival of this community of nations over many years, even after the dissolution of the Soviet threat, suggests a certain widely perceived benefit to the type of international leadership, and protection of the global commons, that the United States provides.[90]

Part of the reason for this community's longevity is surely that it operates in a way that allows individual nations to make their own choices, in real time, about when and how they will employ force in defense of the interests of the broader community of states as a whole. The U.S.-led Western security community is neither a coercive system nor a rigid one. The strategist Joseph Nye writes of the paradox of American power, underscoring that the very success of the United States in leading a large coalition of states arises from the fact that it cannot and generally does not try to do so with a heavy hand.[91] And a global distribution of power aligned in such a unipolar way—with the term "unipolar" referring not to the United States itself but to the broader system of alliance partners—is steadier and probably less conflict-prone than most alternatives.[92] The notion that a "balance of power" helps reduce the chances of war is not borne out by history or by military analysis, partly because it is so hard to construct balances of military power that are truly robust.

None of this prejudges the role that U.S. land power should take in upholding the international order. More specific analyses of various regions of the world and various possible military contingencies are needed for that purpose—a task to which the rest of this book now turns. But I take it as a premise in the chapters to come that U.S. leadership and international engagement are desirable, even as the nation must remain highly selective about how it employs its military power in the upholding of that order and in protecting American interests at home and abroad. To foreshadow the book's conclusions, this is not an argument about whether or how the United States might consider a large military buildup or renew the degree of military activism witnessed in the first dozen years of the new century. Rather, it is about whether the nation should hold the line near current levels—roughly a million-soldier army, of which about half are in the active force and half in the reserve component, as part of an overall U.S. military spending level that will soon decline to 3 percent of GDP—or be cut even further. The latter option, as I attempt to show, would be unwise.

We now turn to a survey of where conflict, or other large-scale disorder or disaster, could plausibly erupt around the world in coming years and decades. With that survey complete, chapters 3 and 4 then sketch out a number of scenarios that might, under certain assumptions, lead to the large-scale use of American ground power—or where a U.S. capacity to deploy such capabilities in extremis might usefully reinforce deterrence. Chapter 5 pulls these pieces together to develop a long-term vision for the future U.S. Army.

CHAPTER TWO

Conflicts Real, Latent, and Imaginable

LET'S LEAVE ASIDE THE United States and its possible role in warfighting for the moment. Where are consequential conflicts, or other large-scale disasters, most plausible in the coming decades around the world—and especially in areas of greatest strategic significance to the international system, and thus to U.S. national security?

Reaching conclusions about future war is, of course, a tricky business. Who would have guessed, in the year 2000, that Afghanistan could soon be the place where 150,000 of the world's best military personnel would be deployed? Or in early 1950 that half a million GIs would soon be fighting in Korea, or in 1960 that another half million American troops would be engaged in combat in Indochina? One must be imaginative in thinking about where war is possible in the future. That is the case even if some such conflicts might, in retrospect, be ones that the United States could have or should have avoided. In fact, ignoring such possibilities in the past did *not* keep the United States out of these conflicts. Ignorance did not produce either bliss or nonintervention.

It is important to underscore at the outset that U.S. ground force operations are not desirable for the good of the country. They drain its coffers, expend its treasure, take the lives of its soldiers, and often polarize its politics. They can cause blowback against American interests as well, if U.S. military operations are seen as illegitimate by even a substantial minority of a given country's or region's population. But this chapter does not prejudge if and when the United States should engage in combat in response to the outbreak of violence elsewhere; such considerations are the subject of later chapters. Here the goal is to survey regional politics in key strategic theaters around the world in an attempt to evaluate the chances that large-scale violence may occur, with or without the United States in the mix.

Some of the cases are fairly obvious, in light of Vladimir Putin's adventures, China's ongoing rise, the Middle East's ongoing volatility, South Asia's combustible mix of huge populations and ongoing territorial disputes, and so forth. In other cases, a bit more imagination is employed.

In the interest of brevity, the approach taken in this chapter and the next is not designed to be comprehensive. Instead, I primarily examine those countries and parts of the world of greatest size, strategic significance, economic potential, and military capability, beginning with the great powers of Russia and China, then working through South Asia and the Middle East before concluding with Africa and Latin America. (See the following tables on world population, GDP, military spending, and ground power distributions, as well as additional tables in appendix D.) The analysis here is generally strategic and political in character, invoking matters of economics and natural resources when appropriate; more detailed background on these latter matters is found in the appendixes to the book.

Table 2-1. Twenty Most Populous Countries, 2012
Population in millions

China	1,350.7	Mexico	120.8
India	1,236.7	Philippines	96.7
United States	313.9	Ethiopia	91.7
Indonesia	246.9	Vietnam	88.8
Brazil	198.6	Egypt	80.7
Pakistan	179.2	Germany	80.4
Nigeria	168.8	Iran	76.4
Bangladesh	154.7	Turkey	74.0
Russia	143.5	Thailand	66.8
Japan	127.6	Congo, Democratic Republic of the	65.7

Source: United Nations, Department of Economic and Social Affairs, "World Population Prospects: The 2012 Revision" (http://esa.un.org/unpd/wpp/Excel-Data/population.htm).

Table 2-2. Twenty Largest Economies Based on GDP, 2014

Billions of current U.S. dollars

United States	16,768.1	Canada	1,839.0
China*	9,469.1	Australia	1,501.9
Japan	4,919.6	Spain	1,393.5
Germany*	3,731.4	Korea	1,304.5
France	2,807.3	Mexico	1,262.3
United Kingdom	2,680.1	Indonesia	912.5
Brazil	2,391.0	Netherlands	853.8
Italy	2,137.6	Turkey*	821.9
Russia*	2,079.1	Saudi Arabia	744.3
India	1,875.2	Switzerland	685.9

Source: International Monetary Fund, "World Economic Outlook Database" (www.imf.org/external/pubs/ft/weo/2013/01/weodata/index.aspx).
*Estimates by the International Monetary Fund.

Table 2-3. Twenty Largest Economies Based on PPP Valuation of Country GDP, 2014

Billions of current international dollars

United States	16,163.2	Italy	2,110.9
China*	14,789.5	Mexico	2,007.7
India	6,252.7	Korea	1,623.8
Japan	4,543.2	Canada	1,477.9
Germany*	3,549.5	Saudi Arabia	1,466.2
Russia*	3,396.2	Spain	1,519.0
Brazil	3,080.6	Turkey*	1,367.0
France	2,490.2	Iran	1,282.9
Indonesia	2,343.8	Australia	1,014.9
United Kingdom	2,374.2	Taiwan	984.0

Source: International Monetary Fund, "World Economic Outlook Database" (www.imf.org/external/pubs/ft/weo/2015/01/weodata/index.aspx).
*Estimates by the International Monetary Fund.
PPP = purchasing power parity

Table 2-4. Twenty Largest Defense Expenditure Countries, 2014

Millions of current U.S. dollars

United States	640,221	Italy	32,657
China	188,460*	Brazil	31,456
Russia	87,836*	Australia	23,963
Saudi Arabia	66,996	Turkey	19,085
France	61,228	Canada	18,460
United Kingdom	57,891	Israel	16,032*
Germany	48,790	Colombia	13,003
Japan	48,604	Spain	12,765
India	47,398	Taiwan	10,530
South Korea	33,937	Algeria	10,402

Source: *SIPRI Yearbook 2014* (www.sipri.org/yearbook/2014/04).
*Estimate.

Table 2-5. Top Ten Active Duty Armies by Country, 2014

Country	Number of personnel
China	1,600,000
India	1,150,900
North Korea	1,020,000
Pakistan	550,000
United States	539,450
South Korea	522,000
Vietnam	412,000
Turkey	402,000
Myanmar	375,000
Iran	350,000

Source: International Institute for Strategic Studies, *The Military Balance 2015* (New York: Routledge Press, 2015).

Table 2-6. Top Twenty Countries with Active Personnel in Armed Forces, 2014

Country	Number of personnel, all forces
China	2,333,000
United States	1,433,000
India	1,346,000
North Korea	1,190,000
Russia	771,000
South Korea	655,000
Pakistan	644,000
Iran	523,000
Turkey	511,000
Vietnam	482,000
Egypt	439,000
Myanmar	406,000
Indonesia	396,000
Thailand	361,000
Brazil	318,000
Colombia	297,000
Taiwan	290,000
Mexico	267,000
Japan	247,000
Sudan	244,000

Source: International Institute for Strategic Studies, *The Military Balance 2015* (New York: Routledge Press, 2015).

RUSSIA AND THE FORMER SOVIET UNION

A survey on the future of land warfare might usefully begin by examining areas in and around the world's largest country, with the longest borders—and the most recent history, among the major powers, of waging interstate war. Indeed, the Russia case should be a reminder of the need to stretch imaginations, because some of the scenarios that now seem all too plausible under Vladimir Putin's Russia might have struck some as purely speculative or even inconceivable just a few years ago. In short, as argued below, it seems necessary to wonder whether Russia might, for many years to come, have aspirations for reclaiming parts of the former Soviet Union populated predominantly by Russian speakers and loyalists, particularly in light of the Kremlin's recent claim to a right to protect ethnic Russians and Russian speakers wherever they may be. That real risk then implies other possible dangers, and the chance of escalation, particularly if the Russian ambitions were someday to extend all the way to NATO members such as the Baltic states.

Vladimir Putin's Russia dominated the international news in 2014 as the Russian strongman invaded and then annexed Crimea, and then stoked trouble in eastern Ukraine. Secretary of State John Kerry aptly described this set of actions as a throwback to the behavior of major powers in the nineteenth century.

But Putin's behavior enjoyed enormous popularity within Russia, with his favorability ratings often in the range of 80 percent—even if those numbers have partly been engineered, and should not be taken entirely at face value. After suppressing dissent and marginalizing many opposition politicians before the election of 2012, he won that race handily. One must wonder whether it was the Russian polity itself, as much as any one man, that was ultimately responsible for the aggression against independent Ukraine. And that leads naturally to the next question: can we really be confident that the twenty-first century will be generally free of the kind of interstate behavior that typified the nineteenth (or eighteenth or twentieth)? In fairness, Putin used a more cunning form of warfare than most leaders in the past, and caused fewer casualties as well—at least in the initial incursion into Crimea, if not in the subsequent conflict in eastern Ukraine. That cunning may have made the action even more popular in Russia. It reflected a certain cleverness in modern military tactics at a time when many Russians had felt humiliated by the West and down on their luck for the previous couple of decades.[1] In other words, it helped restore Russian pride.

These concerns are particularly salient in regard to a large, aggrieved land power like Russia bordering many countries that it formerly controlled and that do not presently have recourse to the protection of an alliance system like NATO. Even leaving aside its own internal Chechnya conflict, with all the brutality associated with that struggle, Russia contributed to violence in Georgia in 2008 and in Ukraine beginning in 2014.[2] What actions, and which victims, may be next? Since Putin has conjured up so many fears and vivid scenarios among his neighbors, the question here may be less theoretical or abstract than it is in regard to other countries in subsequent sections of this chapter and the next. Much of the issue in regard to Russia, therefore, is not which scenarios we can imagine but how much of the broader Russian polity beyond Putin would consider aggression against other neighbors over the longer term. In other words, how durable is the Putin effect, and how deeply rooted in the Russian political mind is the notion of hegemony in central Eurasia?

Focusing on the other former Soviet republics that are not, like the Baltic states, part of NATO today, one might wonder about the fate of a Moldova, Azerbaijan, Kazakhstan, Turkmenistan, or Uzbekistan. There remains as well the possibility of renewed conflict with Georgia and Ukraine—and perhaps even Russian designs on eastern parts of the Baltic states, where Russian speakers are numerous, especially if NATO should be seen to lose its focus or verve in protecting alliance members. At least, it seems fair to ask such questions at this juncture. Putin's behavior, however egregious and brutal in the real world, may have a benefit in the context of this book by jarring us out of any complacency about the supposed permanence of great-power peace in the modern world, forcing us to ask uncomfortable questions about what the future may hold, and spurring thought about where wars that had previously been considered unimaginable may in fact be quite plausible, especially if we lower our collective guard.

None of this discussion is meant to prejudge the question of where, if anywhere, the U.S. Army and Marine Corps may be relevant to conflict scenarios involving Russia. The purpose here is to examine the potential for conflicts in their own right, while withholding judgment about the implications for American military planning until subsequent chapters.

The decade of the 1990s was one of Russian decline. Putin is infamous in the West for calling the dissolution of the Soviet Union the greatest strategic catastrophe of the twentieth century. That is clearly a huge exaggeration by any fair standard. But for Russian nationalists, the 1990s were not only the decade in which the Warsaw Pact fell apart and the Soviet Union dissolved, they were also a period of extreme state weakness. The country's population was cut nearly in half; its military forces declined by two-thirds in size and four-fifths in funding; and the economy went into free-fall, as the transition from communism to capitalism was dominated by corrupt cronies of the ruling elite, who largely plundered the nation for their own selfish ends. The Western world became more concerned about Russian weakness, possible state collapse, and loose nuclear materials than about any new aggression initiated by Moscow. The Chechen war raged off and on as well, and other parts of the former Soviet empire sometimes took up arms too, notably Armenia and Azerbaijan against each other. Given how much of the Russian Federation included minority populations that had been subjugated or assimilated in earlier times, the distinct possibility seemed to exist of centrifugal forces ripping the country apart.[3] And, of course, NATO expanded, not only up to the frontiers of the former Soviet Union but right up to the Russian border, when the Baltic states were incorporated into the Western alliance.

Then came the new century, and Putin. Its early years were characterized by a greater sense of stability at home, as well as hopefulness in relations with the West, especially after the 9/11 attacks and extremist violence on Russian soil seemed to give Washington and Moscow common purpose. George W. Bush famously looked into Putin's eyes and liked what he discerned about the former KGB official's soul. Russian economic recovery was recognized as important, and its energy resources were seen as crucial in an era of Persian Gulf instability.

Russian military recovery in the first instance meant fewer terrible accidents like the tragedy in 2000 aboard the attack submarine *Kursk,* less danger of loose Russian nukes winding up in terrorist hands or of a brain drain of underpaid Russian weapons scientists heading for rogue nations for more remunerative work, and greater stability (however brutally achieved) in Chechnya. The downside of this Russian recovery seemed manageable, especially since Russia was now something of a democracy that limited Putin to two consecutive terms and benefited from a nascent Western-like civil society.

But especially since 2008, this narrative has broken down, culminating in the dual developments of Putin's return to the Russian presidency after a four-year stint as prime minister and now the crisis in Ukraine. Problems began earlier in the decade, of course, with Putin developing a sense of grievance over issues such as the 2002 round of NATO expansion and the 2003 invasion of Iraq. But the Georgia conflict of 2008 may have been the first unambiguous sign of trouble. It was reinforced by a growing suppression of dissent and political debate at home, an ambitious military buildup, and then intense acrimony between Moscow and the West over Libya and Syria policy (see box 2-1 for more about Russia's military). To be sure, the Obama administration's Russia reset policy seemed to achieve certain specific successes in its early years, including greater logistical access to northern entry points into Afghanistan to support the war effort there and cooperation in sanctioning Iran and North Korea, as well as the conclusion of the New START treaty in 2010. But the trend line was never clearly favorable, and the entire momentum of the reset has by now surely been lost, a conclusion few would dispute after the events of early 2014. Nor can the problem be pinned exclusively on Putin. His popularity at home, symbolized by the happily tearful reactions of Russian parliamentarians when he explained the logic behind his actions in Crimea, shows that both the resentments and the aspirations run much deeper within Russia.

Russians are proud of their history and their nation and their state. Such views are not becoming anachronistic; they seem every bit as powerful today in younger generations as in older ones.[4] Russians also tend to think that the state it is still very relevant for ensuring their security. They see a rising China to their east, what they believe to be a highly assertive and sanctimonious America and its allies to their west, and trouble to their south. They also have felt embarrassed and anxious over the decline in their nation's cohesion, power, and standard of living after the cold war. The Russians are not a people who will quickly dismiss the importance of the state. Putin may exemplify this attitude most poignantly. But his popularity, the generally favorable reaction of normal Russians to his assertiveness in Crimea, and the general weakness of civil society and independent media within the country as a whole suggest that it is widespread.[5]

It is difficult to forecast possible future wars involving Russia by reference to specific territorial disputes involving the federation and its neighbors. None of these neighbors appears to be itching for a fight against the great Russian bear, and none of them has particularly obvious salience as the next logical target for Putin or a subsequent leader. Russia is already huge and controls huge resources; it already has ways of reaching various ports and waterways (even more so with Crimea in its grasp, and Black Sea ports therefore under its control).

Therefore, it is probably more helpful to look at broad schools of thought within Russian strategic culture and the Russian national security debate, rather than seek to identify specific flash points for future conflict. Thinking through which of the strategic dispositions might most strongly influence future policy choices in Moscow, under Putin and his successors, could conjure up the most useful visions of where warfare might occur.

It is certainly possible that one paradigm could be a Russia that is not anti-West. Even if it is incredible that a future Russia would ever seek NATO membership, it is not beyond belief that a future Russian state could look to mend fences and develop fundamentally compatible interests with the Western world. Several motivations could drive Russians toward such an outcome. Russia could seek to maximize its interactions with the outside world largely for the sake of economic growth and prosperity. It could also see a strong association with the EU or NATO as a useful hedge against Islamist extremism and China's rise. Put differently, to reach this mental disposition, Russia would not necessarily have to abandon all security fears, real or imagined, but would have to conclude that the greater dangers came from the south or east (or from within) and could be more effectively checked with Western help. Such a conclusion would reflect a decision that may seem obvious to Western observers but is much harder at present for Russians to countenance, in light of the common view that NATO broke its word and took advantage of Russian weakness after the cold war. However, Russians might reach a decision to align with the West partly as a result of the cooling of passions that have been stoked in many minds ever since the cold war ended. NATO expansion, largely a phenomenon of the 1990s and early 2000s, may someday be a more distant memory. If the West in conjunction with Russia can find a solution to ensuring Ukrainian and Georgian security, and that of the other former Soviet republics not currently in the Western alliance, without offering NATO membership to them, it is possible that future generations of Russians will be able to declare a truce in this geostrategic competition (as many Americans probably assumed they already had, prior to the events of 2014).[6]

Box 2-1. Russia's Military Modernization Plan

In late 2008, after a difficult war with Georgia, Russia embarked on military reforms under Defense Minister Anatoliy Serdyukov, building on an earlier phase of reforms the year before. The general improvement in Russia's economy and the desire to reassert national power led to an expansion of available resources to fund the country's armed forces and implement those reforms.

The modernization agenda had several components. A central goal was to create higher-performance, more mobile, and better-equipped units. The military was reduced in size considerably, by about a third, and officer ranks were scaled back as well. As with the U.S. military during this time period, the main unit of ground combat capability was reduced from the division to the brigade, and the remaining brigades were more fully staffed and manned. Most tanks were eliminated or deactivated as well, though some 2,000 remained, out of an initial force ten times that size. Military education was revamped; pay was improved; professionalism was emphasized.[a]

In late 2010, then Prime Minister Vladimir Putin announced a dramatic weapons procurement plan to go along with this earlier set of reforms in personnel, force structure, and readiness. Ambitiously, some $700 billion was projected for weapons modernization over a ten-year time frame. This plan includes a wide range of equipment. For example, in the naval realm it includes Yasen-class nuclear attack submarines, Lada-class and Kilo-class diesel attack submarines, several classes of frigates and corvettes, Borey-class ballistic missile submarines, and two Mistral-class amphibious vessels (from France, in the last case a sale now canceled).[b] Fighter aircraft deliveries have been averaging about two dozen a year and include MiG-29SMT, Su-34, and Su-35S jets.[c]

By 2014, annual military spending levels had reached the range of $70 billion to $80 billion, at least half again as much as the 2008 figure. Projections were for that total to approach $100 billion in the near future.

The essence of this kind of policy would be a return to the calmer days of NATO-Russian relations of the 1990s or the early Putin years, but in the context of a confident and stable Russia. New institutional mechanisms might be created. Or existing vehicles such as the Organization for Security and Cooperation in Europe, the NATO-Russia Council, and the UN Security Council might be deemed adequate (as well as a possible Russian return to the G-7/G-8). Nuclear arms control might resume,

Subsequently, the dramatic drop in oil prices, combined with the imposition of various sanctions on Russia over the Ukraine crisis, reduced these numbers considerably (when denominated in dollars at least, given the rapid decline of the ruble). Thus, Russia may slow down this plan but probably will not terminate it. Indeed, by purchasing power parity metrics, Russian defense expenditures remained above $100 billion in 2014, according to certain estimates, and at a still quite significant 3.4 percent of GDP.[d]

Such large resource increases provided the basis for modernizing most elements of Russian military power. However, the increases are not proportionate across all components of the armed forces. As Russia's 2014 activities in Ukraine suggest, it would appear, for example, that special operators, airborne forces, and cyberunits, among others, may have been preferentially favored, in weapons and training and logistics, among other dimensions of military power.[e] And indeed, there have been some successes already attributable to the military reform and modernization plan.[f]

a. See Jim Nichol, "Russian Military Reform and Defense Policy" (Washington: Congressional Research Service, August 24, 2011); and Rod Thornton, *Military Modernization and the Russian Ground Forces* (Carlisle, Pa.: Strategic Studies Institute, U.S. Army War College, 2011).

b. Christian Le Miere and Jeffrey Mazo, *Arctic Opening: Insecurity and Opportunity* (London: International Institute for Strategic Studies, 2013), p. 84.

c. Tomas Malmlof, Roger Roffey, and Carolina Vendil Pallin, "The Defence Industry," in *Russian Military Capability in a Ten-Year Perspective—2013*, edited by Jakob Hedenskog and Carolina Vendil Pallin (Stockholm: FOI, 2013), pp. 128–29.

d. International Institute for Strategic Studies, *The Military Balance 2015* (London, 2015), pp. 164, 184.

e. Michael R. Gordon, "Russia Displays a New Military Prowess in Ukraine's East," *New York Times*, April 21, 2014; and Anton Lavrov, "Russia Again: The Military Operation for Crimea," in *Brothers Armed: Military Aspects of the Crisis in Ukraine*, edited by Colby Howard and Ruslan Pukhov (Minneapolis, Minn.: East View Press, 2014), pp. 157–84.

f. Bettina Renz, "Russian Military Capabilities after 20 Years of Reform," *Survival* 56, no. 3 (June–July 2014): 61–84.

missile defense negotiations could become less acrimonious, and strategic cooperation on issues such as Iran and North Korea could outweigh disputes over any ongoing problems like Syria. The blocs might cooperate on peacekeeping missions and would presumably strengthen cooperation on counterterrorism as well.

A second possibility, still relatively benign from the standpoint of Russia's neighbors and the West, might be a "minimalist Russia" that seeks to do less in world affairs. While not overmilitarized, it might not be so pro-West either. Indeed, it could result from a somewhat jaundiced Russian view of other states. And yet it might still wind up being fairly benign in the international arena. If Russia concluded that it was not likely to be attacked or otherwise threatened, it could perhaps get by with a modest-sized army and navy and defense budget, coupled with a substantial nuclear arsenal (something that seems a given under any plausible future scenario). This Russian outlook might, for example, result from the simultaneous Russian rejection of both the Western world *and* Vladimir Putin, together with his legacy.

This approach to foreign policy might be based in part on the notion that Russian security was threatened less by interstate conflict or foreign foes and more by internal challenges that required attention and resources. Since the Russian national security strategy for the period to 2020, approved in May 2009, emphasizes the importance of everything from economics to health care to the environment in its list of national security priorities, there is a precedent in modern Russian thought for leavening the importance given to more traditional measures of power and security.[7]

A third possibility is what Cliff Gaddy and I term a "Reaganov Russia."[8] It would be associated with a proud, nationalistic state that in the Russian context might strike many as aggressively motivated and inclined. But if in fact the Russian state could take pride in reestablishing itself as a successful status quo power, it might not see the need for revanchism or other aggression.

The concept builds on some aspects of Ronald Reagan's legacy in the United States. That is not to criticize Reagan's legacy, which was largely positive. But if one reduces Reagan foreign policy to its component parts—a strong military, but a military rarely used, and a confident United States that might have struck some as arrogant but that was led by a generally affable leader—there could be an analogy with a future Russia. Americans might not like that Russia as much as they liked Reagan, and indeed, that future Russian state might or might not measure up favorably against Reagan's America. It might sound rather chauvinistic rhetorically and act that way at times diplomatically. But if it channeled its main national competitiveness and patriotism into relatively benign actions such as improving its armed forces and making progress in economic and scientific realms, the net effect of such a Russia on the region and the world could be tolerable.

This philosophy for the future Russian state might envision the defense sector providing technological innovations that could be spun off to revive the Russian scientific and manufacturing sectors more broadly. The idea is Reaganesque in the American tradition (though spinoffs from the defense world were perhaps even more notable in the United States in the decades just before Reagan). But it is also an idea that has been advanced by Russian defense official Dmitry Rogozin in the modern Russian context.[9] A fourth and less happy possibility is a Russia that feels itself besieged. Perhaps the least needs to be said about this possible future path for Russia because it may be what current events under Putin most evoke. The idea here is that, even if Russia sees the futility of trying to restore previous levels of international grandeur, the wounds to Russian pride are deeper than many have appreciated. Particularly if Vladimir Putin is able to get away with additional adventures in Ukraine, and if Russian economic growth does not suffer unduly as a consequence, Russian leaders may decide there is room to make further mischief in the near abroad for many years to come, and Russian voters may condone their assertiveness.

By this vision, Russia would not relent, even though it could make various tactical adjustments and show restraint when temporarily expedient or necessary. It could at some future time pursue opportunities for expansion or at least reestablishment of a strong sphere of influence in much of Ukraine, Belarus, and Georgia while pursuing potentially hostile policies toward the Baltic states and perhaps Poland and other Central European states. That Vladimir Putin may remain in office a full decade more, and perhaps also shape the selection of his successor, provides further grounds for believing that this model of a future Russia cannot be dismissed.

It is also possible that latter-day notions of a great-power Russia could influence this way of thinking. Harking back to traditions of Russian thought that glorified the country's role as the great Slav nation, the bridge between East and West, and the huge Eurasian land power, this kind of Russia could be inspired by pride as well. It would build on the traditions of earlier Russian leaders such as Peter the Great and Alexander II, and the thinking of intellectuals such as Eduard Limonov and Elgiz Pozdnyakov.

Such a worldview would be not unlike what Gaddy and I describe in our vision of a Reaganov Russia. But it would likely be less benign in this case, as it would be intertwined with a sense of besiegement and perhaps also be inclined toward aggression. Dmitri Trenin describes this outlook

Europe with Parts of Russia, Central Asia, and the Mediterranean Region

Country Abbreviations:
Alb. = Albania
And. = Andorra
Belg. = Belgium
K. = Kosovo
Li. = Liechtenstein
Lux. = Luxembourg
M. = Montenegro
Mac. = Macedonia
Mold. = Moldova
Mon. = Monaco
Neth. = Netherlands
Slov. = Slovenia
S.M. = San Marino
Switz. = Switzerland

as "postimperialist" rather than imperialist or neo-imperialist, still quite assertive in goals even if different from traditional forms of great-power behavior in the means employed. Militarily, its signature behavior might be exemplified by the special operators in unmarked outfits in Crimea in early 2014, in contrast to the classic infantry or tank invasion forces of earlier epochs.[10]

A final and even more concerning possibility, what might be termed a neo-tsarist Russia, takes the idea of a besieged Russia one step further. It postulates a Russian state that seeks not only to gain revenge and restore dominance over near-abroad states but also to maximize national power more generally, and to advance the romantic vision of a Russian state that encompasses and protects all or nearly all Russian speakers throughout Eurasia.[11]

This paradigm could imply even more blatant and aggressive actions against the former Soviet republics in Europe, up to and including complete annexation. It could further include Russian expansionism into the Central Asian republics, where there are some significant ethnic Russian populations, which could provide a Putin-like leader with a pretext for aggression.[12] It could also feature greater use of Russian naval power in the state's exclusive economic zones and beyond, to extract economic benefits through means such as mineral and hydrocarbon exploitation and extensive fishing and dominance of Arctic shipping lanes as they open up as a result of global warming. (Some of these anticipated postures are already evident under Putin, with the September 2013 occupation of the New Siberian Islands in the northern regions above Russia and increased military maneuvers in northern seas.)[13] Finally, such a worldview and the competitive international approach it implies could manifest in further efforts to impede international collaboration on projects of importance to the West, such as nuclear nonproliferation agreements with countries such as Iran and North Korea.

Russia will not be able to restore its previous superpower status under any of the above approaches to national security policy. Its population base and economic strength are too limited, and will remain so even if Russian political leadership makes occasional conquests, as with Crimea. But it can sustain very substantial capabilities. Russia might, for example, spend 3 percent or perhaps an even higher fraction of GDP on the nation's armed forces. That could imply a total of perhaps 5 percent or more of GDP spent on all security capabilities, including internal defense, an area of recent emphasis in light of various internal challenges, among them unrest from growing Muslim populations and exclusionary groups.[14] This level of effort would exceed that of any major Eurasian power and would also exceed projected levels for the United States, as a percentage of national economic output.

Because Russia's economy will remain so much smaller than that of the United States, China, or even Japan or Germany under any realistic extrapolation from today, such a higher level of military spending as a fraction of national economic power would not elevate Russia to superpower status. But Russia would probably be able to retain and indeed solidify its position as the world's number 3 military spender, after the United States and China. And it may be able to create a sense of military momentum over a period in which American and other Western defense spending may continue to decline, a momentum that Russia could seek to translate into favorable strategic outcomes, at least close to home.

Notionally, under this approach, in 2020 U.S. military spending might total around $500 billion to $550 billion. China might tally around $300 billion. Russia's military spending, depending on what happens to its economy in the interim, might range from $100 billion to $150 billion annually, with several major American allies and India ranking next on the list, in the range of $50 billion a year each.

With all of that money, Russia would still be hard-pressed to maintain a military with full capacity to secure all its land borders through conventional military means alone. It would, of course, remain incapable of recreating the kind of military that the Soviet Union once possessed. A million-man force, up modestly from today's, would be a realistic ceiling on the total active duty strength of the armed forces, even with the resources presumed in this scenario.

But Russia could nonetheless aspire to several capabilities that would likely be within its grasp. Its nuclear forces, at least in size and megatonnage, could remain equal to those of the United States. Its navy could be big enough to challenge any neighbor in coastal waters and exclusive economic zones, and in large swaths of the Arctic.[15] Its special forces, of the type seen in Crimea, could remain well trained and well equipped (as they might in the other scenarios too). Its aerospace sectors could be well enough funded that Russian air and space forces would be very well endowed and Russian companies would be competitive in many international arms export markets.

As for the main ground forces, this is the area where the realities of defending a huge and exposed land mass with a military derived from a modest and declining population would cause great trouble for the Russian state. A robust defense capability for Siberia would be out of the question. And to the extent Russia believes that NATO poses an overland threat, maintaining a strong defense in the European parts of the nation would also be challenging when measured against the NATO militaries.

Realistically, however, Russia would have options. It could probably sustain several divisions of strong maneuver forces that could seek to contest and counterattack any hypothetical foreign invasion force that tried to move significantly into Russian territory. Because of the logistical challenges of invasion, even a huge Chinese military would for the foreseeable future have great difficulty sustaining a large fraction of its total armed forces in a distant locale like Siberia. Therefore, while a robust perimeter defense of the country may not be viable, Russia may still be able to build a good enough conventional military capability at least to isolate and counterattack any hypothetical invasion force, particularly from China. Such forces might employ nuclear weapons for certain tactical purposes as well, as Russian doctrine allows. As such, when all the pieces are put together, this more expensive and capable Russian military may hold appeal for future voters and policymakers.

But a Russian military built around such worst-case scenarios and implausible missions would naturally possess the capacity to cause a great deal of trouble against smaller neighbors to its west and south. Indeed, Russia could have viable forces for causing trouble in the neighborhood even at military spending levels well below 3 percent of GDP, given the limited sizes and capabilities of Ukraine, Belarus, Moldova, Georgia, and other nearby countries.

Just where all of this could lead in the future in a plausible worst-case scenario is difficult to discern, of course. If Russia continues its habit of bullying neighbors, and sometimes chipping away at their territories, but confines such behavior to the near abroad and to non-NATO members, the scale of any conflict is likely to remain modest, even if the West and Russia wind up in a mini-cold war in economic terms. If, however, Moscow is tempted to set its sights on Russian-majority areas of the Baltic states or otherwise take action that greatly ups the ante, it is possible to imagine significant and sustained military implications. How this issue might affect the United States is a matter left for subsequent chapters.

Asia

Atlantic Ocean

Barents Sea

EUROPE

RUSSIA

Sea of Okhotsk

Sakhalin (Rus.)

Kuril Islands (Rus.)

Pacific Ocean

JAPAN

Sea of Japan

Manchuria

MONGOLIA

N. KOREA

S. KOREA

East China Sea

Ryukyu Islands (Jap.)

TAIWAN

Northern Mariana Islands (U.S.)

GUAM (U.S.)

Black Sea

Caspian Sea

KAZAKHSTAN

KYRGYZSTAN

Sinkiang

CHINA

Tibet

South China Sea

PHILIPPINES

PALAU

GEORGIA

AZERBAIJAN

ARMENIA

UZBEKISTAN

TAJIKISTAN

TURKEY

TURKMENISTAN

AFGHANISTAN

NEPAL

BHUTAN

VIETNAM

LAOS

BRUNEI

Mediterranean Sea

CYPRUS

LEBANON

ISRAEL

SYRIA

IRAQ

JORDAN

KUWAIT

IRAN

BAHRAIN

QATAR

U.A.E.

OMAN

PAKISTAN

INDIA

BANGLADESH

(MYANMAR)

BURMA

THAILAND

CAMBODIA

MALAYSIA

SINGAPORE

MALAYSIA

Borneo

INDONESIA

Celebes

New Guinea

PAPUA NEW GUINEA

SAUDI ARABIA

YEMEN

Arabian Sea

Andaman & Nicobar Is. (India)

Bay of Bengal

SRI LANKA

Sumatra

AFRICA

MALDIVES

Indian Ocean

0   500   1000   1500 miles

CHINA AND ITS NEIGHBORS

What is the potential for large-scale violence on land in eastern Asia in the early decades of the twenty-first century? Naturally, most scenarios center on China, but there are other important states in the region to consider as well.

It is not all about possible war. The sheer population densities of China's coastal regions make the nation vulnerable to complex natural disasters—earthquakes or typhoons, for example—perhaps leading to nuclear power plant disasters or other breakdowns in infrastructure as a consequence. China would naturally attempt to handle the repercussions of any such disaster on its own, but the international community could be called on for help if the scale of the catastrophe exceeded the People's Republic of China (PRC)'s capacities. Other populous states in the region, such as Indonesia, could be prone to such problems and potentially even less able to handle them independently.

As for the possibility of civil war, the odds within China itself seem very remote. There have been recent increases in the size and frequency of demonstrations against the government, along with rising expectations among the population and natural limits to the economic growth model that the country has adopted in recent decades. Still, the concern seems primarily theoretical. It is also difficult to discern along which regional or ethnic lines a Chinese civil war might be fought. The omnipresence of the Chinese Communist Party (CCP) in all aspects of life for the last sixty-five years makes it hard to see where and how the country could fissure. Moreover, the general pragmatism of the CCP makes it relatively hard to imagine another ideologically based civil war.

Civil warfare may be somewhat more plausible in the Philippines, with the Moro Islamic Front on the island of Mindanao, or in Indonesia in a region like Aceh.[16] Owing to the sheer size of these giant archipelago nations and the relative dearth of infrastructure and connectedness to the main islands of Luzon in the Philippines or Java in Indonesia, future civil unrest is entirely possible (though probably unlikely to resemble cold war–era communist threats).[17] Yet at present it is hard to foresee that the likely scale of the unrest would be massive, insofar as the nations' various separatist groups are largely isolated internally and are relatively weak both militarily and politically. Moreover, ethnic and religious minorities do not constitute large fractions of the population in either place (for example, just over 1 percent of Indonesians are ethnically Chinese and less than 4 percent are Malay; just 5 percent of Filipinos are Muslim).[18] Civil war seems more likely to arise out of state weakness and a descent into anarchy than out of a pitched, large-scale movement that might draw in broader international forces and actors to aid their ethnic or religious kin. The most likely exception to this broad generalization about the region is probably the Korean Peninsula, a subject to which I return below.

At present, the chances for major interstate land wars involving China seem reasonably remote. In contrast to its approach at sea, the PRC has resolved many earlier border disputes with its neighbors and has tightened cooperation with a number, perhaps most notably Russia, in recent times. Indeed, many Chinese argue that, despite the sparks flying of late in maritime regions, China's foreign policy is inherently peaceful and likely to remain that way. They assert that China has a distinctive strategic culture, much different from that of the European imperial powers in particular, derived from Confucian precepts. It largely preaches harmony and the peaceful, cooperative resolution of disputes. Where some form of contention cannot be avoided, it tends toward favoring Sun Tzu's admonition to "win without fight or force."[19]

The standard Chinese portrayal of the Ming-era national hero, Admiral Zheng He, fits with this image. His voyages at the height of Chinese power in the fifteenth century are cited as proof that China does not seek territorial conquest or forcible subjugation. At the official commemoration of the 600th anniversary of Zheng He's travel, a senior Chinese official stated, "During the overall course of six voyages to the western Ocean, Zheng He did not occupy a single piece of land, establish any fortress or seize any wealth from other countries."[20] Other Chinese officials have made similar arguments, grounded in their interpretation of Chinese history and Confucian culture.[21]

In recent times, China has adopted a policy of "peaceful rise" since the Deng Xiaoping era. It has generally sought peace with neighbors and has not used ground force against any other country since 1979. As articulated in the 2013 Defense White Paper:

> It is China's unshakable national commitment and strategic choice to take the road of peaceful development. China unswervingly pursues an independent foreign policy of peace and a national defense policy that is defensive in nature. China opposes any form of

hegemonism or power politics, and does not interfere in the internal affairs of other countries. China will never seek hegemony or behave in a hegemonic manner, nor will it engage in military expansion. China advocates a new security concept featuring mutual trust, mutual benefit, equality and coordination, and pursues comprehensive security, common security and cooperative security.[22]

Under President Hu, advocates of a more assertive China were countered as a matter of state policy.[23] Although some have suggested that the early ideas advanced during the tenure of President Xi Jinping, such as the "China Dream" and "China Revival," point to a more assertive nation, most Chinese officials continue to stress continuity with the core concept of peaceful development.[24] They see it as serving China's fundamental economic and other strategic interests and believe it should be sustained.[25]

But other Chinese voices are becoming more assertive, and with China's ongoing rise, their number as well as their influence could grow.[26] They suggest that the weakening of U.S. economic power following the 2008 financial crisis and the ongoing budget challenges in the United States have led Chinese strategists to conclude that power relations have tilted decisively in China's favor, justifying a new, more assertive approach. They point to what they perceive as increased Chinese assertiveness across a range of foreign policy issues and explicit calls by retired senior People's Liberation Army officials to challenge U.S. hegemony.[27]

Forming the backdrop to current debates about policy is China's view of its own recent past, and specifically its experience in the century preceding the Communist Revolution of 1949, the so-called "century of humiliation." This era began with the European incursions starting around 1839 and culminated in the Japanese invasion and occupation, followed by the expulsion of Chiang Kai-shek's Kuomintang from the mainland by the Red Army and the CCP and the establishment of the PRC in 1949. This sense of vulnerability has deeper roots in Chinese history, for example during the periods when China was subject to invasion by the Mongols. There is disagreement over what it means to "reverse the losses" of these periods, but also little doubt or disagreement that avoiding any such future period of vulnerability is essential to the well-being of the Chinese people and Chinese state.

There is also a perceived imperative to restore lands purportedly taken from China during its period of weakness. In the sixty-plus years since the establishment of the PRC, many of the instances of Chinese use of force have been connected with territorial claims, ranging from actions in India in 1962 and the Soviet Union in 1969 to the episodic use of force in the Taiwan Strait from the 1950s to the missile firings of 1995–96. These areas are routinely identified as "core interests"—consistent with the leadership's oft repeated definition of China's core interest as "sovereignty, unification and territorial integrity."[28] But there are important ambiguities about the scope of this core interest concept, as with the dispute over the Senkaku/Diaoyu Islands.[29] For most of the decades since 1949, the territorial imperative has focused on Hong Kong, Tibet, and Taiwan.[30] Now a crucial additional question is whether the claims could be extended further, to states formerly seen as part of the broader Chinese sphere of influence in distant historical times, or to states and regions located at key strategic junctures where China now has established crucial economic interests on which it depends for its prosperity.

With respect to the South China Sea, China seized the Paracel Islands from Vietnam in 1974 and the Spratly Islands in 1988, as well as Mischief Reef (also claimed by the Philippines) in 1995.[31] In justifying these actions and its broader claims, China has relied on a historical narrative buttressed by a reference to positions taken by Nationalist China prior to the revolution.[32] Although the official territorial claim of the Chinese government appears to be limited to the islands themselves and the immediately surrounding waters, some Chinese have suggested the sovereignty claim extends to all seas within the "9 dash line," which covers most of the South China Sea. China's claim to the Diaoyu Islands is rooted in the assertion that the Ryukyu empire, of which the islands were a part, was a tributary state that Japan illegally sought to annex in 1895, and that the islands were implicitly promised to China as part of the post–World War II settlement at Yalta and Tehran.[33] Some independent Chinese scholars writing in state-run papers have even raised the idea that Okinawa should be viewed as Chinese territory, although this position has been rejected in official statements.[34]

In the first instance, such claims involve maritime interests rather than possible motivations for ground combat. But one can imagine a multistep process in which assertion of maritime claims could lead, possibly, to occupation of not only the small islands of the South China Sea but even some elements of, say, the Philippine archipelago, as a means of dominating and coercing Manila into more acquiescent behavior in the South

China Sea itself. As such, it is difficult to overlook these maritime issues entirely, even in a discussion about land power and land warfare.

From the Qing era on, China had other territorial holdings on the Eurasian mainland of even more direct relevance to the subject at hand. They included what is now Mongolia and part of Russian Manchuria, and were lost to Russia over the period of roughly 1860 to 1920. No Chinese leaders have suggested so far that reclaiming these lands could be a legitimate objective of the state's foreign policy.[35] China's recent history of resolving border disputes with Russia, Kazakhstan, and Vietnam suggests that China values amicable relations with its neighbors over achieving maximalist territorial gains, at least for now.[36] That said, there is some underlying tension in the Russia-China relationship, partly owing to latent worries in Russia that China could be a rival or even a threat. Some Russian officials and scholars have occasionally sounded the clarion call about the potential Chinese threat to Siberia.[37]

Turning back to Southeast Asia, some would argue that recent quarrels between China and Vietnam in maritime domains, however undesirable, should not be confused with any Chinese ambitions or irredentism along Vietnam's land borders. Yet China's long history of invasions of Vietnam—mostly centuries ago, but also in 1979—raises the question of whether things could change.[38] And Beijing has shown the capacity to move ten or more divisions quickly about its own territory during various crises in the past, underscoring the potential to pose significant threats to its land neighbors should it so choose.[39] Were a maritime dispute to escalate, ground combat could not be dismissed as a possibility.

Similarly, China's border with Korea would seem stable at first blush. Yet historically, China has had claims to part of the peninsula, specifically the ancient kingdom of Koguryo, and has viewed Korea as a so-called tributary state. In addition, China likely values the buffer provided by North Korea's existence, meaning that it might not welcome the disappearance of that state in any future change of strategic circumstances on the peninsula.[40] And, of course, the presumed presence of nuclear weapons in North Korea—with apparent ongoing efforts by the regime not only to retain but to expand its arsenal—adds an additional degree of combustibility to the mix, and a degree of risk to the security of the American allies South Korea and Japan as well.[41] As the Georgetown University scholar Victor Cha has argued, moreover, the fact that North Korea is effectively destitute, with few prospects of achieving economic progress or greater political legitimacy and influence, does not guarantee peace, because desperate countries can sometimes become reckless.[42] In the event of another war or major civil disturbance or the collapse of the Pyongyang government on the peninsula, Washington and Seoul would likely pursue reunification of the peninsula that could prove unwelcome in Beijing.[43] While it is surely true that Beijing has a complex relationship with Pyongyang, and very mixed feelings about the North Korean regime, its strategic interests on the peninsula may not lead it naturally to cooperate with Seoul and Washington in a crisis or conflict.

The border dispute with India remains an inflammatory issue within a challenging relationship that China continues to face with one of its most consequential neighbors.[44] China still occupies a part of Indian-claimed Kashmir that it considers important for maintaining control in Tibet.[45] It may have further aspirations about an Indian province further east, Arunachal Pradesh, which it calls South Tibet and considers to have been taken from China a century ago by the British.[46] Were Chinese forces ever to move into that region, the entire eastern zone of India, separated from the main territory of the country by the narrow corridor created by Bangladesh's land mass, would in principle become vulnerable. In response to greater Chinese activity there, the Indian military over the last few years has beefed up ground and air forces and improved road networks in the vicinity.[47] Relations remain tense in the area.[48] On balance, the two sides seem to want to limit the salience of this dispute in their overall relationship, at least for the moment, but it is difficult to know whether the issue might flame up more intensely in the future.[49]

The potential for disputes extends, in theory at least, even further. As China's economy has become increasingly dependent on global trade and access to natural resources, economic issues have come to play a more important role in China's national security debate. Specifically, China's leaders and strategists have increasingly begun to focus on the need to ensure, through military means if necessary, Chinese unimpeded access to vital sea lanes and maritime resources.[50] Some Chinese thinkers have also turned more attention to the need to reduce China's vulnerability to coercion by the United States by virtue of America's current domination of the open seas.[51] This could have implications for Chinese military policy in South Asia and even in areas further west.

In sum, East Asia has the potential for natural disaster and also for civil war, but the greatest concerns have to do with China and its future. The immediate risks for land combat seem rather low, on balance—unless, that is, conflict erupts in Korea, in which case all bets are off about China's possible ensuing role. The longer-term prospects for stability on land in East Asia hinge largely on whether China's relative restraint vis-à-vis land border issues continues or whether the country instead becomes more assertive in these domains, just as it has of late at sea.

INDIA, PAKISTAN, AND SOUTH ASIA

Historically one of the world's great powers, and the jewel in the crown of the British colonial empire in the first half of the twentieth century, India has also been home to nearly half the world's poor for decades and has struggled during most of its independent history since 1947 to establish any kind of significant economic momentum. As the twentieth century wound down, India ranked 128th in the world on the UN's Human Development Index and roughly 160th in per capita income (depending on the exact means of measure), out of fewer than 200 countries in the world. These figures have improved, but only modestly, since then. Yet India has been a fairly peaceful country for several decades, especially in regard to its foreign policy.

Pakistan is, of course, a much different story, with a great deal of internal violence, extremist movements, a history of conflict, what may be the world's fastest-growing nuclear arsenal, and a poor economic track record in recent times. And unfortunately, the Indo-Pakistani relationship remains fraught.

Bangladesh may not present quite the same witches' brew of weapons of mass destruction, extremism, overpopulation, and economic malaise. But it does share the latter two challenges with Pakistan, and perhaps even greater problems than are faced by Islamabad owing to the ever-present threat of natural disaster.

On balance, it is hard to escape the conclusion that South Asia contains major potential for large-scale operations by ground forces, whether in the context of interstate conflict, severe internal violence, or complex humanitarian catastrophe in which the effects of natural disasters are compounded by weak governance and political instability.

To flesh out some of the possibilities more clearly, first consider India. It experienced wars with Pakistan at independence, in 1947, and again in 1965 and 1971. It also faced a major crisis in 1999 over the disputed Kashmir territory (which joined India at independence based on the actions of its Hindu leader, even though it had a Muslim majority), and then endured terrorist attacks by groups with links to Pakistan in 2001–02 and 2008.

Over the course of this period, India gradually built up a nuclear capability, carrying out a "peaceful nuclear explosion" in 1974 and then conducting five more undisguised nuclear tests in May 1998 (which were followed later that same month by Pakistan's six nuclear tests).

India's major military cooperation throughout the cold war was with the Soviet Union. The indigenous defense industry was for the most part underdeveloped. Bureaucratic parochialism, interservice rivalry, and a stultifying form of state capitalism led to what Stephen Cohen and Sunil Dasgupta have called India's "arming without aiming"—that is, a rather vague, unfocused, and diffuse approach to military modernization and strategic planning. This mode was arguably not all bad, as it reflected and also reinforced a general Indian disinterest in foreign wars of aggression or conquest and the relatively modest burden placed by military spending on the overall economy (ranging typically from 3 to 4.5 percent over the previous several decades, closer to 2 percent today). But it also resulted from a multilayered dysfunctionality within the Indian defense community that left it unable to make big decisions or to push the envelope on technology development or force planning.[52]

Whatever dysfunctionalities may have existed in India have been magnified greatly in the case of Pakistan. Arguably, the nation's very existence is predicated on the notion of conflict, as its founder, Muhammad Ali Jinnah, defined the rationale for the Pakistani state largely as a homeland for Muslims—and as a counterweight to India. There was little other central purpose behind the Partition of the Raj. To many Indians, this was the equivalent of original sin, an irrevocable act with tragic consequences far into the future, creating turmoil and antipathy among peoples where none had been necessary, in light of the long-standing mixing of populations on the subcontinent.[53]

Pakistan's persistent focus on Kashmir, an area of limited strategic value, is telling in this regard. As the analyst Arvin Bahl writes,

The ideology that Pakistan was founded on, the two-nation theory, makes ending Indian rule over the Kashmir Valley of utmost national interest. For Pakistan to concede that a Muslim-majority region that is contiguous with it can be a part of India would be for Pakistan to accept that there was no need for the partition of the subcontinent along religious lines and the creation of Pakistan in the first place.[54]

Pakistan has used terrorist groups to further its agenda, aiding and abetting their attacks on India and Indian interests, over the years.[55] Some of these groups may act more autonomously in the future.[56] Pakistan's approaches to this and other disputes with neighbors, including with Afghanistan, are amplified and exacerbated by elements of its national institutions, including the madrassa schools, which often inculcate extremist ideologies and methods in the minds of younger generations.[57]

What does this diagnosis imply about Pakistan and India and their future potential for conflict? At this point, it is hard to believe India would ever wish to rule Pakistan's territory again in a reunified state. Antipathies are too deep and Pakistan's problems vis-à-vis India are too severe at this point in history. It may not always have been so, when the Pakistani territory boasted a stronger economy and a better-educated population base. (Indeed, its economic growth rate averaged 6 percent annually for decades after independence.)[58] But things have changed. Pakistan's scores on human development indices, while improved somewhat, have lagged behind improvements in India's; the typical child in Pakistan now receives three years less education than the average Indian child, and Pakistan's economic production per capita is currently 20 percent less than India's.[59]

So the greater worry is that Pakistan or its surrogates would start a conflict. A solution to the Kashmir issue appears far off at best, meaning that elements in Pakistan will continue to have a specific motivation for engaging in conflict.[60] The Pakistani state has been complicit in aiding groups like Lashkar-e-Taiba, the terrorist organization that carried out the 2008 Mumbai attacks, as well as other extremist organizations. Whether that policy is beginning to change now is unclear.[61]

Delhi's reaction was remarkably restrained in the immediate aftermath of the Mumbai attacks. But as a result of the tragedy, the Indian military gave inklings of formulating a "Cold Start" doctrine, along with associated changes to military organization and weaponry and posture, that would allow it to carry out a quick, punitive response, on up to eight axes, to any similar future Pakistani transgression. Plausible targets might include terrorist training bases and other facilities in Kashmir, or perhaps even in and around Lahore.[62] It is not clear just how codified the Cold Start doctrine has become in Indian military strategy and planning. But any such thinking could be dangerous, since if were actually implemented, it might raise the fear of all-out war in Islamabad, and thus increase the dangers of escalation.[63] For that reason and others, the Cold Start concept has not been totally embraced even within India's government or armed forces.[64] At the same time, there is widespread awareness in South Asia that related ideas may in fact be influencing Indian strategic thought. And if Pakistan began to fear that Indian forces were thinking of marching on Islamabad, Pakistan might consider threatening the limited, localized employment of nuclear weapons.[65] Once the nuclear threshold was crossed, it is far from clear that further escalation could be avoided, whether because India would then find it necessary to avoid appearing weak, and would use nuclear weapons in reply itself, or because doctrinal, organizational, or technical mistakes would produce escalation inadvertently.[66]

Of course, the implications of a general nuclear war in South Asia could be extraordinarily bad. Beyond the direct casualties, which could reach into the low tens of millions at least, one study has estimated the potential for massive famine affecting many hundreds of millions of people (not to mention the general breakdown in state services, infrastructure, and health care that would surely ensue).[67]

In 2013 and 2014, governments changed in both Pakistan and India. There are reasons for hopefulness in these recent political transitions. The return to power in Islamabad of Prime Minister Nawaz Sharif in 2013 may or may not lead to any meaningful improvement in Indian-Pakistani relations. For one thing, Sharif's own desires are only part of the equation; the Pakistani military has a good deal to say about this matter. But Sharif did attend Indian prime minister Narendra Modi's 2014 inauguration. The jury is out, and skeptical, as to whether Sharif can make meaningful headway in reforming his own country's economy or Pakistan's role in the Afghan civil war. Among other things, the country continues to struggle mightily with its own Taliban threat and with huge challenges in terms of energy, infrastructure, and other economic requirements.

Yet as one looks out further into the future, one must contemplate the possibility not only of improved and more moderate governments in the region but of worse ones as well. Pakistan ranks tenth on the Fund for Peace's list of fragile states, a dangerously high position for such a large country possessing nuclear weapons as well as numerous extremist groups on its territory.[68] Bruce Riedel has written of the possibility of a coup by an Islamist military officer in Pakistan. Such a development could usher in greater state support for terrorist groups like Lashkar-e-Taiba, with their apocalyptic visions of provoking an Indo-Pakistani war (perhaps as a means of dismembering India and improving the odds for the formation of a caliphate). Such state-sponsored terrorism could also increase the odds of further attacks against the United States like the Times Square bombing of 2010, conducted by the Pakistani Taliban or some other group, and raise the possibility of a direct American military response against the regions in Pakistan where such groups might be based.[69]

Even short of such dramatic developments, other serious problems could emerge. One category centers on water sources. With the region increasingly densely populated, and with climate change affecting the Himalayan glaciers, the potential for problems between India and Pakistan or India and China or India and Bangladesh clearly exists. To date, the countries have generally been remarkably professional and responsible in keeping water management matters separate from broader political disputes. But there remain frictions, and not only over general matters, such as the Kashmiri origin of most major South Asian rivers, but also in regard to more specific issues, such as China's provisional plan to dam the Tsangpo River in Tibet and change water flows in ways that could affect India.[70]

What of other relationships and other countries on the subcontinent? India has had complex relations with a number of its smaller neighbors too, beyond China and Pakistan. Most of the relationships have been reasonably stable of late, but there have been significant tensions at times. Nepal sometimes resents India's size and ability to dominate the mountainous, landlocked country. Sri Lankan Tamil separatists have sometimes been funded by Tamil communities within India—but some of their more extreme members have also turned their guns and suicide bombs against Indian peacekeepers and politicians at various points in the Sri Lankan civil war (in which the largely Hindu Tamil fought the largely Buddhist Sinhalese). India has also had insurgencies throughout its history, leading to losses that have generally ranged into the low thousands per year—though, with the exception of the Kashmir challenge, India has generally viewed these uprisings on a scale appropriate for its police forces rather than its army.[71]

Bangladesh, though protected by India at the time of secession from Pakistan in 1971, has complex relations with Delhi now. It has also improved relations with China in a way that could potentially implicate it in struggles between South and East Asia's two great powers. Desire for access to ports in Bangladesh by Beijing, or a fear of lost access to eastern India by Delhi, could conceivably result.[72]

Bangladesh certainly does not present the severity of challenges from Islamist extremist organizations witnessed in Pakistan, but it has not been spared all such problems either. Its most severe threats along such lines were countered fairly effectively by Bangladeshi security forces in the early years of the twenty-first century. Yet the extremist groups have sought to rebuild in recent years.[73] Some extremist groups in Bangladesh have links to parallel organizations in Pakistan, such as Harkat-ul-Jihad-al-Islami (or HuJI).[74]

In addition, because of Bangladesh's dense populations, low altitude, and uncertain weather, it is easy to imagine future large-scale refugee flows.[75] By contrast, political problems involving Bangladesh's indigenous tribes, largely in the Chittagong Hill Tracts of the country's southeast near Burma, do not seem likely to be on a scale to cause major consequences for Bangladesh itself or the region (though there were periods when 30,000 Bangladeshi troops helped police the region of some 3 million).[76] But the scale of movement abroad has been considerable, with up to 20 million illegal immigrants from Bangladesh in neighboring Indian provinces as of several years ago.[77]

Many countries in the South Asia region are progressing economically. The subcontinent's superpower has been a relatively peaceful local hegemon over the years. With the exception of conflicts in Afghanistan, there has not been a large-scale war in decades. But the sheer confluence of dangerous elements—including huge and densely packed populations dependent on shaky infrastructure in regions prone to natural disasters, and enduring political grievances within and between states that possess weapons of mass destruction and are home to takfiri/extremist groups bent on overthrowing regimes or causing interstate conflict—makes the region fraught as well.

THE MIDDLE EAST

Many parts of the world face the possibility of irredentism or simple revenge by countries seeking redress for perceived historical slights, or interstate conflicts over disputed resources and territories, or nations trying to protect their dispersed citizens in other countries against threats real or imagined, or civil war.

The Middle East has all these challenges itself, to be sure. But it also faces a basic challenge to the existing state system from Salafist/jihadist extremism and other causes.[78] The post-Ottoman order that arose after World War I is now experiencing severe duress. Sunni-Shia conflicts are intense in numerous places.[79] On top of that, more than in any other part of the world at present, major states have recently experienced or are currently facing large-scale revolution from within. And none of this has even yet involved the shoe that could still fall, and with resounding implications if it did: potential instability of the House of Saud in Saudi Arabia.

In surveying the region's carnage, and its momentous changes now under way, one has to ask which of these will be transformative and which, while still important, may be less tectonic in lasting effect. The world has experienced periods of intense turmoil before, only to realize in retrospect that the crises of the day were perhaps less cataclysmic and less unusual than contemporaries tended to believe. The scholar Yahya Sadowski persuasively argued this point about the 1990s, now often seen as a halcyon period in world history but at the time regarded as a time of unleashed hatreds and rampant violence in many parts of the world.[80]

The debate over what went wrong in the U.S.-led invasion of Iraq in 2003 illustrates the broader analytical conundrum. A considerable body of literature argues, with impressive documentation, that much of the mayhem that ensued after the overthrow of Saddam Hussein was caused by American mistakes that were foreseeable and preventable. This line of reasoning, with which I am in considerable sympathy, holds that the mission's huge problems were largely the result of a lack of proper planning for stabilizing the country through the use of proper constabulary and counterinsurgency techniques after the initial invasion and through rebuilding security institutions quickly, giving former Baathists a path to forgiveness and a sure role in the new Iraq, and creating a sound political system that would be representative of all major sectarian groups.[81] But other analyses underscore the enormous challenges inherent in trying

Middle East and Northern Africa

to rebuild a weak society broken by decades of misrule and afflicted by overwhelming sectarian tension. Even had the United States made most of its decisions wisely and carefully, it is difficult to believe the project would have been particularly straightforward or easy.[82]

Some very learned scholars wind up effectively being on both sides of this debate. For example, the Iraqi exile Kanan Makiya, in his powerful 1989 book, *Republic of Fear: The Politics of Modern Iraq,* wrote of a badly broken and dysfunctional society after years of Baathist rule and Saddam's cruelties.[83] But Makiya was himself one of the most hopeful that, on Saddam's overthrow, the Iraqi citizenry would be so relieved, joyous, and unburdened that they would "greet the troops with sweets and flowers," as Makiya famously told top members of the Bush administration shortly before the 2003 invasion.[84]

The tension in these two views resonates powerfully when one tries to predict the region's future. If prudent and competent decisions by a well-intentioned political leader can set a state on the path to success, all the region arguably needs is a few more leaders of the quality of, say, Ataturk or the King of Jordan or the new leadership in Tunisia—and a few less mistakes from Washington.[85] Admittedly, finding such leaders is no mean task, but it is more tractable, perhaps, than a wholesale transformation of the respective societies. Perhaps Humpty Dumpty can be put back together again; perhaps some of the main drivers of political Islam can move in more moderate directions; perhaps Sunni and Shia can remember how to live together, as they have so often in so many places in the past. Perhaps most insurgents and others causing trouble in these lands are "accidental" guerrillas, in the soldier and scholar David Kilcullen's memorable phrase, willing to revert to a more peaceful life once they sense there are reasonable opportunities available to them.[86] Possibly the positive forces of democratization that have finally begun to take root in Central Europe and Latin America in recent decades can influence the Middle East as well.[87]

Yet if the forces of Salafist extremism, sectarianism, autocracy, and anti-Westernism have now become so strong that they will inevitably create ripple effects for decades to come, hope may be more elusive. In that case, the best we can attain in the near future might be to keep a lid on things and try to prevent threats from getting substantially worse.[88] A number of astute observers, from within the region and outside, underscore the magnitude of the challenge in their various prescriptions for what it will take to fix the Middle East and prevent another round of major tumult. Some have argued that peace between Israelis and Palestinians is central to everything else in the region, suggesting that if such a peace can be achieved, the region will do much better. But that seems a nearly hopeless proposition at present.[89] The Brookings scholar Kenneth Pollack and others see a deeper problem, and suggest that a much broader agenda for political reform will be needed in the region.[90] But the Arab Spring and its aftermath may make many established regimes less, rather than more, willing to countenance opening up, perhaps simply delaying the day when more revolutions will erupt. Centrist voices may have a hard time being heard in the years ahead, and reform efforts may be widely resisted.[91]

And the magnitude of what could still go wrong is hard to exaggerate. For example, a worsening Sunni-Shia regional conflagration could produce a lasting division of Iraq and Syria, with one outcome possibly being an impoverished Sunni Arab zone run by extremists. A negotiated approach to federalism in either or both countries might be perfectly acceptable, but an unmanaged de facto partition that left boundaries and resources in dispute and minority rights in a shambles throughout the region would not be. It would almost surely exacerbate bitterness and extremism, and thereby plant the seeds of future conflict.

Bahrain, with its significant hydrocarbon resources and as the base for the U.S. Fifth Fleet headquarters, might wind up in revolution. Eastern Saudi Arabia, home to most of the kingdom's Shia and possessing much of its oil resources, might be contested, with the hidden hand of Iran playing a more aggressive role. The Persian Gulf itself, with its extensive oil resources and crucial waterways, might be subject to violence, including, in the worst case, prolonged conflict of one type or another pitting Iran against members of the Gulf Cooperation Council. While our main focus here is on land conflict, the Persian Gulf and the Strait of Hormuz are so close to key land areas that any prolonged tension at sea could lead major state actors to try to control crucial littoral zones affording access to the Gulf.

The Iranian acquisition of a nuclear weapons capability somewhere along the way, superimposed on all the above, could quite possibly result in the active pursuit of a nuclear weapons capability by Saudi Arabia or the United Arab Emirates. The path to proliferation would itself be hazardous enough, but once one or more regional countries had the bomb, the stakes in any possible war that might be unleashed would be even higher. Containing a nuclear Iran would not be a hopeless enterprise for the United States and its partners, but it would make life harder and more dangerous.[92]

There is also the possibility of another spectacular attack by al Qaeda or its affiliates, which remain committed to the overthrow of many countries in the broader region to permit the formation of a fundamentalist caliphate.[93] Such attacks could occur within the region or beyond. Important al Qaeda affiliates or kindred spirit organizations exist from Nigeria, Mali, and Libya to Somalia and Yemen, to Syria and Iraq, to Central and South Asia.[94] Egypt too could be affected.[95]

Al Qaeda and its affiliates could strike again in numerous ways. Crucial ports or oil fields in the broader region might be successfully targeted, for example. Several airliners might be brought down in a way that eludes clear diagnosis and response and thereby discourages normal commerce in the region for months or years thereafter. Key political leaders might be assassinated, with ensuing instability in a place like Jordan or Saudi Arabia. The foreign fighters now cultivating their networks, radical worldviews, and fighting tactics in Syria—perhaps approaching 20,000 individuals from ninety foreign countries, including the United States and other Western nations—could return home to attempt such attacks.[96]

From the vantage point of 2015, none of the above scenarios seems particularly far-fetched. Sketching out what could go wrong in the Middle East need not involve a great deal of imagination at this stage. Of greater intellectual difficulty is thinking through how plausible future scenarios could potentially implicate American armed forces, a subject addressed in the following chapters.

SUB-SAHARAN AFRICA AND ITS PIVOTAL STATES

Africa as a whole is showing promise. Indeed, it is showing more promise than at any time since the independence movements swept the continent in the late 1950s and early 1960s, only to be followed by a prolonged period of autocratic rulers, frequent coups, civil wars, cold war proxy conflicts, and economic mismanagement.[97] All that has begun to change. In economic terms, nearly half the continent's economies have found their way to sound policies featuring modest budget deficits, reduced trade barriers, and less bureaucratic resistance to the creation and functioning of business. Promising growth rates have ensued in that group of some twenty countries. In political terms, there are also now some twenty democracies. The continent is less mired in largely fruitless north-south debates about colonialism and neocolonialism and is taking more responsibility for its own well-being, as reflected in, for example, the growth of African military participation in UN as well as African Union peacekeeping operations. In military terms, despite the increased threat of extremism and terrorism in places such as Nigeria, the continent as a whole is now substantially less violent than it was in all other postindependence decades. Promising signs are evident from Ethiopia, and even Somalia, in the Horn of Africa, to the western part of the continent, including Ivory Coast, Ghana, Sierra Leone, and Liberia (despite the Ebola outbreak), to Angola and Mozambique. Even the Democratic Republic of the Congo (DRC) is showing some glimmers of relative progress.

Yet all of this progress is fragile. It is highly uneven across the continent. And it is juxtaposed with a growing terrorist threat that is exacerbating Christian-Muslim relations in much of sub-Saharan Africa's northern tier of states as well.

As with other regions, it is logical to begin with the large states. The analysis below focuses largely on two countries, the DRC, because of its size and central location, its potential for sparking interstate conflict, and its resource wealth; and Nigeria, because of its enormous population and therefore its huge role in shaping all of West Africa's future, as well as its new challenges from extremism in the form of Boko Haram. South Africa and Ethiopia, because of their size and stature, also merit some attention. All of these countries have rapidly growing populations, with Nigeria's heading toward some 400 million by 2050, Congo's and Ethiopia's each likely to exceed 150 million then, and South Africa's expected to reach about 65 million, according to recent projections.[98]

Nigeria is a country that, like Congo, experienced major internal unrest in the 1960s, but then stabilized somewhat in ensuing decades. That said, it has faced a host of challenges, from mediocre economic growth and inequities across regions to north-south competition across fault lines that are both ethnic and religious, enormous amounts of criminality, and now Boko Haram, with its al Qaeda-like ideology and extremely violent ways.[99]

Nigeria's population is dominated by three main ethnic groups, the Yoruba, the Igbo, and the Hausa-Fulani. The last, the main Muslim group, predominates in the north; the Yoruba are centered in the country's west, and the Igbo in the east. It was an Igbo-based revolt and attempted secession in 1967 that led to the deadly Biafra civil war. The nation was an amalgamation of otherwise disjointed and distinct British colonial possessions that had little political glue holding it together. Politics since independence in 1960 have largely amounted to internal competition among these three groups, with numerous centrifugal forces threatening and perhaps still imperiling the cohesion of the nation. Indeed, as with most of Africa, further civil conflict seems substantially more likely than interstate conflict.[100] That is true even though Nigeria has sometimes employed its military regionally during various security challenges in West Africa, often through the Economic Community of West African States, or ECOWAS.[101]

Boko Haram is a serious force to be reckoned with. It is responsible for several thousand deaths in Nigeria since 2010 and has also kidnapped many hundreds, including more than 200 schoolgirls in a single episode in 2014. It has shown some interest in extending operations to states such as Niger and Cameroon as well.[102]

Trends in economics, population, and employment are mixed. Nigeria's economy has been growing at 6 to 7 percent a year in real terms of late, but this rate may not be enough to improve employment prospects for a population still growing rapidly and projected to reach U.S. levels by mid-century.[103] At that time, Nigeria's population could exceed 400 million, as noted, more than twice the current figure.[104]

These observations, when woven together, suggest that the prospects for future conflict in Nigeria are mixed. Interstate war seems unlikely. All-out civil war is not imminent but is possible over time. Extremism is serious, even if probably less worrisome than in the heart of the Middle East or South Asia. Some economic trends are hopeful. Yet the witches' brew of transnational crime, north-south tensions fueled by sectarianism and unequal access to resources—and, of late, terrorist and counterterrorist operations—as well as a rapidly growing population would seem to make the country of significant potential international security concern.

Next to be considered is the Democratic Republic of the Congo, or Congo/Kinshasa, the former Zaire—and sub-Saharan Africa's largest country. On the African continent, only Algeria is larger by land mass, and much of Algeria's land is desert. The DRC is also sub-Saharan Africa's third most populous state, after Nigeria and Ethiopia, with some 75 million people (Nigeria has more than 175 million, Ethiopia some 85 million). It ranks fourth on the Fragile States Index of the Fund for Peace, making the DRC by this measure the most threatened large state in the world.[105]

Like many African states, Congo has spent most of its postcolonial period engaged in internal conflicts of one sort or another. It was one of the poster children for what the renowned political scientist Crawford Young described in his book, *The Politics of Cultural Pluralism,* as artificial multiethnic countries constructed by outside powers and held together by little more than a short colonial history, a common currency, and a strongman as leader.[106]

The Mobotu period, from the mid-1960s through the mid-1990s, provided a respite of sorts from conflict—though only at the price of severe repression, enormous corruption, and economic mismanagement, which planted the seeds for future warfare over the last two decades. In recent times, internal combat in the country's eastern highlands merged with the spillover effects from Rwanda's conflicts to create a stew of violent militia groups and other armed factions. Congo became the site of Africa's first true complex interstate war, with several other regional countries at least partly implicated in helping one side or another.[107]

The conflict was characterized by a great deal of sexual violence and the virtual disappearance of the state, with the result that huge numbers of deaths occurred from lack of basic nutrition and health care, despite the region's fertile soils and plentiful rains. A UN peacekeeping force, present in Congo since 1999, has been unable to make many inroads against this mayhem, despite totaling around 20,000 soldiers, which makes it the UN's largest mission. But while large in one sense, the mission is very modest in scale in another. It attempts to address the needs of a country of 75 million—more than the population of Iraq and Afghanistan combined, or ten times the combined population of Bosnia and Kosovo—with force densities less than one-tenth as great. (Congo's own military of some 135,000 is of quite mediocre quality and dependability.)

Though the international community has not marshaled a particularly strong response to Congo's war, there has been more hope in recent times. The 2013 deployment of a UN rapid intervention force consisting of troops from Tanzania, South Africa, and Malawi, and some overdue diplomatic cooperation between Rwanda and Congo, produced a moderate improvement in 2013.[108] Were there better political leadership in Kinshasa, including a greater willingness to tackle corruption and institutional reform in the security forces,[109] the world might sense an opportunity to do even more.

Should the horrible humanitarian tolls of the late 1990s and early 2000s resume, on the other hand, the pressure to do more could also increase.[110] To be sure, the world might choose to ignore the situation, as it often has in the past in Africa. Then again, doing so would fly in the face of the supposed global consensus about a responsibility to protect, arrived at through UN auspices through such signature efforts as the 2000 Brahimi Report and the 2005 High-Level Panel.[111] This responsibility to safeguard human life applies in the first instance to sovereign nations themselves, but then falls into the lap of the international community should sovereign nations prove unwilling or unable to uphold their own duties to their own peoples.[112] Beyond such norm-based arguments, there could also be more direct challenges that emerge from Central Africa in the future that engage the more immediate security interests of the broader international community, such as new outbreaks of contagious disease with the potential to spread globally.[113]

The broader Horn of Africa region merits some attention in any brief survey of Africa's potential future conflict spots as well. Current conflicts in the region center largely on Sudan. In fact, there are three UN peacekeeping missions related to Sudan today (as of mid-2015)—addressing Darfur as well as the Sudan/South Sudan split and internal issues within South Sudan. The separation of Sudan into two states was a long, arduous, bloody process. Conflicts in Darfur and in the new South Sudan have continued to the present. All have the potential again to intensify.[114]

Ethiopia is a key epicenter of many of the issues discussed here because of its size, its role as home to the African Union, headquartered in in Addis Ababa, and its location, straddling the Arab and sub-Saharan regions. Partly as a result, it has been involved in more regional struggles with neighbors than the typical African state. Beyond that, it continues to experience enduring internal conflicts, even if they are not presently severe. It is doing well at the moment, but that may not last.

Ethiopia's interstate challenges in recent decades have numbered at least three. First, it fought a very bloody war at the end of the twentieth century against Eritrea, which seceded (thereby also depriving Ethiopia of any seacoast). That war remains unresolved because of ongoing border disputes, not to mention ongoing rancor, and one also has to wonder whether Ethiopia has fully accepted its lack of direct access to international waterways.[115]

Second, Addis Ababa's plans to build a major dam on the Nile River potentially implicate Ethiopia in complex water issues with the Sudans and Egypt. This is a new development in regional water issues, which have always been complex and fraught.[116]

Third, the country has had historical struggles with Somalia too, and its ongoing problems with its own Ogaden region near Somalia have the potential for further flare-ups. Most recently, however, Ethiopia has been contributing in important and constructive ways to the African Union's mission in support of the Transitional Federal Government in Somalia, under Somali president Hassan Sheikh Mohamud.[117]

On balance, despite currently peaceful conditions and a reasonably robust economy, Ethiopia has its share of potential issues, not to mention a very rapidly growing population. Future regional conflicts, if severe enough, could conceivably complicate navigation in the Suez Canal or the Red Sea as well.

Finally, a word is in order about South Africa, the continent's wealthiest country in per capita terms and also its most industrialized and advanced. Despite these advantages, South Africa cannot easily escape the history and legacy of apartheid, most evident in its endemic high rates of unemployment, misery, and crime in many of the nation's black townships. Even though murder rates have been declining, they remain among the highest in the world.[118] This volatile set of ingredients has the potential to cause considerable future unrest within the country. Fortunately, civil wars or interstate conflicts seem relatively unlikely; it is hard to imagine over what fault lines, territorial disputes, or other specific causes they would erupt and be waged.

On balance, Africa seems less likely to produce major wars of globally strategic significance than many other parts of the world. But there are enough looming stresses from population trends, crime and terrorism, ongoing civil conflicts, and disease such as the terrible Ebola outbreak of 2014 to keep its problems on the radar screen in any assessment of global trends in land warfare.

LATIN AMERICA

Once a global epicenter of cold war struggles, with frequent coups, leftist insurgencies, and rightist strongman rulers, Latin America has made remarkable progress in recent decades. Starting in the early 1970s, it gradually became quite democratic, with twenty-two of its thirty-three countries now rated "free" by Freedom House. There has been only one successful military coup in the last two decades.[119] There has not been a war between different states in the region since the nineteen-day border fight in 1995 between Peru and Ecuador; indeed, the occasional struggle between those two states has produced the region's only real interstate conflicts since World War II.[120] Economic growth, even if uneven in time and space, has accompanied this political progress as well.

Yet the region is not out of the woods, and its proximity to the United States raises the stakes for America. Severe income inequality is a blight on the region's economic improvement, and severe poverty remains endemic. Partly as a result, violence—not so much between states but, as in Africa, within them—is a constant scourge in the lives of many. Much of the violence is not random but related to broader challenges posed by transnational criminal syndicates.

Along with southern Africa, Central America and Latin America have the highest homicide rates in the world. Moreover, even as democracy has spread and solidified its hold on politics, the trend lines for violence have pointed in the wrong direction. Between 1996 and 2010, the percentage of the region's citizens who identified security as their greatest concern in life grew from 7 percent to 27 percent. Between 1990 and 2008, homicide rates across the region increased by 20 percent overall, and much more in some countries, such as Brazil and most states of Central America. In the 2000s, violence has greatly intensified in Mexico as well.[121]

The prognosis for various countries in the region varies greatly from case to case. From the perspective of U.S. national security, it makes sense to examine the case of Brazil, far and away the largest country, and the axis extending roughly from Colombia through Central America and into Mexico—the area most implicated in criminal narcotics activities, the part of Latin America closest to the United States, and the part with the fastest changes in violence rates in the region (for the better of late in Colombia, for the worse in areas further north).

Northern Latin America

Atlantic Ocean

UNITED STATES

MEXICO

Gulf of Mexico

Bermuda (U.K.)

BAHAMAS

Cayman Islands (U.K.)

CUBA

Turks & Caicos
Islands (U.K.)

DOMINICAN
REPUBLIC

HAITI

JAMAICA

BELIZE

GUATEMALA

HONDURAS

EL SALVADOR

NICARAGUA

COSTA RICA

PANAMA

Caribbean Sea

Puerto
Rico

ST. KITTS & NEVIS

Netherlands
Antilles

Aruba (Neth.)

Virgin Islands (U.S.)

Virgin Islands (U.K.)
Anguilla (U.K.)
ANTIGUA &
BARBUDA
Guadeloupe (Fr.)
DOMINICA
Martinique (Fr.)
ST. LUCIA
BARBADOS
GRENADA
ST. VINCENT
TRINIDAD
& TOBAGO

VENEZUELA

COLOMBIA

ECUADOR

Galapagos
(Ecuador)

Pacific Ocean

GUYANA

SURINAME

French Guiana

BRAZIL

Amazon

PERU

BOLIVIA

0   500   1000 miles

Colombia has progressed enormously since the administration of President Álvaro Uribe Vèlez starting in the early 2000s. Its rates of violence and crime have dropped by at least half, if not closer to two-thirds by now, and the FARC insurgency has been put on the ropes. Yet Colombia also has the second highest number of internally displaced persons in the world, some 5 million, as the toxic mix of right-wing militias, leftist insurgencies, and narcotraffickers has driven many ordinary citizens off their land.[122] Its crime rates, while much improved, remain very high by global standards. Its justice system remains troubled, and local economic development is mediocre in many remote areas of the country. On balance, the trends are hopeful. Indeed, it is possible that Colombia will be an increasingly important ally of the United States in the region, among other things training partner militaries in counterinsurgency and counter-crime tactics in a way that is often difficult for the United States to carry out. But it is too soon to declare Colombia definitively and permanently a success story.[123]

Venezuela has been very troubled under presidents Hugo Chávez and Nicolás Maduro. Despite the charisma of Chávez and the momentum his leftist leadership created for a time in the region, Caracas hardly seems to be building a strong revolutionary or rejectionist axis in the region (despite ongoing close relationships with countries such as Cuba).[124] Yet Venezuela's authoritarian political leadership, overdependence on oil revenues, and very high crime rates mean that the country itself is very stressed, with a real potential for civil conflict or even partial state collapse.[125]

As for Central America, and particularly the "northern triangle" countries of Honduras, Guatemala, and El Salvador, violence fueled by drug-trafficking organizations and other criminal gangs has been a terrible burden, resulting in large numbers of homicides in the region, as well as the recent influx of child refugees into the United States. Various approaches have been taken to deal with the problem, some building on ideas from Colombia and Mexico. They range from greater use of the military in law enforcement to broader-ranging development strategies focusing on economics and at-risk youth, to attempts at government-sponsored mediation with various gangs and syndicates. In broad brush, little has worked to date, at least relative to the scale of the problem. The resolutions of the region's civil wars in past decades have so far produced limited benefits.[126] Nor does economic growth promise a rapid rescue:

even where it has occurred, it has not significantly alleviated the extreme poverty afflicting much of the region. The northern triangle region of Central America of nearly 30 million inhabitants remains among the most troubled parts of the world, a virtual war zone in many ways.[127]

Mexico has been on a roller coaster in recent years. The country has made considerable economic progress, and reforms are under way in important sectors such as energy.[128] The nation's levels of violence got far worse starting around 2008, before peaking in 2011. President Enrique Peña Nieto's continuation of a policy of using the military, strengthened over the years in part through the Mérida Initiative, conducted in partnership with the United States, to target top drug and crime leaders, has had some success. Nonetheless, the country remains much more violent than a decade ago, and regions along the Pacific coast have not enjoyed even the limited progress that areas closer to the United States have experienced. Criminal groups with military-grade weaponry pose a serious potential threat to the state. Vigilante groups, however well intentioned and however effective in some cases, create the risk of a more warlord-like society in which the state would lose much of its monopoly on the use of force. Judicial systems and police forces remain weak and uncoordinated in much of the country.[129]

It is entirely possible that the fragile progress of recent years will not be sustained and indeed could even be reversed. In that light, and because of its proximity to the United States and its size, Mexico bears watching as a potential high-end security problem for its northern neighbor.

Brazil is the regional behemoth, with a population roughly equal to all the above Latin American states combined. Its prognosis appears decidedly mixed. Brazil has long been a focal point of American business interests because of its size and potential.[130] In the twenty-first century it has moved beyond its past troubles to have earned what the scholar and former ambassador Lincoln Gordon called a "second chance" to join the "first world."[131] It made considerable progress in the early years of the new century in particular.[132] But it remains very troubled by corruption, worsening violence, deep poverty, and virtually all the other problems facing major Latin American states.

Latin America is doing better, overall. But many of the parts of the continent closest to the United States are not. And in parts of the region, internal violence and drug-related criminality remain severe threats.

CONCLUSION

How best to sum up the prospects for large-scale conflict, or other major challenges to global order, that may emerge on the world's main land formations in the years and decades ahead?

Referring to table 2-7, which is based on the analyses of this chapter, as well as on my survey of the world's natural resources and the potential for resource-related conflicts and disasters (discussed in appendix A), I begin with the following broad observations. In areas in and near Russia, natural disasters and demographic pressures are relatively unlikely to sow the seeds of possible trouble. But many other causes and factors could contribute, including revanchist politics and conflicts over natural resources. In and around China, disputes over hydrocarbons do not seem likely to cause severe tensions, except perhaps at sea. But other issues could, including the scarcity of certain key resources, such as water; and in political and military terms, the Korean Peninsula remains a tinderbox. The Indian subcontinent is perhaps most vulnerable to complex catastrophes that could be caused in part by natural disasters (or nuclear reactor catastrophes) and faces the added challenges of severe internal and interstate tensions, centered in particular on Pakistan. The Middle East is spared very few possible causes of unrest and violence. It may be less prone to storm damage or to fights over metals and minerals, but otherwise it displays vulnerabilities on multiple axes. Both Africa and Latin America may be less vulnerable to classic interstate conflict and somewhat less vulnerable than Asian rim states to massive storms or most other natural disasters, but they are very vulnerable to internal schisms resulting from poverty, criminality, and other problems associated with weak states.

Two competing themes emerge from this overview of the world. The planet is not becoming more violent or unstable on balance, at least not as far as the eye can easily see in 2015. But neither is there any inexorable trajectory apparent toward a more harmonious global society in which war somehow becomes obsolete or even rare. One can hope for the latter over time, and there are some grounds for optimism, but such a world will have to be created—it is not now here, and it is not on the horizon. With these general considerations in hand, we now turn to specific scenarios that could, under some circumstances, be relevant for U.S. military planning in general, and for American ground forces in particular.

Table 2-7. High-Probability Causes or Motivations for War and Unrest, by Key Region[a]

	Region					
Cause	Russia and neighbors	China and neighbors	Indian subcontinent	Middle East	Sub-Saharan Africa	Latin America
Population (and growth)	Yes	Yes	Yes	Yes	Yes	Yes (Central America most)
Farmland, food, fisheries, forests, water (or floods or shortages)	Yes	Yes (especially China)	Yes (less glacial flow into major rivers)	Yes (Levant, Iraq, Egypt)	Yes (Nigeria, Sahel, Congo)	Yes (Andes, Mexico, Central America)
Hydrocarbons	Yes			Yes	Yes	
Metals/minerals	Yes	Yes			Yes	
Natural disaster (besides drought, flood)		Yes	Yes			
Nuclear power (and possible accidents)	Yes	Yes	Yes			
Interstate politics	Yes	Yes	Yes	Yes		
Civil discord, crime, and terrorism	Yes (aided, abetted by Russia)	Yes (the Koreas in particular)	Yes (Pakistan, Bangladesh)	Yes (continuation of current troubles)	Yes	Yes (Central America and Mexico)

a. Not all conflicts would be within regions, of course. There could be conflicts, for example, pitting Russia against China, China against India, the United States against China, or the United States against Iran. Those cells with "Yes" are assessed as places where conflict could be caused by the noted factors.

CHAPTER THREE

Scenarios with Russia or China

HAVING CONSIDERED IN CHAPTER 2 where the world's most likely strategic fault lines on land may lie, in this chapter I begin to narrow down this book's discussion of land warfare writ large to a more specific set of scenarios of relevance to American force planning.

This chapter and the next do not offer a comprehensive list of plausible scenarios. There are clearly too many, if we consider the entire planet and project several decades into the future. Nor is it realistic to think that somehow the U.S. intelligence community will find the tools to narrow the list to the point that the future becomes inherently more predictable. Any such expectation ignores the fundamentally contingent nature of future world events and of human history.[1] Rather, my goal is to examine all, or at least most, major types of potential conflicts. The goal is also to be sure that relatively more demanding scenarios are considered. This methodology is designed to attempt to bound the demands and complexities of other possible scenarios that may not be foreseen or easily foreseeable.

How can one know whether a given possible intervention or mission is in the national security interest of the United States? Richard Haass's distinction between wars of necessity and wars of choice provides a very useful analytical springboard.[2] Yet there is often considerable challenge in determining which type of possible war is which. As such, I do not expect all of my own scenarios to be equally compelling to all readers. Indeed, by including them here, I do not mean to prejudge the need for possible American military intervention in any, only to acknowledge the possibility.

This chapter does not attempt to resolve the question of simultaneity, that is, the issue of determining how many conflicts at a time U.S. forces should be capable of handling. That matter is considered in chapter 5, which deals with general principles for future U.S. force planning and with a proposal for a specific force posture for the U.S. ground forces.

The scenarios considered in this chapter involving Russia and China are quite unlikely, one hopes, and are analyzed with that premise in mind. Many contingencies in the next chapter are more plausible examples of where force might actually be employed. Those involving Russia or China are viewed as important primarily for ensuring successful deterrence—indeed, for keeping certain scenarios virtually unthinkable for potential adversaries. That said, some type of Russian challenge to nations such as the Baltic states in the months and years ahead seems less unthinkable now than it may have just a couple of years ago. There is a spectrum of likelihood associated with these scenarios, and no simple and easy categorization scheme.

No sweeping assumptions are made about the roles of allies and other security partners. These are assessed on a case-by-case basis. Nor is a certain standard international legal framework assumed for any and all possible operations. However useful UN Security Council approval of a given mission might be, I do not presume it as an absolute prerequisite to action for all cases.

Overseas military scenarios are not the only concern when building an army or a marine corps, of course. Peacetime engagement, forward presence, regular exercises, crisis response capabilities, and numerous other activities contribute in important ways to the deterrence of would-be adversaries and the assurance of allies. Domestic emergency contingencies must be part of the mix, too, and one such scenario is considered in the next chapter. Smaller operations than discussed here are also important to bear in mind. But this chapter and the next focus primarily on larger-scale responses to violence abroad that could involve major roles for U.S. ground forces, since such responses will do the most to determine the broad size, shape, and character of the nation's Army and Marine Corps.

The scenarios that follow involve a wide range of needed capabilities. Even though the assumed missions are large, the goal is not to emphasize only traditional high-end combat as the main scenario for future U.S. Army and Marine Corps planning while somehow treating all other operations as lesser included or less important cases.

My approach in analyzing scenarios in this chapter and the next is to provide enough texture of the challenges of a given case so as to give some meaningful way of doing rough force sizing, without getting bogged down in detail or prejudging the specific characteristics of weapons and warfare as they might exist in 2020 or 2030 or 2040.

Some similar scenarios are undoubtedly being analyzed within the Department of Defense already. But there is value in assessing them independently in a book like this nonetheless. First of all, much DOD thinking on such scenarios is classified, meaning that it cannot easily inform the broader policy debate about future military strategy, missions, and budgets. Second, some of the missions considered here may be too sensitive for a government agency to investigate, even in a classified context, for fear of leaks. Third, independent analysts using their own methods and imaginations may think of certain ideas that official Pentagon assessments do not (and vice versa). Fourth, the government's current disillusionment with large-scale stabilization missions may discourage creative thinking about certain categories of scenarios, or at least may keep such thinking from being particularly influential when fundamental decisions are made about U.S. military force posture, as happened, for example, in past periods of U.S. history, such as the post-Vietnam era.

Following the same basic geographic sequence as in chapter 2, the scenarios proposed here are as follows. The first three, which could involve Russia or China, are addressed separately in this chapter. The remaining seven are examined in the next chapter.

—A Russian invasion threat to the Baltic states.

—A second Korean war, including possible Chinese involvement.

—A maritime conflict between China and Japan or China and the Philippines that spills over onto land.

—A fissioning of Pakistan, perhaps combined with a complex humanitarian emergency sparked by a major natural disaster in South Asia.

—Indo-Pakistani war, perhaps over a terrorist strike, with Kashmir providing the spark.

—Iranian use or threatened use of nuclear weapons against a neighbor.

—A major international stabilization operation in the Middle East—perhaps in Syria after a negotiated peace.

—Civil war accompanied by terrorism and perhaps a biological pandemic in Nigeria.

—An increase in the brutality and reach of criminal networks in Central America.

—A major domestic emergency in the United States.

A RUSSIAN INVASION THREAT TO THE BALTIC STATES

The behavior of Vladimir Putin in 2014 in regard to Ukraine, including the claim to a right to protect ethnic Russians wherever they may be, raises serious questions. Could Russian ambitions extend to areas that were once part of the Warsaw Pact—or at least the Soviet Union, especially those parts inhabited by large numbers of Russian speakers? Putin and successors must have no doubt about the credibility of NATO's Article 5 commitments to all its members, lest they be tempted to use force in such places.[3] Of course, maintaining adequate military capacity is only one part of the equation; America must project the credibility and the resolve to use that force in defense of its allies to create the necessary deterrent effect. But military capacity is an essential ingredient.

Whether one supported the expansion of NATO to include these countries in the first place or not (and I have argued against it over the years myself), the validity of any Russian claims to neighboring NATO territories must not be countenanced. There can and should be major efforts to find a diplomatic solution to the Russia-Ukraine crisis of recent times (if these comments are still germane when this book is published). But the clarity of the NATO commitment to the Baltic states and other NATO members must be sustained, in light of the dangers associated with any other path.[4] The United States and its allies need to have a credible capacity to defend these forward nations. Investigating just what that entails is the subject of the analysis for this scenario. Over time, the United States and allies could consider alternative security structures to perhaps supersede NATO.[5] But it certainly seems ill-advised to undertake such thinking at the point of a Russian gun. Hence, NATO must be sustained for the foreseeable future, and America's combat capacity must be kept robust as well. And even a successor organization would need credible combat power backstopped by the U.S. military against possible contingencies, like the one addressed here.

Russia could threaten one or more of the Baltic states in numerous ways, including everything from cyberattacks, to the "little green men" used in the stealthy invasion of Crimea in 2014, to some type of partial naval blockade against key shipping in and out of Latvia, Lithuania, and Estonia. But for planning the main ground forces of the future U.S. military, the most stressful case is probably a classic overland invasion, though it could be coupled with one or more of these other types of limited attacks as well.

As such, my military analysis begins with an examination of how much force Russia could realistically employ against one of the Baltic states, and how quickly it could use it. I start from the premise that the United States and NATO should not rely exclusively on nuclear deterrence to address a possible Russian threat to the Baltics. Indeed, Russia's aims might not be complete conquest of such a state so much as "liberation" of the eastern swaths of the targeted country, where many ethnic Russians and Russian speakers live. Threatening a nuclear reprisal to deter Russia from carrying out such a conquest and annexation—or, perhaps even harder, to force it to remove troops once they have already taken a chunk of Baltic territory and created a fait accompli—might not be a wise course.[6] The history of the cold war underscores the difficulty of effecting such extended deterrence and compellence as well.[7]

The NATO charter's binding Article 5 mutual defense pledge reads as follows:

> The Parties agree that an armed attack against one or more of them in Europe or North America shall be considered an attack against them all and consequently they agree that, if such an armed attack occurs, each of them, in exercise of the right of individual or collective self-defense recognized by Article 51 of the Charter of the United Nations, will assist the Party or Parties so attacked by taking forthwith, individually and in concert with the other Parties, such action as it deems necessary, including the use of armed force, to restore and maintain the security of the North Atlantic area.[8]

Thus, American military force may not be an automatic consequence of an attack on a NATO ally, but the option of such a military response is important to retain.

Ideally, NATO would be capable of a reinforcement capacity that would allow the establishment of a fairly robust defense at the first

serious sign of possible trouble.[9] Failing that, a credible if limited counteroffensive capability, perhaps to cut off the resupply of Russian forces
in the Baltic regions with an operation along the Baltic-Russian borders,
might be a useful capability. It would require more time to deploy to the
region, and more verve to employ, than a strictly defensive operation, but
it would also offer a much more restrained and proportionate response
than would large-scale conventional or nuclear escalation.

What size force could Russia realistically use against the Baltic states
on short notice? Alas, geography works against NATO in this case. The
region presents relatively open terrain for the movement of large armies,[10]
and Russia is much better positioned to act quickly. As the presumed
aggressor in this scenario, it could have the added advantage of surprise.

In the cold war, although estimates varied, it was generally believed
that the Soviet Union could move at least forty divisions (out of 200 total),
and thus around half a million soldiers, into Central Europe within perhaps two to three months of beginning to mobilize, reinforcing the dozens of divisions the Warsaw Pact already had there.[11]

Today, Russia could not reach that same standard. Its military is just
a quarter the size of cold war levels and has also experienced more than
two decades of relative privation.[12] But projecting one to two decades
into the future, the situation could change to a degree.

Much of the infrastructure that would have facilitated Warsaw Pact
reinforcements is either still intact and in operation or within the capacity
of the future Russian state to repair and refurbish. As such, the physical
capacity of Russia's internal lines of communication, in the western part
of the country and on into the Baltic region, could in theory allow the
movement of tens to hundreds of thousands of Russian troops into Latvia,
Lithuania, or Estonia—if the units were maintained in a sufficiently high
state of readiness or if Russia took the time to mobilize and prepare them.

It is unrealistic to think that NATO could permanently station enough
forces on the territories of its eastern members to have a reliable counter
to any such hypothetical Russian threat. What, then, is the realistic standard that the alliance should seek to attain? At its Wales summit in September 2014, NATO proposed creating a rapid reaction force of 4,000.[13]
Such a force, however useful for trip-wire deterrence, would constitute a
meager combat capability against plausible Russian threats.[14]

What would it take to mount a more stalwart defense?[15] And what
kind of counteroffensive capacity would make Russia think that, even if

it secured initial control of elements of the Baltic nations, it could lose them as supply lines from western Russia were threatened by a NATO maneuver operation that cut them off?

NATO would almost surely not need quantitative parity with Russia for the defensive mission, if its goal was simply to deny the Russians any guarantee of a quick and easy win. As the late Trevor Dupuy found in his examination of numerous cases, an attacking country with simple quantitative parity had a slightly better than 50 percent chance of winning a given battle. If it had a three-to-one advantage, its prospects of success improved to something closer to 65 to 75 percent—but still nowhere near 100 percent.[16] So if NATO's goal was simply to complicate the calculations of Russian planners and make victory seem less than guaranteed, being able to rapidly deploy one-third as much defensive capability in the Baltics as Russia was thought capable of mustering for an offensive might be deemed adequate, especially in light of NATO's technological advantages.

Continuing in broad strokes and with rough numbers, Russia might be able to deploy 300,000 troops to its borders with the Baltic states on short notice in the years ahead, as a ballpark estimate, plus or minus several tens of thousands. Of the total, perhaps three-fourths to four-fifths of them might be ground troops. This would be a major undertaking and major achievement, including in terms of logistics and sustainment, and may or may not be realistically achievable for the Russia of 2015. But as a credible worst-case scenario for U.S. force planning it represents a reasonable standard against which to plan for the medium-term future.

According to the above logic, NATO might elect to have the capacity to deploy 100,000 to 150,000 of its own forces there quickly, in order to have a reasonably good prospect of successful defense.[17] I will assume for the sake of conservatism that it might be 150,000. The associated number of NATO ground troops might be two-thirds of that total, given recent precedent, or about 100,000.[18] Depending on the future course of events, NATO might choose to station some fraction of this total on the Baltic state territories permanently, especially if Russian behavior became even more threatening. An additional fraction of the troops could reside elsewhere as long as their equipment was prestationed on the potentially endangered territory and plans were in place to fly them in during a crisis (assuming enough NATO forces were permanently present in the Baltics to protect the equipment depots and staging areas while they awaited the arrival of reinforcements).

The above represents one option. However, it puts a premium on either permanent stationing of large NATO forces in the Baltics or a large capacity for rapid reinforcement, or both.

If these measures were not feasible, NATO would need a different approach to ensuring the safety of its allies. That might take the form of a counteroffensive capability of several divisions, as in the canonical "major theater war" construct the Pentagon has used since the 1990s. The idea might be to liberate any territory that Russia had taken.

In preparing for such an operation, NATO would need to ensure not only enough force to defeat Russian units in the field but also enough to protect its own supply lines. If, for example, it envisioned a movement of 100 miles along the Russian border with one or more Baltic states, and sought to secure its internal lines of communication throughout the process, an additional two to four divisions might be required to sustain logistics lines. (This estimate is based loosely on the notion that a modern division is often expected to be able to hold 25 to 50 kilometers of front per division—though such numbers are extremely rough at best, as Joshua Epstein has persuasively argued).[19] Bearing in mind that divisions of some 15,000 soldiers generally require at least as many additional forces to help sustain and enable them, the overall troop requirement associated with two to four divisions could grow further, making for a total NATO ground force capability of 200,000 (these figures include helicopters for both Army and Marines, and fixed-wing aircraft as well for the Marine Corps, so they are not strictly just ground troops). Again, given the ratios of ground forces to Air Force and Navy capabilities witnessed in recent major U.S. wars, an aggregate ground force of 200,000 implies a total force in the range of perhaps 300,000.

One can also check these same points with one version or another of formal—or at least approximate—combat modeling. There is little point in attempting to be particularly precise about a scenario that may unfold in, say, 2025 or 2030, with different weapons than are in use today, along with other changes in the strategic landscape. However, a back-of-the envelope approach is a useful validation of the above, more qualitative argument.

One way of doing this is with a modified version of Trevor Dupuy's combat model. Although several unclassified models have been usefully employed over recent decades, including those contributed by distinguished scholars such as Richard Kugler, Barry Posen, and Joshua Epstein, the Dupuy method is probably the simplest, without sacrificing accuracy. The actual formula developed by Dupuy has a number of factors associated with it that can make it somewhat difficult to employ; I choose, therefore, to simplify it, as noted below.[20]

The Dupuy method first requires that one calculate the "power" of each side's relevant forces. This power factor can be represented as the product of three terms: the size of the forces in terms of numbers of troops; their overall quality, including equipment and training; and the situational factors that may influence their effectiveness in a given situation, such as surprise, terrain, and weather conditions.

The crucial variable here for this scenario is probably making a fair assessment of the second of these, or the relative quality of NATO forces compared with those of Russia (as the units are arbitrary, the quality of Russian forces can be arbitrarily defined as being equal to 1, so the question becomes how good NATO forces are on this same scale). For example, historically, Israeli forces have usually displayed a relative quality of at least 3:1 relative to Arab adversaries.[21] The United States and coalition partners probably exceeded 10:1 in the maneuver phases of the 1991 and 2003 wars against Iraq.[22] In the cold war, NATO tended to assume little or no such advantage against Warsaw Pact forces when doing its war planning, though that may have been the result of excessive conservatism.[23]

As these types of calculations are inherently imprecise, it is best to avoid pursuit of a single estimate and instead seek to establish a plausible range of outcomes by using two sets of assumptions about performance, one of them optimistic, the other more pessimistic.[24] As such, I would propose assuming a 1.5:1 NATO advantage in the conservative or pessimistic case and a 2:1 advantage in the optimistic case. There is a good argument to make the 2:1 figure even higher, to reflect the improvements in technology that NATO forces, led by the United States, have achieved in recent decades.[25] But for the sake of conservatism, and because Russia may close the technology gap in coming years, no greater advantage than this is assumed, even in the optimistic case—especially in light of the fact that the airfields and ports the United States and allies would need to reinforce their initial positions could become vulnerable to the very same precision munitions that in recent decades have improved net American advantages in certain types of conflicts. (Ships carrying U.S. supplies across the ocean could also be vulnerable to submarine interdiction.)[26]

Cyberattacks could slow down reinforcements as well, particularly if targeted on certain underprotected civilian infrastructure crucial to the war effort, such as key transportation hubs. Even chemical attacks by Russian forces against such infrastructure or against deployed NATO troops cannot be excluded. Since chemical agents have caused 10 percent or more of the total casualties in previous wars in which they were widely used, their effects on combat performance and power would likely be at least that great in quantitative terms, especially if one considers all the precautionary and protective measures that even fears of their possible use can require.[27]

As for the situational term, historically this variable can double (or halve) combat performance under a typical range of circumstances. Taking it as equal to 1 for Russia, it is then reasonable to vary it from 0.75 to 1.25 for NATO. The lower figure implies that NATO forces suffer from being surprised, the higher figure assumes that they benefit from fighting from defensive positions, with the reverse applying to the case in which NATO forces go on the counteroffensive.[28]

So, for the case in which Russia has 300,000 troops and NATO just 100,000, the optimistic and pessimistic cases look like this:

Optimistic Case
Russian Power: (300,000)(1)(1) = 300,000
U.S./Baltics/NATO Power: (100,000)(2)(1.25) = 250,000

Pessimistic Case
Russian Power: (300,000)(1)(1) = 300,000
U.S./NATO Allies' Power: (100,000)(1.5)(0.75) = 112,500

The next step in the Dupuy method is to estimate a daily loss rate for each side. This will change with time, and therefore the method requires an iterative series of calculations to be completed properly. However, for our present back-of-the-envelope purposes, simply comparing the initial loss rates relative to initial force size gives an adequate sense of where the direction of battle is headed. The loss rate for each side is, in my simplified approach, the product of a normalizing factor (the same for each side, and designed as a rough gauge of the intensity of combat and thus of daily loss rates), that same side's troop size, and the ratio of the power terms for the two sides:

Optimistic Case

U.S./NATO Allies' Loss Rate: (0.01)(100,000)(300,000/250,000) = 1,200 casualties per day

Russian Loss Rate: (0.01)(300,000)(250,000/300,000) = 2,500 casualties per day

Pessimistic Case

U.S./NATO Allies' Loss Rate : (0.01)(100,000)(300,000/112,500) = 2,666 casualties per day

Russian Loss Rate: (0.01)(300,000)(112,500/300,000) = 1,125 casualties per day

In the optimistic case, the two sides fight to an effective standstill, as the U.S./allies' loss rate is less than half Russia's, and the allies could presumably muster some reinforcements during this period too, given the huge standing size of their land armies. In the pessimistic case, by contrast, Russia clearly wins, especially because it begins with a much larger force and so can afford to suffer attrition more than NATO forces could tolerate.

Put differently, a NATO defensive force of 100,000 might be adequate for a forward defense, especially if it can get into position well enough that it suffers few downsides from being surprised and benefits from the natural tactical and terrain advantages of a defender. But it is a close call, and this calculation suggests that it might not be prudent to count on it.

As for the case in which NATO might mount a counteroffensive, this kind of operation would leave NATO forces quite vulnerable if it failed. As such, it is appropriate to focus the calculation on the case in which NATO's advantages are less strong—specifically, where it has only a 1.5:1 quality advantage (even if we assume it does benefit from surprise in this case). Then, considering those 300,000 Russian forces in the theater to be available for opposing the U.S./allied forces' counterattack, aided by perhaps 100,000 more reservists and other later deployers, the equations would be:

Russian Power: (400,000)(1)(1) = 400,000

U.S./NATO Allies' Power: (300,000)(1.5)(1.25) = 562,500

Russian Loss Rate: (0.01)(400,000)(562,500/400,000) = 5,625 per day

U.S./NATO Allies' Loss Rate: (0.01)(300,000)(400,000/562,500) = about 2,000 per day

This is an acceptable result from NATO's perspective, as the Alliance's loss rate is much less than half of Russia's even in this conservative case, and the NATO force is three-fourths the size of Russia's. One would want a decisive advantage as evidenced above, in light of the risks of operating near Russian territory (and the possibility that Russia might be able to reinforce more easily than NATO in the longer term, should the battle bog down).

Of that figure of 300,000, perhaps three-fourths, or 225,000, would have to be American. It would be ideal if European and Canadian contributions could be larger, but that may not be realistic. The front-line Baltic nations, while modest in size and military strength, would nonetheless be able to devote virtually all of their forces to the fight. Other NATO nations might collectively provide the other 50,000 troops, based largely on a rough estimate of their capacities by reference to the Afghanistan mission (where their collective contributions peaked at somewhat less than that level). It is also roughly consistent with the aggregate size of the various EU and NATO response forces that exist today.[29] Perhaps Europeans could muster closer to 75,000 troops, and presumably they could mobilize larger forces over time, but a prompt response capacity of 50,000 seems a safer estimate.

Of the total of 225,000 or more Americans, based on the precedent of previous major conflicts, some 150,000 would likely be U.S. soldiers and Marines.

Again, these calculations are notional and very rough. The use of several significant figures in the above results should not be taken literally, and the numbers employed are clearly approximate.

I do not truly anticipate a war with Russia. Indeed, under certain types of worst-case Russian attacks of one type or another on a country like Latvia, Estonia, or Lithuania, it might be more prudent to employ indirect or asymmetric economic or military responses rather than a direct counteroffensive. But it is important that Russia not perceive itself as the undisputed preeminent land power of Central and Eastern Europe.

WAR IN KOREA—AND POSSIBLE CHINESE INVOLVEMENT

American ground force planning currently emphasizes Korean contingencies, as it rightly should. But an even broader range of contingencies in that region could be relevant to long-term U.S. military planning.

Another Korean war is perhaps the only case where a large-scale encounter could credibly occur between Chinese and American land armies in the future. I do not predict such an outcome. It would take a complete breakdown of diplomacy, and much more, for such a direct confrontation between the twenty-first century's superpowers to happen. But there are plausible paths by which it could occur in the context of a war pitting the Democratic People's Republic of Korea (DPRK, North Korea) against the Republic of Korea (ROK, South Korea) and the United States. Even if the peninsula were someday reunified, the United States might wish to maintain the capacity, when combined with ROK capabilities, of a credible land defense option for Korea against any possible Chinese threat—in this case, less because of the likelihood of an actual use of force and more to keep such thoughts unthinkable in Beijing.

Thankfully, another Korean war seems very unlikely. But events in recent years on the Korean Peninsula, including the sinking of the Korean frigate *Cheonan* and the shelling of Yeonpyeong Island, demonstrate that even relatively small incidents risk triggering a wider conflict.

Consider how a Korean scenario could unfold in the near future. According to the so-called 5027 War Plan for the United States, North Korea might have initiated another major attack on South Korea, presumably without Chinese help, which would then require a major South Korean and American response. The North Korean attack might not begin as the earlier one did in 1950 but could grow out of a more limited exchange of lethal force—for example, something like that 2010 *Cheonan* sinking, in which North Korea murdered forty-six South Korean sailors in cold blood, but in this case followed by a South Korean retaliatory strike. South Korean military rules of engagement issued after that incident, as well as political realities, make it less likely that a subsequent North Korean provocation would be tolerated.[30] Such dynamics could lead to all-out war—not as their most likely outcome but as a possibility, however remote, after a series of escalatory steps by both sides.

It is also at least possible, if less likely than in the nuclear crisis of 1994, that if North Korea continues to construct a new nuclear reactor suitable for producing large amounts of plutonium, the United States and South Korea will preemptively destroy it. That could of course lead to possible DPRK retaliation against them.[31]

Alternatively, as envisioned in the 5029 plans developed by the Combined Forces Command in Seoul, North Korean collapse or another type of internal chaos could create a situation of unrest adequate to justify a major response by ROK and American forces. This might result largely from fear that the DPRK's nuclear materials could wind up in the wrong hands.[32]

Either one of these scenarios could lead to a major conflict. Large elements of North Korea's million-man armed forces, and ultimately many reservists, would be pitted against South Korea's half-million-strong active duty military, the nearly 30,000 American troops in Korea, and a similar number perhaps from Japan (though some of the American forces now in Japan would surely stay there to help with the protection of Japan itself, as well as with logistical support and possible refugee issues related to the Korea conflict). Over time, Korean reservists and U.S. reinforcements would enter the fight as well. The latter might ultimately number in the hundreds of thousands, depending on the course of the conflict. The presumed goals for the Combined Forces Command would be to eliminate the North Korean threat to South Korea in general and Seoul in particular in the first instance, to neutralize the North Korean army, and to control the territory and population centers of North Korea, with an eye toward restoring order while also securing weapons of mass destruction. These goals would probably be most realistically achieved by also overthrowing the North Korean government.

There would be a premium on rapid and substantial American response in this case. Some argue that today's military balance on the Korean Peninsula no longer necessitates significant contributions by U.S. ground forces. They assert that, with South Korea's military just over half a million strong and North Korea's twice that size but far less well prepared, the South now has military superiority over the DPRK and can handle any conflict on its own without much more than U.S. airpower in support. The logic of this thinking is part of what has driven the idea that Operational Command of Combined Forces can change, with the United States no longer playing the top role in an integrated hierarchy but the two sides essentially sharing different elements of the command responsibilities in any conflict. However, this thinking is flawed. North Korea's nuclear capacities, combined with its preexisting conventional forces, put a premium on rapid and comprehensive defeat of the DPRK regime—quite likely necessitating a major U.S. role and a tightly integrated allied effort.

To apply the Dupuy method here, I begin by assuming that South Korea has a military edge over the North comparable to what Israel has had against Arab neighbors over recent decades, roughly 3:1 in quality. I further assume that North Korea enjoys no net benefit from surprise (that is, any North Korean benefit of surprise would be modest and at least offset by allied forces' advantages in fighting from defensive positions). Nor do I assume that either Korea benefits from its many reservists, if the scenario is an attack on South Korea, since those reservists are generally not equipped with a great deal more equipment than small weaponry and take some time to mobilize. The calculation is then:

South Korean Power: (500,000)(3)(1) = 1,500,000
North Korean Power: (1,000,000)(1)(1) = 1,000,000
South Korean Loss Rate: (.01)(500,000)(1,000,000/1,500,000) = 3,667 per day
North Korean Loss Rate: (.01)(1,000,000)(1,500,000/1,000,000) = 15,000 per day

By this calculus, even with the United States left out entirely, South Korea successfully defends its own territory, in that its daily casualty rate is only about one-fourth of North Korea's and it begins with a force half as large. And again, this is meant as a conservative calculation from the point of view of the U.S. allies.

However, this assumes a protracted war of attrition during which Seoul could be bombarded repeatedly—and after which the North Korean regime would likely remain in place. Neither of these circumstances is likely to be acceptable to Seoul or Washington. A counterattack by allied forces into North Korea would likely be their response, not a simple defensive holding action.

In any ROK-U.S. counterattack, North Korea's 6 million reservists could come into the equation. They are poorly equipped, but many are well indoctrinated and likely to be tenacious.

North Korea's nuclear arsenal creates huge uncertainties for the analysis. Above, I assumed that it would not be used in an attack on South Korea, perhaps out of fear of retaliation. But if allied forces moved northward toward Pyongyang, North Korean calculations could change, and incentives to employ nuclear weapons could grow. Might the DPRK then use a nuclear weapon or two to blow a hole in allied defenses in one sector of the front lines by using an airburst that would minimize fall-out—and thus permit fairly rapid North Korean exploitation of the subsequent weakness in Combined Forces lines? Nuclear attack to generate electromagnetic pulse to damage U.S. and ROK electronics would also be plausible.

The American Dimension

These latter considerations would put a premium on U.S. maneuver forces. While South Korea has a fine army—perhaps one of the five best in the world, in quantity and quality—its capacities for amphibious and aerial movement are limited. As such, and as the above Dupuy equations imply, its success in a future war would likely be largely a matter of defeating North Korean forces in detail by attrition. But that approach would allow lots of time for North Korean fissile materials to move about, for North Korean reservists to be mobilized, for Seoul to be threatened, and for China to weigh multiple options for its own role (see below).

Thus, an American maneuver capability would be hugely advantageous. It could in theory help secure the perimeter of much of North Korean territory, to make it hard for nuclear weapons and fissile materials and any leaders bent on escape to depart. It could also help create the capacity for a victory achieved less by defeat in detail of the enemy than by a pincer movement that would cut off many of its forces from their leadership and capital. The U.S. force could be spearheaded by the 101st Air Assault division, with its helicopter mobility, and by a U.S. Marine division deploying by amphibious ships and maritime prepositioning ships. It could further include an army division or more also marrying up with equipment from prepositioning ships and deploying by fast sealift. Together, this would constitute a corps-level capability that would be robust against North Korean counterattack even when deployed on North Korean soil.

Such a U.S. force would have a size of up to 150,000 ground forces, perhaps, and be complemented by another 75,000 naval and air personnel. They could thus possess a combined power by the Dupuy equations of 2,250,000—assuming a quality advantage of 10:1 against DPRK soldiers, not unlike what was observed in U.S. air-ground engagements against Iraqi forces in recent decades. This could roughly equal the realistic capacities of those 6 million North Korean reservists, many of whom might never make it to the fight and most of whom might not fight well—but nonetheless a force whose sheer numbers require some degree of balancing by the allies.

The Nuclear Dimension

Further reinforcing the case for a strong U.S. capability of the size and type outlined above is the North Korean nuclear arsenal. American nuclear weapons would provide a strong deterrent against this capability, as well as a hedge in the event that North Korean use of weapons of mass destruction complicated any conventional effort. But it is too simple to assume that U.S. nuclear weapons would fully counter and checkmate any possible North Korean employment of the DPRK's own nuclear arsenal. First of all, given the presumed stakes in this scenario—overthrow of the North Korean regime—there is little reason to think that DPRK leaders would be dissuaded from resorting to any and all means of halting an invasion of their country, according to standard deterrent logic. Perhaps they could be told that, while their unseating from power was the inevitable goal of any such military effort, they might be spared the death penalty or even offered eventual asylum if they desisted from such abominable actions. Yet the credibility of such a pledge in the middle of wartime operations could be difficult to establish. Moreover, North Korean leaders might really think that by using a nuclear weapon or two in a battlefield mode to slow an advancing army, while implicitly or explicitly threatening the use of other nuclear weapons against Seoul, they might find a credible pathway toward a negotiated settlement. Former Combined Forces commander General B. B. Bell has argued persuasively that to think North Korea would be fundamentally averse to using its nuclear weapons in war is wishful thinking, were regime survival on the line, especially when one bears in mind that the United States itself used nuclear weapons in the past.[33]

Simply retaliating with nuclear weapons, in a proportionate manner, against North Korean forces or other targets might not be a full answer to the dilemma either. Beyond the humanitarian implications, it is doubtful that North Korea's armed forces would be as concentrated geographically or as dependent on specific targetable assets such as airfields, major ports, highways, and command centers as the Combined Forces would be. The North Korean nuclear strikes might be airbursts near key military assets and units, detonated high enough to avoid the creation of large amounts of fallout—that is, at roughly 1,700 to 1,800 feet of altitude, as with the roughly 20-kiloton Hiroshima and Nagasaki bombs.[34] To achieve comparable effects, the United States might need to employ a dozen or more nuclear weapons of its own. It would have the capacity to do this, to be sure, but might not have the will in light of the likely repercussions in terms of human costs and in broader political and strategic terms. It also might wish, initially at least, to withhold use of nuclear weapons in order to deter further North Korean escalation. Perhaps most credibly, it could use a nuclear weapon or two in response to signal to Pyongyang that it would not be intimidated from responding in kind, but it might choose the location of the attack in such a way as to minimize the lethal effects, especially on civilians. This might mean that the military benefits would be limited as well, and U.S. force planning would therefore wisely proceed from the assumption that the key response to North Korean nuclear aggression would be conventional.

As such, the allied forces would need a margin of error. They would also need to operate in a sufficiently dispersed way that they limited their vulnerability to a single nuclear burst or two. In rough terms, a weapon of Hiroshima or Nagasaki force could severely damage most vehicles out to about half a mile to a mile distance and kill or severely injure most people out to 2 to 3 kilometers from ground zero, below the point of detonation.[35] In a major offensive, a modern military might concentrate its forces such that a brigade was placed every 5 to 10 kilometers within a general zone of advance.[36] That might not be prudent in a potentially nuclear environment.

On balance, in light of the normal geographic zones over which advancing mechanized forces generally would operate, it is prudent to assume that perhaps a brigade of unsuspecting Combined Forces Command ground forces plus corresponding support could be destroyed or severely degraded for each nuclear weapon used. This is a very notional and rough estimate, clearly. But assuming a rough rule of 10,000 allied forces lost for every North Korean nuclear weapon employed is probably a reasonable guide. As such, perhaps 30,000 to 50,000 additional allied troops should be built into planning requirements to cover this contingency. Some fraction of those could be South Korean reservists, but this kind of concern again validates the case for a robust American contribution to the allied war capability of at least the size discussed above. Indeed, a 250,000-strong U.S. force, with up to 175,000 of them Army and Marine Corps personnel, is hardly an excessive estimate of the U.S. military personnel that might be needed in such a scenario.

The China Dimension

How would China likely respond to all of this? The presumption among many American analysts has been that, recognizing North Korea as the chief source of the conflict, China would do everything possible to limit its own involvement. Why implicate itself in the mistakes of the world's last bastion of Stalinism? Why risk direct war with the United States? The idea that the People's Republic of China (PRC) in its modern guise would behave in a manner analogous to what Mao had done in the early days of the cold war would seem to smack of absurdity.

However, there are reasons to be concerned that China would not simply stand by. Fearing refugee flows, if not the leakage of nuclear or chemical materials from the DPRK, China might wish to seal its border with North Korea. And if protecting the border were the goal, doing so from a forward position could strike many Chinese military minds as sound policy.[37] Creating a buffer zone 50 or 100 kilometers into North Korea might appeal. In short, there are reasons to think the People's Liberation Army (PLA) might wish to intervene in a Korea contingency.[38]

Chinese decisionmaking would also be influenced by assessment of the longer-term consequences of North Korea's collapse. Beyond concerns about border security, Chinese leaders could be thinking about postconflict force dispositions on the peninsula. Expecting that the United States might try to retain forces in Korea even after reunification and stabilization efforts were complete, they might seek to establish leverage against that possibility. This scenario is particularly credible in light of two Chinese views. The first view is that an American military presence on the Asian mainland is inimical to the long-term Chinese interests of creating a greater sphere of influence and security for itself while avoiding encirclement by a pro-U.S. coalition.[39] The second is that Korea historically falls within any such Chinese sphere as a "tributary" state.[40]

Creating a fait accompli of tens of thousands (or more) of Chinese troops on Korean territory might seem a good bargaining chip in this context. Beijing's argument, explicit or implicit, might be that it would of course be happy to remove its troops from Korean soil once the peninsula was again stable—provided that the United States agreed to remove its own forces as well. Such a motivation might lead China to seek to deploy its forces further south than was required for a border-related operation, and perhaps to employ larger numbers of troops than it otherwise would have. It is also possible that China would hope to retain some kind of rump North Korean state after hostilities, as a buffer between itself and the United States and Republic of Korea, even if it recognized that such a North Korean state could require a new government.

China's military modernization efforts in recent years have focused more on maritime domains, but a number of its programs could empower—and perhaps embolden—PRC leaders to consider a direct role in a conflict in Korea. The most notorious Chinese programs in modern times include the DF-21 antiship ballistic missile, Kilo attack submarines and Sovremenny destroyers purchased from Russia, aircraft, including the J-11B and J-20 and perhaps now the J-31 too, and the PLA's first operational aircraft carrier, the *Liaoning*.[41] But while the overall thrust of these and other programs is probably to address disputed territories and waterways in the western Pacific, a number of the relevant systems, including the aircraft, could also be very helpful in a major overland operation. More generally, China's army has been streamlined and professionalized in recent decades, making it an even more formidable potential foe on the peninsula than it was from 1950 through 1953. In recent times it has emphasized greater use of information, combined-arms and joint operations, and mobility, while improving training and logistics as well. The PLA still has a way to go in many of these areas, of course.[42] That said, even before all these recent innovations and improvements, it showed in the 1950s that it was well capable of deploying large forces to the Korean Peninsula.

A PLA intervention in Korea could be a prescription for disaster. That is especially true as the U.S. and Chinese militaries have had very little contact or discussion about Korea over the years. Some hard-liners in both South Korea and the United States could be expected to call for a firm, even forceful response by the Combined Forces Command to such a Chinese encroachment.[43] Inadvertent escalation owing to miscommunication or the assertive actions of local commanders could also result. Even if top-level political leaders did not advocate or authorize it, any ambiguity they conveyed in their orders might allow a direct clash.

For a Chinese military that has not gone to war in a generation, it is possible that the dangers of combat might be downplayed or underappreciated. As the scholar Andrew Erickson has pointed out, the modern

Chinese military has not gone through its own version of a "Cuban missile crisis"—meaning it has not been sobered by a deeply unsettling and frightening experience.[44] Overconfidence could result. So could an inadequate appreciation of the dangers of war, or a hope that new technologies would permit shorter and more decisive wars than in the past—a tendency of many militaries and many leaders over the generations.[45]

The above considerations also suggest that both sides not only have much to lose by failure to coordinate their response to crisis but indeed, might have a lot to gain through coordination. The United States and the Republic of Korea should consider that a Chinese role in a future Korea scenario might in fact be helpful rather than threatening. It could lower the risks of inadvertent war. It could also reduce U.S. and ROK troop requirements for stabilizing the northern part of North Korea and provide reassurance to the North Korean people that their legitimate interests would be protected in a unified Korea. China too has much to gain from prior coordination with the Republic of Korea and the United States, although this would necessarily need to be highly confidential, given the likely anxiety it would cause in Pyongyang.

But none of this sort of cooperative endeavor can work absent a strong American capability, including the capacity to deploy corps-scale forces rapidly. The United States needs to be in a strong position vis-à-vis China to maintain the kind of leverage and influence required to make collaboration with the PLA a truly sound idea. Beijing should not gain the perception that it would be the most important and influential outside player in a future Korean war. Should China come to such a conclusion, its incentives for asserting its own prerogative to act as it saw fit might increase. This logic provides additional grounds for favoring a U.S. capacity for Korea in the range of a corps of ground forces—three to four divisions, plus support—complemented by substantial airpower and other assets, for a net strength of some 250,000 GIs, as argued earlier. Again, the logic is not to assume the need to defeat China in battle, only to have Seoul and Washington in a strong position to set the main parameters by which the PLA might credibly contribute to a positive outcome in a future war scenario.

It is also important not to trivialize the difficulty of the operation once acute hostilities and combined-arms maneuvers are complete. Sporadic resistance from North Korean units might continue for a time; land mines, chemical weapons, and other dangerous materials could remain strewn throughout much of the country; not all nuclear materials might be quickly accounted for. Stabilizing a population of some 25 million, as North Korea may boast at the time of the postulated conflict, would in theory require 500,000 to 600,000 forces, according to the Amos-Petraeus criteria from the U.S. military's counterinsurgency manual.[46] (In fact, the plausible range is wider, based on historical cases; for example, in post–World War II Japan, force levels were much lower and in post–World War II Germany they were much higher, by way of historical perspective.)[47] Again, South Korea would provide most of this stabilizing force over time, but it could have its own country to worry about, too, given the likely casualties and damage a war could cause to Seoul and environs. A substantial U.S. role should not be ruled out.

U.S. Requirements after Possible Korean Reunification

What about the longer term? If Korea is someday reunified, whatever the mechanism or the pathway, what would be the implications for U.S. force planning? For the purposes of this book, such a question is just as important as the immediate issue of the U.S. government's 5027 or 5029 War Plans.

Of course, the primary voice in any future decision about long-term peninsular security must be Seoul's, and that of the Korean people. It is entirely plausible that, if and when the peninsula is reunified, Koreans will decide that they are best off without any enduring military alliances, and take a path forward, not unlike, say, Finland, or Vietnam. In this case, the United States can wish the Korean people well, viewing them fundamentally as an economic partner, a friend, and a security partner for out-of-area missions rather than as a formal ally bound by a mutual defense accord. If the Koreans decide to go it alone, they may have to accept that doing so will be a permanent decision, with no wartime rescue from America (as in 1950) in the event that the calculation proves erroneous. It would simply be too hard for the United States to project power to that location, especially if one assumes the future aggressor against Korea might be China.

Just as plausibly, therefore, Seoul may decide that a sustained alliance with the United States does indeed serve its interests even in the absence of a North Korean threat. If so, the United States should consider retaining the alliance too, assuming that South Korea remains serious about providing for its own security and remains a stalwart ally of the United

States in the region and the world in general. Such circumstances seem likely. Few allies around the world have been as dependable friends of the United States, or as impressive in their own accomplishments. Korea is now a major international economic player that contributes substantially to the world economy, even if it possesses no particular resources that make it irreplaceable as such. It is also an important exemplar of global democratic and human rights norms, and of nuclear nonproliferation norms as well.

If a reunified Republic of Korea and the United States of America decide to sustain their formal alliance after the DPRK threat is no more, the question remains of how that should be done. Specifically, should the United States consider the territorial defense of Korea to be a realistic and desirable defining mission for its future ground forces?

There are two main ways to think about U.S. ground force planning in regard to a reunified Korea and a possible Chinese threat to it. One way is to think of deploying a trip-wire force that would make it nearly inevitable that any attack would cause American casualties and therefore, quite likely, entrain further American responses—be it a major reinforcement of its initial positions on the peninsula, a sustained bombing campaign against lines of communication into and out of Korea, an asymmetric attack on Chinese interests elsewhere in the world, or the possibility of nuclear escalation. Such a trip-wire force could be deployed in a relatively nonprovocative way. Given likely Chinese concern over the possibility of U.S. troops stationed on its land border, the United States could agree to keep any future American forces south of the 38th parallel and to reduce their number and capabilities relative to prewar totals, drawing on the model adopted in the post-unification arrangements for Germany in NATO. The remaining forces, say 10,000 strong, could be focused on multilateral missions such as training for peace operations that could involve Chinese and other regional forces, perhaps at some kind of a regional peace operations training center in the general vicinity of the current Korean DMZ.

The other approach would seek to have a sufficiently strong U.S. Army and Marine Corps that, in the event of Chinese attack, a reunified Korea and the United States would be capable of defending Korean territory even without the use of nuclear weapons. This is a very demanding requirement, but one worth examining. The motivation would be less any concern that such a conflict might someday actually happen and more to discourage Beijing from ever thinking that it was the only outside power with credible ground-combat capability on the peninsula.

As such, a military calculation is informative, even if it applies to a scenario that almost surely would never play out. Assume that China could benefit from proximity to deploy 2 million military personnel to the peninsula, out of a 2014 active duty force of 2.3 million.[48] Korea would have its entire force, presently about 650,000, as noted, with many more in reserve. For the sake of conservatism, assume further the U.S.-unified Korean qualitative advantage to be 1.5:1. Then, if the United States could manage to get half a million personnel to the peninsula, the math would look roughly like this:

Allies' Power: $(1,150,000)(1.5)(1) = 1,725,000$
Chinese Power: $2,000,000$
Allies' Loss Rate: $(0.01)(1,150,000)(2,000,000/1,725,000) =$
    13,333 per day
Chinese Loss Rate: $(0.01)(2,000,000)(1,725,000/2,000,000) =$
    17,250 per day

By this math, the outcome is a win for China, but not an easy or inevitable one. And if unified Korean reservists are worth anything, their enormous numbers might at least be able to make China pay a huge price for trying to occupy the peninsula (whether or not the reservists could prevent the initial invasion). As such, if the goal here was to create doubt in the minds of Chinese planners about the chances for a successful invasion attempt, it might be attainable, for a force of the presumed size.

The above would require deploying most American forces to the peninsula quickly, before Korea had been overrun. It would require large numbers of U.S. forces that were either on active duty or in a high state of readiness within the National Guard, able to be mobilized within weeks. Even assuming ready units, two to three months would be needed to get the majority of forces across the ocean, and the full deployment might take three to six months. Loading and unloading most ships can easily take a week per vessel; the ocean voyage is typically two weeks; getting equipment to the port of debarkation in the first place is often time-consuming, with preparations measured in weeks; sometimes two or more trips must be made by a given ship since transport assets are limited in number.[49] So success in this mission would require maintaining very capable and ready transport assets as well.

China could, of course, oppose the movement of these U.S. reinforcements across the ocean, using its submarines and other assets. It is not an unreasonable estimate to think that, even with antisubmarine warfare convoys protecting the shipping, submarines could penetrate the barriers and typically achieve several torpedo shots before being destroyed. Moreover, barrages of antiship cruise missiles from submarines, ships, or aircraft could saturate the defenses of incoming U.S. ships and cause significant numbers of losses, if reliable targeting information was available. There are various ways to get at estimates of losses. Simple historical analogies from World War II convoy loss rates, when reconnaissance technologies and precision strike assets were far more primitive, suggest that loss rates for surface shipping could reach 5 to 10 percent, depending on the specific balance of measures and countermeasures available to attacker and defender.[50] Loss rates today could be higher. In recent decades, antiship missiles aimed at ships with working defenses have typically found their way to their target 25 percent of the time.[51]

The PLA could seek to disable or destroy major infrastructure in Korea—ports, airfields, rail lines, marshaling yards—needed to absorb this incoming equipment and material. Such attacks are far more foreboding in the modern era of precision missiles than in the past. They could, at a minimum, significantly slow the arrival of reinforcements. To some extent, air bases can be repaired quickly, if fuel and command and control capabilities are underground, aircraft shelters are available, and runway repair equipment is adequate to the task. But there would still be considerable risks to large transport aircraft, which commonly do not have access to shelters of sufficient size, and in any event, these kinds of threats could significantly slow operations. A similar observation can be offered about ports and unloading infrastructure: even if roll-on/roll-off ships are employed, ships need access to harbors, wharves, and safe marshaling yards where unloaded equipment can be temporarily stored. Again, likely loss rates for ships, planes, and thus supplies could be in the range of some 5 to 25 percent for many scenarios.[52] If China or North Korea chose to employ tactical nuclear weapons as well—however unlikely the odds of Beijing electing to do so, for what would be for the PRC a limited war—these uncertainties would increase.

To be sure, the United States would not be the only party vulnerable to such attacks. Chinese forces, even if moving largely through their own territory, would still depend on certain ports, airfields, railway marshaling yards, bridges across the Yalu, and other crucial infrastructure. And the United States would likely still have the most advanced weaponry in the world for engaging targets through such deep interdiction campaigns. Fighters and bombers flying from Japan and Guam and other locations, perhaps to include Alaska, as well as other long-range systems that could include conventionally armed ballistic missiles, as well as America's extremely potent submarine forces and its surface Navy, could approach Chinese targets and exact punishment. So some of the uncertainties sketched out above would cut both ways.

The bottom line in rough numbers might be that, to generate a presence of one-half million U.S. uniformed personnel on the peninsula, the United States might need to send 600,000 or more personnel, to allow for possible losses in transit. Roughly two-thirds of the total forces might be ground troops, as with the previous estimates for the Russia case, meaning 400,000 soldiers and Marines. This scenario stretches the limits of a realistic criterion for future U.S. Army and Marine Corps force sizing, given its extreme unlikelihood, but it may be worth keeping in the back of one's mind.

A SOUTH CHINA SEA SCENARIO:
A MAJOR CHINESE THREAT TO THE PHILIPPINES

There may be other ways in which American land power could be relevant to military scenarios involving China. Specifically, if Chinese tensions with a U.S. treaty ally such as the Philippines or even Japan dramatically intensified, one could imagine Chinese threats to some of the islands making up those nations today. Perhaps China would use missiles and raids to destabilize or punish the islands, such as Okinawa, or Palawan in the Philippines—islands relatively near areas where maritime disputes could intensify. Or perhaps Beijing would attempt to seize one of these islands, to prevent its military use by the sovereign country against Chinese maritime interests or as punishment of the other state, as well as to project an implied threat that other national territory could be threatened as well. In this kind of situation, U.S. ground forces might be relevant to garrison the same or other islands and to protect military and civilian assets on them.

Because Chinese writers have sometimes raised the possibility of challenging Japan for control of the Ryukyu Islands, that scenario could be considered. One could ask what size Japanese and American deployment would be adequate to maintain a robust defense of Okinawa from a plausible invasion force, or what size force would be needed to liberate the island from PRC control if somehow China was able to seize it. (Of course, any comprehensive military analysis would need to consider air and naval aspects of such a scenario as well.)

However, on balance, this scenario strikes me as very implausible. China's own government does not lay claim to Okinawa, or any other islands now controlled or administered by Japan beyond the Senkaku/Diaoyu, and the difficulty of amphibious operations against a high-technology defender in the modern era is enormous. Moreover, Beijing could hardly doubt Tokyo's and Washington's willingness to fight for what is an important part of Japan, where more than 1 million inhabitants now live.

By contrast, the Philippines might represent a more believable target for Chinese aggression. While Manila and Washington do have a formal alliance, it is less rock-solid than the U.S.-Japan relationship. As such, America's willingness to defend its ally might be less credible in Chinese eyes. Main U.S. forces are not based in the Philippines today, either. The Philippines have a small defense budget and a fairly small military to defend a huge land mass with many islands. It is doubtful that China would see any of those islands as useful prizes of war in their own right. But if a sustained maritime campaign developed between the two countries over islands, fishing beds, and underwater resources, China might consider seizing an island from the Philippine archipelago to punish Manila and deter any further Filipino uses of armed force. Palawan island, for example, a long island running north-south in the western part of the Philippine archipelago, with only a modest indigenous population, might be a tempting target. By holding it, China would prevent the Philippines from using any bases there against its own forces, would punish Manila for what Beijing perceived as bad behavior, and would potentially deter further such behavior by implicitly showing the Philippines what could happen if it retaliated (more islands could be seized).

Most of what is discussed below could ensue even if China did not try to seize Palawan but simply acted increasingly aggressively in the vicinity near the western edges of the Philippine archipelago. As such, even though a Chinese invasion of that island is assumed in the following discussion, many of the implications for U.S. ground forces in other types of South China Sea scenarios might be similar to what is estimated in the following pages. If maritime domains in Southeast Asia became contested in some way, the United States, working with Manila, might have to consider establishing airfields and other facilities in the Philippines, and garrisoning a number of islands in the Philippines with ground forces to help protect these assets.

China does not have a large power projection force at present, and it may not have a large one in the time when this scenario is contemplated—say, in the 2020s or 2030s. Its amphibious fleet is expanding somewhat at present, but not radically so.[53] As such, it might have only the equivalent of roughly a division's worth of amphibious lift and a comparable amount of air assault capability in this scenario (about 15,000 troops each).[54] But that might be of limited comfort. First of all, Palawan is not heavily defended. Second, even if U.S. naval and air assets were in the region, not knowing the destination of Chinese amphibious and airborne forces, they might choose not to shoot at them—thereby essentially conceding the initial victory to the PLA. Third, unless the United States immediately changed its approach thereafter, China could build up airfield and port facilities and reinforce its initial positions with adequate forces to solidify control of the island and create the rudiments of an island defense against a possible counterassault led by the U.S. military.

Depending on how far this scenario progressed before a reaction was considered, the United States and the Philippines would, together with any other countries supporting them, have a number of options. One would be to prepare, over a period of months if necessary, a massive flotilla from Luzon or another major Philippine island and ultimately set sail to attempt to retake Palawan (with much of the necessary air support coming from planes based on other Philippine islands). This approach would have the disadvantage, however, of being vulnerable to possible Chinese interdiction with attack submarines and other assets—and would necessitate in the end a bloody liberation of the island. A second would be to attempt a naval quarantine of Palawan, though that would have the effect of punishing the islanders along with the occupying Chinese troops.

A third and potentially more appealing option would be to garrison some of the other nearby Philippine islands to prevent any further Chinese conquests while building an international coalition to apply asymmetric pressure on China, through military interdiction of sea lanes and/or a regime of international economic sanctions. To put it differently, and bluntly, this would amount to the containment strategy of China that

Beijing complains about even today—but in this case, China would be right that it was truly being applied.[55]

What might such garrisoning entail? American and Philippine ground forces would likely focus on protecting key bases, including airfields, against missile attack, special operations raids, and the like. They could also conduct offensive operations in the broader maritime domains. Army forces could play a role in the latter activities with shore batteries capable of ranging targets at various distances at sea, as then Secretary of Defense Chuck Hagel and Deputy Secretary Robert Work both have discussed in more generic terms in recent years.[56] Protection of main civilian population centers on Luzon and elsewhere in the central Philippine archipelago could be left to the Philippine armed forces, given the unlikelihood of a Chinese assault over such distances.

How many bases might be needed? It is difficult to know in advance, absent precise information on what kind of a force China might be able to sustain on Palawan, and in its vicinity. One point of reference, however, might be to consider the number of airfields used in recent major U.S.-led military operations. Presumably, even if a campaign against Chinese military assets and perhaps shipping assets in the region were less intensive in many ways than, say, the 1999 Kosovo War or Operation Desert Storm in 1991, there would be an even greater expanse of territory to monitor, and even greater worries about airfield vulnerability in this case. The Kosovo War involved some twenty to twenty-five air bases, as did Desert Storm.[57] As of the fairly recent past, the Philippines had about a dozen airfields throughout its archipelago, though more could be constructed if need be, of course.[58] Take these various numbers as rough guides, it is plausible that the United States and the Philippines would seek to establish one to two dozen bases to establish superiority in air and naval domains against anything China could realistically sustain at such a distance (it is just under 1,000 miles from Hainan Island to Palawan).

Standard army doctrine would suggest using roughly a brigade, of perhaps several thousand troops, for each such facility.[59] That is enough to maintain perimeter monitoring, rapid-reaction capability, air and missile defense, and command and control for a base that could be several miles long on a dimension, and thus with a perimeter of 10 to 20 miles. Assuming a roughly equal mix of U.S. and Philippine army units suggests a total of up to twelve U.S. brigades at a time for the operation. That could mean a total of 40,000 soldiers and Marines in the brigades themselves and a grand total of some 100,000 ground forces, including support.

Then there is the matter of a rotation base. This defensive operation could last some time, as other tools of national power, including air and naval forces, pressured China in other ways. In theory, unless the brigades were to be simply stationed on the islands and left there for the duration of any standoff, without relief, sustaining twelve brigades could involve a force structure three times as large. That could include elements of the National Guard, since there would be time to prepare for such rotations.

CONCLUSION

The scenarios considered in this chapter are almost surely less likely to occur than those that follow in the next. At least, one hopes that to be the case, since they could involve hostilities against nuclear-armed major powers. Indeed, the possibility of the actual use of weapons of mass destruction is an additional reason why the types of calculations offered here are imprecise: the possible mushroom clouds of war must be added to Clausewitz's fog of war, and all the other realities that make military force planning difficult and inaccurate. As such, U.S. planners need to remember the importance of building in a cushion when carrying out force sizing analyses.

Despite the various problems that have plagued U.S.-China and especially U.S.-Russia relations in recent years, I see no particular evidence that the premises driving these contingency analyses—namely, a direct Russian threat to the Baltic states or large-scale Chinese threats against Korea or the Philippines—are acute worries at present. But the goal of force planning should be, in part, to keep them unthinkable.

The scenarios considered here imply the need for anywhere from several tens of thousands to several hundreds of thousands of U.S. ground troops, depending on circumstances and specifics. Once force requirements are estimated for the seven contingencies examined in chapter 4, we will then have the grist for proposing a future force structure for the Total Force of the U.S. Army and the U.S. Marine Corps.

CHAPTER FOUR

Scenarios in South Asia, the Middle East, Africa, and the Americas

WHILE THE POSSIBLE SCENARIOS considered in chapter 3 may be the most challenging for American planners, and pose the greatest risks of either nuclear war or other fundamental threat to the integrity of the global order as well, they are probably not the most likely for the United States in the decades to come. This chapter considers those areas of the world where war might be slightly less apocalyptic for American interests if it happened but where, alas, it is also more likely to occur—or even occurring already, in some cases.

To recapitulate, this chapter considers the final seven scenarios on my list from chapter 3:

—A fissioning of Pakistan.

—Indo-Pakistani war.

—Iranian use or threatened use of nuclear weapons against a neighbor.

—A major international stabilization operation in the Middle East—perhaps in Syria after a negotiated peace.

—Civil war accompanied by other challenges in Nigeria.

—Increased brutality against Americans by criminal networks in Central America.

—A major domestic emergency in the United States.

A FISSIONING OF PAKISTAN

I start by considering Pakistan in the unlikely scenario in which it begins to fall apart. Pakistan is hardly the only state in the region that faces major internal challenges. But it is among the largest. And not only does it have nuclear weapons, it is the staging ground for a number of terrorist groups bent on doing great harm to India in particular, and to U.S. interests from Afghanistan to other parts of the world as well.

On balance, the Pakistani state is likely to survive, and its circumstances may be somewhat better now than just a few years ago. Still, Pakistan could face threats to its cohesion, perhaps arising out of a combination of insurgencies in places such as Balochistan, together with the internal threat of Islamic extremism.

Imagine, for example, if such a political crisis coincided with a major natural disaster striking a megacity such as Karachi or Lahore, laying waste to much of its infrastructure and perhaps threatening nearby nuclear reactors—and also, quite possibly, the physical security of some nuclear weapons storage sites. When looking out two to three decades and considering scenarios that stretch the imagination as well as the likely capacities of U.S. and other international forces, it is important to do more than extrapolate linearly from today's baseline level of problems and challenges in South Asia.

Under such extreme circumstances, it strikes me as entirely plausible that whatever remnants of a Pakistani government still existed might solicit international aid to help reestablish order, aid in relief efforts, and help secure—or recover—nuclear materials. At present, such a scenario is nearly inconceivable. But if the situation became truly dire, Pakistani leaders might elect to try to hide whatever part of their nuclear arsenal was still intact (so that Americans and other outsiders could not access it) while asking for help with the rest of it, and with other challenges to the nation's security and integrity. Because of the potential for nuclear weapons to fall into terrorist hands, the stakes here could be very high for the United States and its allies as well.

For all the challenges facing the country, it is important to note that today, Pakistan does not appear on the verge of collapse. It is also important to underscore, especially in this period of fraught U.S.-Pakistan relations, that any international effort to help Pakistan restore order to its own territory could only be carried out with the full acquiescence and at the invitation of its government. That is because there is probably no realistic scenario in which Pakistan's army would truly melt away. It is also because the country is so huge that the task of completely stabilizing it with outside forces would be unthinkably demanding, even with today's military—indeed, even with a force twice as large as that of the current U.S. armed forces.

This subject is a very sensitive one with Pakistanis, who tend to be confident about the cohesion of their country and mistrustful of outside powers that would offer "help" in scenarios like the one I have just sketched out. Many Pakistanis suspect that any such assistance would be a means of gaining control of Pakistan's nuclear weapons and fissile materials, among other concerns. The May 2011 killing of Osama bin Laden, done without any American warning to Pakistan, only exacerbated Pakistani sensitivities to any discussion of scenarios that would infringe on the nation's sovereignty.

But of all the military scenarios that undoubtedly would involve U.S. vital interests, a collapsed Pakistan ranks very high on the list. The combination of Islamic extremists and nuclear weapons in that country is extremely worrisome. Were parts of Pakistan's nuclear arsenal ever to fall into the wrong hands, al Qaeda could conceivably gain access to a nuclear device, with terrifying possible results. The Pakistan collapse scenario does appear unlikely, in light of the country's traditionally moderate officer corps and other factors.[1] However, some parts of the country's military as well as its intelligence services, which created the Taliban and other extremist groups, are becoming less moderate and less dependable. The country as a whole is sufficiently infiltrated by fundamentalist groups—as evidenced by the assassination attempts directed against President Pervez Musharraf in earlier days, the killing of Benazir Bhutto in 2007, and other incidents—that this terrifying scenario should not be dismissed.[2]

Were Pakistan to fracture, it is unclear what the United States and like-minded states would or should do. As with North Korea, it is highly unlikely that "surgical strikes" to destroy the nuclear weapons could be conducted successfully. The United States probably would not know their location—at a minimum, scores of sites controlled by special forces or elite army units would be presumed candidates—and no Pakistani government would likely help external forces with targeting information. The chances of learning the locations would probably be greater than in the North Korean case, owing to the greater openness of Pakistani society and its ties with the outside world. But U.S.-Pakistani military cooperation, cut off for a decade in the 1990s, is still quite modest, and the likelihood that Washington would be provided such information or otherwise obtain it should be considered low.

Rather than expect a great deal from surgical strikes or commando-style raids, therefore, a wiser option would be to try to restore order before nuclear weapons could be taken by extremists and transferred to terrorists. If the international community could act fast enough, it might help defeat an insurrection. Another option would be to protect Pakistan's borders, thereby making it harder to sneak nuclear weapons out of the country, while providing technical support to the Pakistani armed forces as they tried to quell the insurrection internally.

Given the enormous stakes, the United States would literally have to do anything it could to prevent nuclear weapons from getting into the wrong hands. Even in the event that China aided in the effort too, as it might well, the scale of the plausible undertaking would be daunting. Pakistan is a very large country. Its population of 200 million is more than six times Iraq's; its land area is roughly twice that of Iraq; its perimeter is about 50 percent longer in total than Iraq's. Stabilizing an entire country of this size could easily require several times as many troops as the Iraq mission (which topped out at about 170,000 Americans). According to the criteria outlined in the U.S. military's counterinsurgency manual, 4 million to 5 million total "counterinsurgents" could be required for a population of 200 million—including indigenous police, gendarmes, and soldiers, as well as any outside forces.[3] Even if one assumes the lower ratios from past operations, history suggests that at least 2 million counterinsurgents would be needed.[4]

Beyond the enormous scale of the stabilization operation itself, there is the matter of transportation and timing. Today, the time frame required for a force of even 100,000 foreign troops to be deployed intercontinentally would likely be two to three months. This is evident from past deployments for Operation Desert Storm and Operation Iraqi Freedom, among others—as well as the simple military realities that even fast roll-on/roll-off ships typically take a month for loading, traversing the oceans, and unloading. Beyond that month is the time needed to get equipment from interior U.S. bases to ports, and from receiving ports in Pakistan to where they might be needed in that country.[5]

But any fissioning of Pakistan would likely be gradual and partial, not immediate and nationwide. One way to guesstimate the scale of a possible operation is through an examination of the ethnic breakdowns of the nation. Pakistan is about 15 percent Sindh, about 15 percent Pashtun, and about 4 percent Baloch.[6] Rather than splintering across ethnic lines, Pakistan could also fray between secularists and jihadists, even within the armed forces themselves. It is difficult to estimate what fraction of the military and intelligence services may be so hard line as to be capable of breaking off from the rest of the state.[7] Either way, however, it does not seem unreasonable to assume that up to roughly one-third of Pakistan or its armed forces could wind up in revolt at some future date. If that occurred, a region of several tens of millions could descend into chaos or civil war—a fraction of the country not unlike Iraq or Afghanistan in the size of the affected population.

One could also imagine a city such as Karachi experiencing a meltdown as a result of a combination of prolonged weak governance and increased criminality, and the city environs then possibly being affected by a terrible natural catastrophe such as a huge earthquake. Perhaps the earthquake would even create a second catastrophe, such as a major accident at a nuclear power plant, with cascading and snowballing repercussions.

Such a situation could bring an urban area and surrounding region of 20 to 40 million people to its knees, while knocking out electricity and other infrastructure and bringing economic activity largely to a halt. (Indeed, a separate analysis estimating the possible effects of a single nuclear reactor accident in South Asia independently calculated that the health of some 30 million individuals could be threatened.)[8] In such circumstances, military forces could be needed not only to restore order but also to provide some minimal level of human necessities—food, water, basic medical care—to a huge population. This massive relief operation, the greatest in history, would occur, moreover, in a potentially hostile and violent environment. The magnitude of the possible effort can be guesstimated by observing that a typical division of some 15,000 soldiers, along with support in the form of additional units again as numerous, might have the trucking capacity for moving up to 10,000 tons or 20,000,000 pounds of supplies.[9] Assuming, say, two round trips a day from a central depot area, to allow time for loading and unloading and distribution, such a contingent of 30,000 troops might provide two pounds of supplies per person to a population of 20 million.[10] If the typical requirement were five pounds a day, 75,000 or more troops could be needed just for providing sustenance, to say nothing of security, at least until water purification systems could be made operational and provided with adequate fuel.[11]

Scaling from the response to the 2010 earthquake in Haiti provides another reference point. That operation involved up to 22,000 American military personnel and at least several thousand more from other countries, making for roughly 30,000 at peak. It also involved many thousands of civilian relief workers—quite possibly comparable in number to the military response. In round numbers, the total was perhaps 50,000 individuals.[12] In a future case like the one considered here, those civilian aid workers might not be able to move about safely, meaning that they would have to be replaced by military or police personnel. As such, a disaster affecting ten times as many people could require, in rough terms, some half million responders (indigenous and foreign) to provide for basic relief, sustenance, and ultimately shelter and recovery.

It seems credible that the foreign troop requirements in these types of Pakistan scenarios could exceed 100,000. An estimate of 30,000 to 50,000 U.S. ground troops does not seem unrealistic for a sufficiently bad and demanding scenario.

INDO-PAKISTANI WAR

An Indo-Pakistani war remains a real possibility in today's world, and quite probably throughout the time frame of this study.[13] There have already been three or four, depending on whether one counts the Kargil crisis of 1999, and it is remarkable that there have not been more, especially after the 2008 Mumbai attack, when India chose not to respond militarily. If in the next possible war the nuclear weapons threshold were crossed, the plausibility of a foreign military role could increase dramatically. This would not necessarily entail taking sides in the fighting or forcibly imposing a peace, but reinforcing a cease-fire once it was negotiated. To date, Delhi in particular has eschewed any and all foreign role in diplomacy over Kashmir or related matters dividing the two countries. But in the aftermath of the near use or actual use of nuclear weapons, calculations could change dramatically—such a world could be characterized by a far different political psychology than today's.

The path to war could begin, perhaps, with a more extremist leader coming to power in Pakistan. It is troubling to imagine the dangers associated with a country of 200 million and the world's fastest-growing nuclear arsenal, antipathy toward both India and America, numerous extremist groups, with some possibly still supported by the nation's intelligence forces, and claims on land currently controlled by India.[14] It is straightforward to see how such an extremist state could take South Asia to the brink of nuclear war by provoking conflict with India, perhaps through another Mumbai-like attack. Were that to happen, and if perhaps a nuclear weapon or two were detonated above an airbase or other such military facility, the world could be faced with the specter of all-out nuclear war in the most densely populated part of the planet.

It is important to understand why nuclear weapons really could be employed, even after seventy years of nonuse globally. First, even if it was the original provocateur, Pakistan could come to fear very gravely for its own survival in the course of this type of scenario. Having aided and abetted a group like Lashkar-e-Taiba, with its extremist anti-Indian views and ruthless brutality, Pakistan would have given India ample grounds for retaliation.[15] That would be true even if Lashkar-e-Taiba had in effect become by then a Frankenstein's monster, no longer obeying its initial creator, Pakistani Inter-Services Intelligence. Yet even a limited Indian conventional counterattack, perhaps influenced by its Cold Start military thinking, could very quickly put the capital at risk, owing to the narrowness of Pakistan in the northern part of the country.[16] Islamabad and Rawalpindi are a scant 200 kilometers from the Indian border—meaning that in theory, they could be reached within days by a successful Indian maneuver operation. This worry could be the Pakistani perception even if it were not the Indian intent. And, of course, Lahore, with its considerable strategic significance (and its role as occasional sanctuary for the leader of Lashkar-e-Taiba), is just over the border.

In such a situation, Pakistan might well see military logic in the use of several nuclear weapons against Indian troop concentrations, marshaling facilities, choke points, bridges, military airfields, or other tactical targets. Presumably Pakistan would prefer to conduct such attacks over Indian soil, though it is not out of the question that it could conduct some over its own territory, too. If airbursts were employed, meaning that the weapons were detonated say a half-kilometer or so up in the air (depending on their precise yield), the effects of the explosions could be catastrophic to people and military equipment immediately below and over an area of roughly 3 to 5 kilometers' radius, without creating much fallout that would later descend on populated areas downwind. That is because such fallout is created mostly when dirt and rock are heaved up into the atmosphere when the fireball of a nuclear detonation makes contact with the ground—as it will do for low-altitude bursts but not higher-altitude ones. Because the Hiroshima and Nagasaki bombs were detonated nearly 2,000 feet above the ground, there were no casualties from fallout from either.[17]

Beyond their immediate military effects, such attacks would simultaneously signal Islamabad's willingness to escalate if the advance did not cease. Despite the huge risks, there would be few better ways of making a threat to attack Delhi credible than to cross the nuclear threshold in attacks against tactical military targets. This approach could, in the minds of Pakistani planners, hold out the hope of simultaneously slowing the Indian advance, showing resolve, and yet at the same time displaying enough restraint that India would not have an incentive to attack Pakistani cities with nuclear weapons in the first instance. Presumably, Pakistanis would have to assume the possibility of Indian attacks against Pakistani armed forces. But that might be a risk the country's leadership would be willing to accept, if the alternative seemed to be defeat and forced surrender after a conventional battle.

Whether such a finely graduated nuclear attack would impress Indians as having been restrained in any meaningful sense can be debated. That might be especially true if any of the Pakistani attacks went off course and caused more damage than intended. Thus, the danger of inadvertent escalation in this kind of scenario could be quite real. It might not even take nuclear attacks by Pakistan to cause nuclear dangers. Even conventional attacks against warning and command systems could create dangers that India or Pakistan would believe it was under nuclear attack by the other when in fact it was not—raising the possibility of a nuclear response.[18]

It is imaginable in such circumstances that, if such an Indo-Pakistani war with nuclear implications began, and international negotiators were trying to figure out how to end it, an international force could be proposed to help stabilize the situation for a number of years. The notion might be based on the concept of trusteeship. Kashmir, perhaps still the original casus belli of the conflict, might be administered under a UN mandate and protected by a UN-legitimated force for a number of years, prior to the holding of a plebiscite that would determine the region's future political status, whether independence, association with India, association with Pakistan, or partition.[19] There might be no other compromise that both India and Pakistan would accept. That nuclear conflict might have occurred by this point would have raised the stakes enormously for both sides, making it hard for any leader to accept a simple cease-fire absent a credible political process to go along with it. A time horizon of roughly a decade or more might be appropriate for such a mission, time enough to allow for a calming of tensions as well as political transitions in both countries, and for Pakistan to demonstrate a willingness to clamp down on terrorist groups that it had previously supported.

India in particular would be adamantly against this idea today. But things could change fundamentally if such a settlement, and such a force, seemed the only way to reverse the momentum toward all-out nuclear war in South Asia. American forces would quite likely need to play a key role, as others might not have the capacity or the political confidence to handle the mission on their own.[20]

If a peacekeeping mission could be limited to Kashmir itself, with a population of about 15 million, standard doctrine would suggest up to 300,000 personnel for a fairly robust capability.[21] However, because of the importance of securing borders and maintaining a muscular margin of insurance against the unexpected, a somewhat larger force might be considered. In addition to securing Kashmir, that mission might monitor much of the Indo-Pakistani border, with enough capacity for active patrolling and monitoring. That could include the entirety of the nearly 3,000-kilometer border, but it might be more likely that it would seek to monitor the roughly 1,200 kilometers of cease-fire line dating back to 1972 and known as the Line of Control.[22] How much force might be needed to maintain a patrol along, say, 1,200 kilometers? It is difficult to give a figure, but the UN mission in Abyei, on the border between the two Sudans, stretches over roughly 100 kilometers of border and involves some 4,000 troops.[23] (And, of course, the Sudans are much less militarily capable than India and Pakistan.) Applied to this case, that ratio would imply about 50,000 additional troops, based on linear extrapolation. Another possible model, the UN Disengagement Observer Force along the Golan Heights, involves about 1,000 troops for a border between Israel and Syria of some 65 kilometers' length.

That figure, when extrapolated, would imply a requirement for something like 20,000 troops along the Line of Control, if similar force densities were deemed adequate.[24]

The U.S. role in such an operation could range from moderate to quite substantial. Recent operations, from Bosnia and Kosovo to Iraq and Afghanistan, suggest a plausible range of 20 percent to 50 percent or more of the total force. If the foreign force requirement were 350,000 and if most U.S. troops were ground forces, the U.S. Army and Marine Corps contribution could range from perhaps 60,000 to 150,000.

It is worth noting that, even if the above scenario seems rather apocalyptic, it is far from the most challenging for U.S. forces that can be imagined in the aftermath of another Indo-Pakistani war. Should such a conflict go beyond the potential threatened use or actual employment of a nuclear weapon or two and escalate to the exchange of many warheads, perhaps even the targeting of parts of cities (say, those with key military command and control centers), the world could be confronted with a situation in which millions were immediately dead—and worse yet, tens of millions were trying to survive without working infrastructure in areas contaminated by radioactivity. Such a specter could dwarf even the previous contingency of a complex catastrophe afflicting a single city like Karachi.

In short, the scenarios advanced here may or may not be the right ones, and may or may not reach the threshold of plausibility in the eyes of all readers. But they are not being gamed to deliberately overstate the scale of potential danger. Substantially worse cases can easily be imagined.[25]

ADDRESSING A NUCLEAR IRAN—
AN IN EXTREMIS U.S. INVASION CAPACITY

A scenario involving Iran's possible acquisition and possible use of nuclear weapons against a neighboring state is designed less as a high-probability scenario than as a "stress test" for future American force planning. My contention here is that, in such a situation, the United States might wish to retain an implied or latent capability to mount a ground invasion that could overthrow the Iranian government that had carried out such a strike or that seemed willing to do so. This is not a preventive war scenario; I am not proposing that the United States seriously consider a major ground war to stop Iran from getting the bomb or to overthrow an Iranian government that might be seeking such a capability. Rather, the exercise is designed with an eye toward a crisis or conflict that Iran might generate while seeking, or after having obtained, such a nuclear capability.

The first premise of the scenario, that Iran someday chooses to pursue or acquire the bomb, is hard to dismiss. The second premise, that a U.S. ground invasion capability could be relevant to handling a future threatened use or actual use of Iran's own nuclear arsenal against a regional ally of the United States, is less obvious and requires explanation.

To be sure, there are scenarios in which the United States would almost surely not respond to an Iranian nuclear threat or attack with a counterattack using conventional ground forces. Most likely in this situation would be a proportionate U.S. nuclear response. Threatening to overthrow the Iranian regime could be exactly what the United States might *not* wish to do in a given instance, if trying to deter Teheran from any further nuclear use, since Iran would have little reason to hold back as it watched American armies march on its capital city.

Still, there are dimensions to a possible scenario that could make it desirable for the United States to have options. For example, if Iran only had one or two deliverable weapons, and had already employed them, the United States (and any coalition partners) might decide that the dangers of leaving in place a regime that had carried out such a heinous attack would be great over the longer term, and that, in the short term, there would be relatively little danger of marching on Teheran, in terms of associated nuclear risk. Or if Iran was believed to have a number of tactical weapons in a specific location or two, but those locations were not known, it could be sensible to look for them rather than to grant Iran the time to build more delivery vehicles, which could dramatically increase the danger they posed to the region. This might particularly be the case if it was known that Teheran was planning to carry out an attack with such warheads, perhaps through stealthy means such as smuggling them into a major Middle Eastern port on a cargo ship.

This scenario is proposed less as a likely U.S. recourse than as a capability U.S. ground forces should seek to retain for the sake of deterrence. An ability to invade and overthrow the Iranian government, even without a corresponding capacity to stabilize and govern the Iranian state thereafter, could be a useful if unspoken additional deterrent, making it less likely that leaders in Teheran would ever contemplate nuclear aggression, knowing the full range of retaliatory options that might befall them if they did.

Leaders in Teheran might convince themselves that the United States would not respond to an Iranian nuclear attack in kind because of the American fear of causing casualties to innocent civilians. If Iranian hardliners could embed themselves within their nation's cities, they might believe themselves to be relatively impervious to the possibility of U.S. nuclear retaliation against their command and control assets and main headquarters. It would be in the United States' interest not to allow Iranian leaders the option of subscribing to a theory that seemed to promise them impunity since any such sentiment, even if wrongly grounded, could make them more reckless and aggressive. It would also be in the United States' interest to reassure its regional allies that it had multiple credible options for responding to any Iranian nuclear coercion or aggression—partly to dissuade those allies from pursuing their own nuclear weapons.[26]

The force requirements for this scenario would mimic fairly closely the standard estimates of what it takes to win a major regional contingency or major theater war of the classic post–cold war definition. Iran is much larger and more populous than Iraq (or Afghanistan, or North Korea), to be sure, but its armed forces are not unlike those of Saddam's Iraq in size, resources, technology, and general capability. That is no surprise at one level, since Iran and Iraq fought to a standstill over nearly a decade of war in the 1980s.

According to the TASCFORM methodology employed frequently in the 1990s by the Congressional Budget Office and the House Armed Services Committee, Iran was notably weaker in the early post–cold war years than either Iraq after Desert Storm or North Korea.[27] Since then, Iran has attempted to rearm, but its purchases have been constrained by various forms of sanctions, and its net capabilities have probably improved only modestly.

Iran, 1992

—530,000 active-duty military personnel, with 305,000 in the army.

—Four armored divisions and seven infantry divisions.

—Key ground weaponry including some 700 tanks (mostly of T-54/T-55 vintage).

—700 armored personnel carriers (largely BTR-50 and BTR-60 models).

—About 1,300 large-bore artillery.

—100 or so AH-1 attack helicopters, and an estimated 262 fixed-wing combat aircraft of variable but mediocre levels of serviceability (a mix of F-4, F-5, F-14, and MiG-29, among other types).

—According to TASCFORM methodology, less than 2.0 U.S. armored divisional equivalents and 2.0 tactical fighter wing equivalents (less than half the capabilities of either post–Desert-Storm Iraq or North Korea).[28]

Iran, 2015

—523,000 active-duty personnel, of which 350,000 are army.

—About 1,700 tanks (including about 500 T-72 tanks from Russia).

—Nearly 9,000 large-bore artillery tubes.

—Some 640 armored personnel carriers.

—About 50 attack helicopters.

—About 334 fixed-wing combat aircraft (with the increase largely the result of acquiring Su-24 jets from Russia).

—Resulting TASCFORM scores approaching 4.0 American armored divisional equivalents and 3.0 equivalent tactical fighter wings.[29]

Of course, this mission would be very demanding and risky whatever the simple math might suggest. First of all, reliably unseating the regime implies more than a Persian equivalent of the U.S.-led coalition's Thunder Run in Baghdad in April 2003. It means staying around long enough to ensure that most top leaders of the government, especially the Revolutionary Guard and QODS force, were tracked down. It took several months to find Saddam in Iraq, and a good deal of great intelligence work and luck as well. Elements of the Iranian regime might attempt to hide in the remote northern mountains of the country, for example.[30] Second, Iran's very size increases the chances that a maneuver operation designed to reach the capital might bog down in one way or another. This difficulty could be amplified if U.S.-led coalition forces felt they needed to come ashore in southern Iran to eliminate the kinds of naval threats that Iran could pose to shipping in the Persian Gulf itself. Third, Iran's weapons of mass destruction could cause the same kinds of problems that were considered in the discussion of a Korea scenario: they could weaken or slow U.S. invasion forces.

These considerations leave aside the herculean task of actually stabilizing a country of nearly 100 million. Simply invading and overthrowing a regime that planned or had committed abominable nuclear transgressions would almost surely be at least as difficult as past Iraq wars were, and comparably demanding to a prospective North Korean contingency. As in that case, the U.S. ground force requirements could surely reach 175,000 uniformed personnel.

A PEACEKEEPING OR STABILIZATION OPERATION IN THE MIDDLE EAST

Despite the understandable aversion of Americans to putting significant numbers of boots on the ground in the Middle East again, there are scenarios that could make it a serious option for the United States, even in the relatively near future. This category of scenarios is probably the single most probable of any considered in this book.

One relatively simpler and smaller operation—though hardly an easy one—could be to undergird an implementation force for an Israeli-Palestinian peace deal. Such a deal is not in the immediate offing, but could still happen someday. President Obama's and Secretary Kerry's effort, in the 2013–14 time period, to help promote an Israeli-Palestinian peace deal involved not only the dedicated efforts of Ambassador Martin Indyk on the political and diplomatic aspects of the challenge but also a parallel effort led by retired General John Allen on the security side. Both tracks were kept generally quiet and private, so available details are limited. But the thrust of the latter effort was clearly to provide Israel in particular with confidence that its security would not be compromised in any deal, which would presumably have required it to pull back its own forces from the occupied West Bank and allow them to be replaced with some kind of international capability. The international force would presumably have had to secure borders against possible arms shipments by regional powers such as Iran to would-be spoilers, carry out targeted counterterrorism operations if and when needed in the Palestinian territories (perhaps in conjunction with Palestinian forces), and help police the population until proper Palestinian security forces could be fully recruited, trained, and vouched for. The international force might also help build those competent and capable Palestinian forces.[31] With a population of around 5 million, the Palestinian regions of the Levant might be policed with roughly one-fifth the assets devoted to either Iraq or Afghanistan. In rough terms, this means that an international force might number 30,000 to 50,000 uniformed personnel. The U.S. share of that total might be 10,000 to 20,000, in rough numbers, or one to three brigades and associated support capability, for a period of several years to a decade or more.

Another operation could be a deterrent mission to help backstop the security of countries of the Gulf Cooperation Council against possible Iranian threats in the aftermath of a U.S. bombing campaign against Iranian nuclear facilities. U.S. ground forces could participate in such a mission. They could also provide protection for U.S. air and naval assets in the region, depending on the nature and duration of any Iranian response to the postulated bombing campaign. They could provide air defense and missile defense and base security for key naval and air assets the United States deployed in the region, and for U.S. partners and allies as well.

But here I focus primarily on two potentially more difficult and dangerous missions. The central scenario is implementation of a possible peace agreement that could ultimately emerge out of the civil war in Syria. A second possibility might be an effort to help restore stability in Saudi Arabia, and to its oil production, in the event of severe violence or a breakdown of the state there.

It is of course possible to imagine other cases where large-scale counterinsurgency or stabilization missions could be considered too. One might be after a major terrorist strike against the United States emanating from a country such as Yemen, which could raise similar questions to those confronted by the United States in the immediate aftermath of the 9/11 attacks as to how to respond and how to root out the longer-term threat.

Take the Saudi case first. A civil war in Saudi Arabia is the kind of scenario that, despite the United States' aversion to large-scale counterinsurgency in the aftermath of the Iraq and Afghanistan conflicts, could lead to another major U.S. ground force deployment to the Middle East. The stakes for Western security and the global economy could be too high to ignore. Most of Saudi Arabia's oil production is in the east; that is also where most of the nation's million-plus Shia reside, in close proximity to Iran (and Shia populations in Bahrain as well). If the widening Sunni-Shia split in the Middle East, perhaps further inflamed by Iranian instigation, led to a major period of violence that also affected oil production and shipment, the implications for the global economy could be quite considerable. Indeed, Iran's interest in stoking such a conflict could be reinforced by such economic considerations, since a higher price for oil could help Iran, assuming that it could still find a way to ship its own production to market. Iran might also try to sow mayhem in this area after a U.S.-led aerial attack on its nuclear facilities, rather than contenting itself with a simple one-off retaliation through terrorism. Perhaps the ensuing violence would also extend to attacks in Riyadh and even near Mecca or Medina.

To be sure, even under the kinds of extreme circumstances presumed here, it would be important to design any military mission very carefully. Clearly, Western forces would not be the optimal units to retake Mecca from an al Qaeda offshoot, for example. Even Western boots on the ground further east in the kingdom could be portrayed as apostasy by many, and could lead to various kinds of violence. Riyadh would be highly unlikely to countenance any Western role on Saudi soil, so this scenario is perhaps plausible only if the current regime either had collapsed or had lost control of most of the country and feared acutely for its future survival. In these circumstances, it might be credible to imagine an international coalition, with Muslim states providing units to handle religious sites while a U.S.-led coalition handled the central and eastern parts of the country.

A related and perhaps more plausible mission, particularly over the next five years or so, could be a negotiated peace followed by a stabilization mission in Syria. The deal might be analogous to the Bosnia peace deal, creating one or more autonomous zones for each of the three major ethnic groups, combined in this case with an additional zone for the intermixed cities of the country's center. This type of hybrid model may offer the only plausible way out of this terrible war, given the strong desire of Turkey and the Gulf states to see President Assad overthrown but the strong resistance to such an outcome by Iran and Russia.[32] A federalist model could help each party to the war attain its core security objectives. It could conceivably grow out of some of the local cease-fires already being attempted in various parts of the country today.[33]

It is too soon to know whether the parties to any peace agreement would want an outside force to help stabilize the situation. But given the likely existence of would-be spoilers to any deal, including perhaps residual elements of ISIL/ISIS, the local parties probably would not be able to secure the peace themselves.[34] And because of the large danger associated with extremist elements involved in the war today, any such peacekeeping force would need to be rather capable.[35] Among the threats one could anticipate would be chemical weapons, jihadist suicide bombers, and the frequent use of roadside bombs and other improvised explosive devices.[36]

Scaling from Bosnia, or employing standard force-sizing methods often used to size counterinsurgency operations, this mission could be very large. Syria's population is approaching 25 million. In theory, it could require 500,000 peacekeepers/counterinsurgents. It is possible that most of them might need to be foreign troops in the early going, as Syrian security forces would probably need to be rebuilt largely from scratch. Alternatively, scaling from the Bosnia precedent would imply more than 300,000 troops, at least in the early going. Either way, the numbers are striking.

Given the extremist presence in Syria, the risk of significant numbers of casualties would be much greater than in the Bosnia mission, making the likely need for high-end U.S. troops even more compelling, if other countries were to be persuaded to send their own soldiers as well. Even the lower of the above figures suggests an American contingent in the range of perhaps 50,000 to 100,000, if one assumes a U.S. contribution of 20 to 35 percent of the total.

COMPLEX TRAGEDY IN NIGERIA—BOKO HARAM PLUS EBOLA

As bad as the Middle East has become, Africa is still the continent where the world has witnessed the most frequent—and, in their aggregate effect, also the most deadly—ground wars of the last couple of decades. But for most periods, this violence has involved African states themselves, and international peacekeepers under UN or African Union auspices, to help end the carnage, much more than U.S. troops. This tendency is unlikely to change very much, even in the era of Africa Command (or AFRICOM) and related institutional improvements in how the United States addresses security challenges in Africa. The United States will most likely prefer to employ modest, indirect leverage through special forces, military trainers, and the like.[37]

Yet there are certain scenarios that could change the calculus for Washington. When the issues have been purely humanitarian, the United States has tended to opt for minimal American engagement. But a sufficiently serious conflict could make a larger American role plausible. Indeed, two of the nation's most recent presidents, Bill Clinton and Barack Obama, have expressed regret about not doing more with American power to address acute security challenges, the former in Rwanda in 1994, the latter in Libya since 2011.

There is a serious case that the prevention of genocide is itself a major national security interest of the United States.[38] However, genocides and civil wars of a character similar to those of the past are not the only possible contingencies. It is also possible to imagine situations that could directly engage other, very important U.S. national security priorities.

The spread of al Qaedaism to Africa creates the potential for a humanitarian crisis juxtaposed with a major security threat to the United States. This dynamic has been seen already to an extent, from Libya to Mali to Somalia. To date, it has generally afflicted smaller states. Salafist extremism has, of course, affected Nigeria too, in the form of the Boko Haram movement, but not yet at a level that has required consideration of major outside help. That could change.

One additional compounding threat is the possibility that a severe epidemic like the 2014 Ebola outbreaks in West Africa could occur in a place already affected by such extremist violence. This could truly make for a horrible situation that would be hard for outside powers to ignore, given the risks of a massive spreading of the disease worldwide. That scenario might include the pandemonium that could result from suicide bombers causing massive casualties in a crowd of people, many of them already affected by an Ebola-like disease. Caring for the kinds of patient caseload seen in such outbreaks, in the context of a security environment in which health care workers and other public servants could be targeted by terrorists, could make for a remarkably difficult situation. It could greatly heighten the risks of an epidemic going out of control, making it harder for the outside world to rely exclusively on local actors to handle the disease, even if it wished to. Indeed, Ebola has already been witnessed in Nigeria, even if the 2014 outbreak there was well controlled.[39]

Boko Haram may now field 10,000 fighters, substantially more than a couple of years ago, and may still be growing.[40] At present, Boko Haram would appear to pose limited direct threat to the West. It is made up largely of disparate cells with only local reach. That said, its extreme ideology and past suspected associations with the broader al Qaeda movement raise the possibility that its capacities, and ambitions, could expand.[41]

The threat of Ebola (or similar contagious diseases, many of which have originated in Africa over the years) could also potentially grow a great deal. The wave of anxiety that its arrival on American shores elicited in 2014 could foreshadow a far more serious situation if the number of cases ever became so great as to escape the immediate control of authorities. Certainly, the prospect of such an epidemic becoming a prevalent worry in much of the world could dramatically change the perceived threat. It is difficult to know how seriously to take such a potential concern. But as one indication, it is worth recalling that in September 2014, the World Health Organization estimated that Ebola could infect up to 20,000, with about half of all victims dying.[42] The same month, the Centers for Disease Control offered a separate estimate and increased the number of projected cases—by a factor of 70, to 1.4 million, by the end of January—if practices did not change.[43] Thankfully, health measures were improved enough in West Africa that the toll from the outbreak will likely be much closer to the lower bound of this range than the higher bound. But the higher end could very well apply in a hypothetical Nigerian case like the one postulated here, if health care could not be properly provided in the context of an ongoing war.

In such a multidimensional crisis, Nigerian armed forces could survive intact but still find themselves overwhelmed by the scale of the crisis. The military has at times shown hesitancy, and at other times mediocre tactics and competency, in its fight against Boko Haram to date.[44] Nigerian armed forces, with 150,000 active duty soldiers, are simply not very large when measured against the scale of the potential problem—they are, for example, substantially smaller than the armed forces of either Iraq or Afghanistan, even though Nigeria has six to seven times the population of either of those countries. Even when the police forces are added in, Nigeria's total uniformed security personnel number about 500,000, for a population approaching 200 million.

In theory, U.S. military doctrine would suggest a need for perhaps 4 million police and counterinsurgents to stabilize the entire country against a significant internal threat. In practice, as noted earlier, these metrics are crude and imprecise, and may err on the side of conservatism for many operations. That said, a complex mission of the type postulated here could involve a number of forced quarantines, regulation of the perimeters of a certain area to control any movement into and out of it, and specific tasks associated with medical or humanitarian relief. These tasks could drive the numbers up.

For the scenarios imagined here, it does not seem likely that the entire country of Nigeria would be equally threatened in such a future operation. If the crisis at hand involved a blend of regional politics, insurgency, and al Qaeda-ist extremism, perhaps it would affect large swaths of Nigeria's Hausa and Fulani populations—ethnic groups that are primarily Muslim and that account for some 30 percent of the population, or more than 50 million individuals. If the violence affected half of this population, the mission could be roughly comparable in scale to those in Iraq or Afghanistan in this century. That in turn could imply a potential need for perhaps 600,000 total counterinsurgents/police in this part of the country. Nigeria has 500,000 of its own security personnel, as noted, but most of these are police, with limited ability to deploy beyond their immediate areas of responsibility—and ongoing obligations in these other areas, too. As such, it seems entirely credible that the international community might need to provide at least 100,000 to 200,000 forces, and to provide them in a fairly remote part of the country, where logistics support could be quite difficult.

The United States would hardly need to provide the majority of the personnel. But its unique capacities in logistics, health care, and planning would be essential ingredients of any successful mission and probably imply a need for 30,000 to 50,000 U.S. Army and Marine Corps uniformed personnel on the ground, in keeping with the typical proportionate American contribution to other demanding stabilization missions in places like the Balkans.

STRENGTHENING THE STATE IN CENTRAL AMERICA

Imagine the possibility that several countries in Central America, already among the most violent and corrupt regions in the world, could experience an escalation of violence not unlike that seen by Colombia in the 1980s and 1990s. Should criminal cartels take the gloves off, attacking the state and perhaps even attacking Americans in an effort to deter the United States from coming to the aid of governments in the region, a much more threatening situation could emerge. It is plausible that Washington then might, in conjunction with beleaguered governments of the region and allies such as Colombia and Mexico, consider a broad stabilization mission. Such a mission could be intended first to attack the criminal syndicates that had escalated the violence and then to build up the region's states so they could fend off future such challenges on their own.[45]

For example, if prominent Americans began to be assassinated by criminal groups gone berserk, the threat to U.S. national security could quickly seem much more acute than today. One would not have to impugn complete irrationality to a criminal group to worry about this scenario. Perhaps a group that felt the noose of the state tightening around its neck, or that had a leader in an American prison that it wished to free, would use violence in the hope that this would lead Washington to relent rather than retaliate. Under certain circumstances, it could seem a credible gamble. After all, some counternarcotics strategies envision the arrest or killing of top leaders of drug cartels—meaning that they raise the stakes very high. To make an analogy with nuclear strategy, it is precisely when one's "regime" is at risk (in this case, one's drug empire, personal wealth, personal freedom, and very survival) that a leader may be prepared to risk it all. A threatened leader of a country might contemplate the use of nuclear weapons if he felt there was no other way to stop a foreign power bent on overthrowing him. In this case, analogously, a drug leader might try to kill (or kidnap) prominent Americans in a long-shot hope to stymie a campaign that clearly had him in its crosshairs.

This problem could be worsened if transnational criminal groups teamed up with terrorists in an unholy alliance of some sort. Perhaps a personal vendetta by a drug syndicate against a political or law enforcement figure would lead to a desire for weaponry that a terrorist group possessed—and perhaps the terrorist group would be willing to exchange the weaponry if offered help with accessing North America and specifically the United States through the various means that many criminal groups have developed over the years. Such a deal would presumably be avoided by drug cartels in North America under most circumstances, since they would have to appreciate the risks involved in being complicit in a direct attack on the United States. But a sufficiently risk-prone and vengeance-seeking group might throw caution to the wind. There is little reason to think that criminals will be perfectly rational all the time. We know from examples such as Pablo Escobar in Colombia that there are groups that choose to escalate their use of violence against the state out of a desire for vengeance or in an attempt to create a climate of fear that they can exploit. Some, like Escobar, may also think that they can gain popularity locally through various forms of charity and patronage, providing additional protection and cover should authorities try to close in, and mitigating their worries about being tracked down.[46] However, Escobar did not undertake major attacks against the United States, and over time, Colombia proved to have most of the capacity to deal with him itself. In a future Central American contingency, it is at least remotely conceivable that a criminal group would not show the same restraint, and that the indigenous government would need outside help to respond.

What type of military mission might the United States and its allies consider in such a scenario? The first instinct would likely be a series of raids directly against the offending group's leadership. But carrying out such raids effectively could prove a major challenge; limited uses of force in general have a spotty record of achieving their goals.[47] And in the case of limited strikes on terrorist groups in particular, the effects of decapitation strategies are typically quite mixed.[48] If the problem became severe enough, therefore, going to its source might seem advisable—meaning trying to help some of the states where the criminals had enjoyed effective sanctuary develop the tools to root them out. Some aspects of the operations could resemble muscular counterinsurgency of the 2000s variety in Iraq and Afghanistan.

Thus, this type of scenario could ultimately lead to a type of stabilization mission in Central America. The goal would not be counterinsurgency per se, as in Iraq or Afghanistan, but short-term law enforcement and longer-term state building. The mission could seek to repeat the kinds of successes achieved in Colombia in recent decades, for example. The goals might be to root out the offending cartels and their networks and leaders and safe houses and weapons caches while strengthening local law enforcement capacities so that the indigenous countries at issue could sustain the progress in the future.

The scale of any such mission would of course be a function of which regions in which countries needed to be handled through such a systematic military, law enforcement, and state-building operation. But a rough sense of the scale can be developed by noting that the combined populations of the three countries in Central America facing the worst of the drug and crime problem today—and suffering from among the very highest rates of homicide in the world as a result—have a combined population of about 30 million. Thus, if the operation were to include El Salvador, Honduras, and Guatemala together, the magnitude of the effort might be comparable to the Iraq or Afghanistan mission, by that population metric at least. The United States might undertake the effort in conjunction with Colombia and other key regional states such as Mexico or Brazil. But it could also expect that it might have to provide a very substantial fraction of the total outside force on its own.

Standard force-sizing algorithms as reflected in the *U.S. Army/Marine Corps Counterinsurgency Field Manual,* for example, could imply up to 600,000 "counterinsurgents" in such a mission. Assuming that some fraction of indigenous capacity was initially available to help with the effort, foreign troops might have to constitute one-third to one-half of the total. The necessary U.S. ground force contribution might reach the rough range of 50,000 to 150,000. More likely, any such mission would not have to address all three countries at once, and the scale of the operation would decline accordingly, so I estimate ultimately a range more like 30,000 to 100,000. Yet it could still be considerable.

Of course, attention should not be limited to Central America. Certainly, large-scale uprisings or major drug-related violence could threaten countries from Venezuela to Cuba to parts of Mexico in the years ahead, as well.[49]

A MAJOR DOMESTIC DISASTER AND EMERGENCY RESPONSE

Hurricanes Sandy and Katrina reminded Americans of the potential for huge natural disasters at home, beyond the usual threats from hurricanes, forest fires, tornadoes, earthquakes, and floods. Further back in memory, the Three Mile Island nuclear accident conjured up fears of what could have happened had the reactor malfunction been even more severe.

The early period after the 9/11 attacks witnessed a range of discussion and analysis on this general subject. The types of disasters that could cause huge damage and major ensuing disruption to life in America include terrorist attacks on nuclear reactors or major chemical facilities, dirty bomb attacks with nuclear-waste-laced weapons, and the spread of a biological pathogen. Other cases include the possibility that a nuclear weapon might be loose within the country or known to be en route to the United States. One might also add scenarios in which a breakdown in electrical or computer systems, perhaps caused by cyberattacks or a high-altitude nuclear weapons burst designed to maximize the effects of electromagnetic pulse, plunges much of the country into a period of protracted darkness. Mayhem could result.[50] The resulting large-scale responses needed to ensure safety for the population—not to mention food, water, and health care if infrastructure were incapacitated for an extended time—could go far beyond the capacity of local police or limited numbers of National Guard troops to handle.

What is the plausible scale of the resulting challenges to response and law and order? The challenge intellectually, as always when carrying out scenario analysis, is to stretch the imagination while maintaining credibility. Asteroid strikes and invasions by extraterrestrials or cannibalistic humanoid underground dwellers are not included here. Nor is a sequence of multiple independent disasters, each of them individually conceivable in isolation but collectively improbable in the extreme.

Even without such truly apocalyptic scenarios, many unexpected events could transpire. The 9/11 attacks really did happen, as did a very long U.S. military engagement in Afghanistan thereafter—and neither of these possibilities would have been easy to predict within the bounds of previous experience beforehand. Moreover, attacks involving weapons of mass destruction that could quite credibly cause many hundreds of thousands of fatalities are not difficult to imagine at all.[51]

Another way to sketch out the realm of the plausible is to think of how large a geographic area of the country could be affected at once by a major disaster or challenge. The most natural scale of possible tragedy is probably a single metropolitan area. A region of such size could be affected by a nuclear or chemical plant disaster, an actual detonation of a nuclear weapon, a huge earthquake, or another such event. However, it is also possible to imagine plausible events that could affect larger areas. A major electricity outage brought on by a system failure, or a solar storm, or an enemy attack with a high-altitude nuclear burst designed to create a major electromagnetic pulse could condemn a whole swath of the country to a lack of power for weeks or months. Fear of a nuclear weapon on the loose in a certain part of the country could require intensive monitoring of movement into and out of several cities. Fear that such a weapon was inbound on a ship could lead to huge search operations at several major ports at once.

The requirements for forces to provide security and relief would of course vary enormously from case to case. But policing cities with a combined population of, say, 20 to 30 million, when blackouts and intense fear and other breakdowns in normal life risk producing pandemonium and thereby necessitating very intense domestic stabilization efforts, could in theory demand more than half a million responders, according to classic counterinsurgency or stabilization algorithms. Inspecting all vehicular traffic into cities, assuming 20 to 100 major entry points per city, could require a mission that would dwarf the call-up of some 20,000 Army reserve component personnel after 9/11.[52] And, heaven forbid, should a nuclear weapon actually go off in a U.S. city, the scale of the needed cleanup effort could be difficult to imagine, certainly exceeding by tenfold or more the scale of the post-9/11 cleanup, with its cost of some $5 billion and the involvement of several tens of thousands of workers, or the response to Katrina, which included 45,000 National Guard personnel and some 20,000 active-duty forces.[53] It would be quite credible that hundreds of thousands could be required for such a task.

CONCLUSION

Numerous military scenarios could each require many tens of thousands and even several hundred thousand U.S. soldiers and Marines for periods of months to years. The plausibility of individual scenarios can be debated, but there are enough imaginable cases to make the possibility of such a scale of response seem quite real and credible. The United States would be right to attempt to limit its involvement in many if not most of them. But in a number of cases, the strategic stakes could be high enough, and the difficulty of the mission great enough, that an effective response would require a major U.S. military role.

Calculating requirements for how to handle various scenarios is a very difficult enterprise. Combat modeling is an inherently imprecise science, and planning war is an inherently mistake-prone human endeavor.[54] That is true even when one can focus on a specific and real scenario. Here the task is necessarily more speculative, and more imprecise. But when planning for the long term, there is no alternative.

As the George W. Bush administration learned in the early 2000s, preemptive and preventive wars are difficult to make legitimate in the eyes of international public opinion—and in the eyes of other states. The logical consequence of this situation is that a country with the avowed purpose of upholding international stability will often wind up having to absorb the first blow in war before it is able to respond decisively, thus conceding some degree of initiative to the enemy.[55]

For all these reasons, an element of caution and a margin of insurance need to be introduced into planning efforts for the U.S. Army and Marine Corps. The next chapter turns to the issue of how many of these scenarios should be prepared for at once, and with what types of forces.

CHAPTER FIVE

Toward an Army of the Future for the United States

WHAT DOES THE LIKELY future of land warfare augur for the U.S. Army, and the Marine Corps? This question will become especially salient if and when the Korea challenge is defused or demilitarized, because the elimination of a credible and massive North Korean military threat to American global interests would remove the single most robust plank from the foundation presently upholding the force structure of the U.S. Army in particular. What would be good for the region and the world would create an existential crisis for the Army. Even without such a transformation in Korea, the American strategic debate may soon be asking fundamental questions about the need for large standing ground forces. Indeed, to an extent, it already is.

Table 5-1 summarizes my estimates of what the scenarios examined in chapters 3 and 4 might entail for U.S. ground forces. Not all of these scenarios may be equally important or credible, and even if many of the circumstances on which some are based transpire in the real world, it should hardly be taken as automatic or axiomatic that the United States should become militarily involved with its Army and Marines. In addition, other considerations besides scenario analysis must be introduced into future force-planning exercises. Yet most or all of the below do seem relevant to planning American forces.

Table 5-1. Possible Scenarios of Relevance for Ground Force Planning

Scenario	U.S. ground force requirements (for deterrence or operations)
Russia/Baltics	150,000
Korea	175,000 without China combat role; 400,000 with China
Southeast Asia basing	100,000
Pakistan in civil war or after disaster	30,000 to 50,000
Kashmir trusteeship	60,000 to 150,000
Iran invasion threat	175,000
Syria stabilization	50,000 to 100,000
Nigeria in civil war, terrorism, Ebola	30,000 to 50,000
Central America stabilization	30,000 to 100,000
Major domestic disaster	300,000 to 500,000

Note: The above figures do not include rotation bases; they represent the estimated requirements at any given moment at the peak of operations. They also assume coalition operations and indicate only the estimated U.S. ground force levels (Army plus Marines).

With these estimates in hand, it is now necessary to wrestle with several broad conceptual issues relevant to the future of U.S. ground forces. These issues range from which types of missions and skills may be most important for the future U.S. soldier and Marine, to how many large operations at a time the United States should be ready to conduct, to what balance of active duty forces with National Guard and Army Reserve troops will be optimal, to technology and modernization matters. My purpose is less to chart a detailed five-year plan than to work through fundamental questions affecting U.S. ground force planning for the next one to three decades.

The emphasis here is on large-scale operations that the U.S. military might carry out. None of this is to disparage or minimize the importance of various other activities that the U.S. Army, Marine Corps, and other U.S. military forces routinely conduct, ranging from joint exercises with allies to forward presence and deterrence missions to building up the capacity of foreign partners through training and other mentoring.

For example, today the U.S. Army has some 25,000 soldiers in Germany, almost 20,000 in South Korea, almost 4,000 in Italy, more than 2,000 in Japan, and several thousand in both Kuwait and Afghanistan (see appendix C for more detail). Just as important, it deploys dozens or

Table 5-2. U.S. Army Basics

Type of unit	Number of soldiers	Type of unit	Number of soldiers
Squad	4–12	Brigade	3,000–5,000
Platoon	16–50	Division	10,000–18,000
Company	60–200	Corps	40,000–100,000
Battalion	400–1,000	Army	100,000–300,000

Type of brigade	
Brigade Combat Teams	*Support brigades*
Armored brigade combat teams	Aviation — Biological
Stryker brigade combat teams	Fires — Radiological
Infantry brigade combat teams	Air defense — Nuclear and
(including airborne variants)	Intelligence — explosive
	Battlefield sur- — Military police
	veillance — Civil Affairs
	Cyber — Medical
	Engineer — Transportation
	Maneuver — Field support
	enhancement — Sustainment
	Chemical — Contracting

hundreds of personnel at any given time in myriad other places around the globe. The Marines are concentrated in Japan, with some 15,000 still on Okinawa; an additional presence of some 1,000 at most times in Australia; and small deployments in many other places.[1] It is worth noting that for the established locations—Germany, Japan, Italy, Korea, Okinawa—the additional costs per soldier or Marine of being stationed abroad are modest. These costs are typically measured in the low tens of thousands of dollars a year per person, perhaps 10 percent of the average cost of having a soldier or Marine in the U.S. military force structure in the first place. In other words, the costs of overseas basing are modest (except in war zones, where the incremental costs per person can reach $1 million annually). Thus, decisions on overseas basing need not and should not be viewed as a main driver of the army budget. Nor, when durable facilities can be constructed, are they typically a major strain on people, at the level of the individual and the family (again excepting war zones and combat deployments).[2]

All these activities and missions, including not only the larger ones, dominated by main combat forces (as summarized in table 5-2), but also the smaller ones, which may emphasize special forces, foreign area officers, civil affairs units, and the like, are important. Some may benefit considerably from greater resources than are now devoted to them or from a higher concentration of personnel in the military occupational specialties associated with aspects of these endeavors. But these activities, however important, do not account for the preponderance of army forces. Rather, it is the reputation, and the reality, of the U.S. Army and Marine Corps as the world's finest operational land forces that make everything else possible. It is largely because those two services are the finest fighting organizations in the world, with many other capacities as well, that partners want to work with them. It is because forward-deployed forces can be reinforced with other forms of American national power in times of crisis, including quite possibly larger concentrations of U.S. ground power, that they are effective. In other words, it is large-scale missions that remain the core competencies of the Army and Marine Corps and that define their organizational cultures and identities. They are ultimately the main issue and the main question for the remainder of this book.

MISSIONS AND SKILLS

After the U.S. Army's long, difficult wars in Iraq and Afghanistan, some critics have argued that the entire notion of attempting to prepare America's ground forces for such complex missions is a fruitless or even counterproductive exercise. Harking back in some ways to the Army's attitude of the late 1970s and 1980s, when in the aftermath of the Vietnam War the Army eschewed counterinsurgency campaigns and focused instead on high-end maneuver warfare operations of the type eventually employed against Iraq in both 1991 and 2003, they favor a force with a more limited orientation.[3] Indeed, the 2012 Defense Strategic Guidance dismissed the plausibility of large-scale counterinsurgency campaigns or other stability operations. It stated, "U.S. forces will retain and continue to refine the lessons learned, expertise, and specialized capabilities that have been developed over the past ten years of counterinsurgency and stability operations in Iraq and Afghanistan. However, U.S. forces will no longer be sized to conduct large-scale, prolonged stability operations."[4]

In 2011, then Secretary of Defense Robert Gates asserted, paraphrasing General Douglas MacArthur, that any future secretary of defense proposing another large land operation in Asia, the Middle East, or Africa "should have his head examined."[5] In a 2013 speech, Vice Chairman of the Joint Chiefs of Staff Admiral James Winnefeld stated that "we've seen very recently that the American people are very wary of getting into an extended war of any type. . . . We should take to heart three principles that Major General Fox Connor imparted to Eisenhower and Marshall when they were both young officers: never fight unless you have to, never fight alone, and never fight for long."[6] President Obama told troops in New Jersey in December 2014 that "the time of deploying large ground forces with big military footprints to engage in nation-building overseas, that's coming to an end."[7]

This type of logic might seem to build on the spirit of the so-called Weinberger doctrine and the Powell doctrine, both of which advocated employing decisive amounts of force whenever the United States might go to war. Some interpret these doctrines as focusing the Army on traditional missions and on a warrior culture aimed at closing with and killing the enemy.

It is important first to note that some of the narrative surrounding this type of vision for the Army is frequently inaccurate. To start with the obvious, General Conner's admonition to Eisenhower and Marshall did not prevent—and could not plausibly have prevented—World War II. Gates made his statement even as the Department of Defense (DOD) continued to wage a major combat mission in Afghanistan that he supported. Both he and President Obama made their respective remarks cited above even as the Pentagon continued planning for a possible Korean conflict, among other contingencies.

However adamantly leaders in Washington declare their lack of interest in large-scale land operations, and most specifically in counterinsurgency and stabilization missions, the enemy gets a vote as well. Put differently, to paraphrase the Bolshevik adage, the United States may not have an interest in such missions, but they may have an interest in us.

To depict high-end, decisive maneuver warfare as the "traditional" U.S. Army or Marine Corps mission is to forget the history of American ground forces, which began with an irregular battle against the British in the Revolutionary War, spent much of the nineteenth century in battles against Native Americans that were far from classic high-end combat, conducted major operations from the Philippines to Cuba and Central America in the late nineteenth and early twentieth centuries, and engaged in complex missions in Vietnam, Iraq, and Afghanistan. More generally, the notion that ground combat between or within states ever was typified by gentlemanly or otherwise highly regularized standards and protocols is inconsistent with much if not most of human history, as Max Boot and others have cogently argued. Guerrilla and irregular warfare are the norm more than the exception. It is true that, especially in World War II, and to a degree World War I and Operation Desert Storm, an ethos of decisive battlefield triumph in "traditional" combat missions permeated much American military thinking.[8] But it was not even a continuous reality from the 1910s through the 1990s, as noted. And when oversimplified thinking about future war did carry the day, the nation often went astray into costly and sometimes bloody blunders.[9]

Moreover, the Weinberger and Powell doctrines are often misinterpreted. Weinberger emphasized the need to limit the nation's military operations to the defense of vital interests. Powell emphasized the need to have means match (or exceed) the ends that they sought to achieve, and to beware of incrementalism in planning and sizing military missions. But it is not hard to imagine complex missions that would occur in defense of core national interests. Helping a fraying Pakistan secure its nuclear materials before they could fall into the hands of jihadists, or shoring up a disintegrating Saudi Arabia, or addressing one of the other contingencies considered in chapters 3 and 4 could address absolutely crucial U.S. national security interests.[10]

Some have even argued, in the other direction, that high-end combat is obsolescent and that the future U.S. military should emphasize missions besides such traditional wars.[11] But this argument is hard to sustain in a world of a revanchist Russia, rising China, and disruptive Iran. It is true that the future U.S. military will spend more time actually conducting missions that have variously been called low-intensity operations, military missions other than war, "lesser included cases" of major regional contingencies, and a wide range of other names. But it must be ready, at least for the sake of deterrence and global stability, to win larger battles as well. Among its other implications, this perspective also suggests strongly that the Army should not discard its heavy forces, as it seemed prepared to do for a time in the early 2000s with its pursuit of the Future Combat Systems program.

A useful and pithy summary of the arguments in favor of retaining a substantial, multidimensional U.S. Army was offered by Major General

H. R. McMaster at a public event in early 2014 at the Brookings Institution.[12] He critiqued four common fallacies about future war:

—"the return of the revolution of military affairs,"

—"the zero-dark-thirty fallacy . . . really all we need are tremendously capable Special Operations Forces,"

—"the Mutual of Omaha Wild Kingdom fallacy . . . other armies will do our fighting for us," and

—"you can opt out of it."

These thoughts echo those General David Petraeus articulated in a speech at his August 2011 retirement ceremony:

> It will be imperative to maintain a force that not only capitalizes on the extraordinary experience and expertise in our ranks today, but also maintains the versatility and flexibility that have been developed over the past decade in particular. Now, please rest assured that I'm not out to give one last boost to the *Counterinsurgency Field Manual*, or to try to recruit all of you for COINdinista nation. I do believe, however, that we have relearned since 9/11 the timeless lesson that we don't always get to fight the wars for which we are most prepared or most inclined. . . . Given that reality, we will need to maintain the full-spectrum capability that we have developed over this last decade of conflict in Iraq, Afghanistan and elsewhere.[13]

The U.S. Army's 2014 Operating Concept, "Win in a Complex World," reflects a similar perspective, namely, that the current and future Army must be ready to handle a wide range of possible challenges.[14] It accords with General David Petraeus's view that the modern soldier must in effect be a "pentathlete," with skills across a wide range of domains that apply to many possible types of operations.[15] General Raymond Odierno, Army Chief of Staff from 2011 through 2015, also frequently underscored his view that the "velocity of instability" in the world has increased—even as major land wars in the broader Central Command region have declined in scale. In late 2014, for example, the Army participated in named contingency operations on five continents, all at once. It had seven of its ten division headquarters deployed in support of these operations.[16] Beyond their sheer number, what was also striking was the varied character of these missions.

The Bush administration, though initially averse to missions that smacked of nation building, came to understand these realities. Its thinking was reflected, among other places, in the DOD's Directive 3000.05, issued in 2005, which stated that "stability operations are a core U.S. military mission. . . . They shall be given priority comparable to combat operations."[17] It was largely in the aftermath of this change in official doctrine that U.S. forces dramatically improved their battlefield performance in the counterinsurgencies of the 2000s, most notably with the Iraq surge of 2007–08. Even though there were many frustrations with the conflicts in Iraq and Afghanistan, the U.S. military achieved one of the great operational comebacks in its history in Iraq in particular, once it truly took counterinsurgency seriously. Moreover, the difficulties encountered in these wars were largely due to strategic mistakes, including poor civilian guidance on how to stabilize Iraq after Saddam's overthrow; wholesale disbanding of the Iraqi army and an overly sweeping purge of Baathists from future Iraqi political life, which gave many Sunnis incentive to rebel; and inattention to the development of viable state institutions in Afghanistan during the period of relative calm there from 2002 through 2006, which might have left Kabul better positioned to fend off the Taliban itself. It is important not to conflate the setbacks in these conflicts with some presumed American military incapacity to handle insurgencies effectively. As John Nagl has argued persuasively, counterinsurgency has always been akin to "eating soup with a knife," and not just for the U.S. military.[18] Counterinsurgency operations are very difficult, slow, costly, and undesirable when a viable alternative approach is available. But they are not a type of mission beyond the reach of U.S. military competence—and they are sometimes not a type of mission that is easily avoidable on strategic grounds.

In any event, it is important that future administrations retain the counterinsurgency and stabilization skill sets developed at such cost and with such effort during the George W. Bush years in particular. Indeed, as the Clinton, Bush, and Obama administrations have realized, these challenges go well beyond DOD to involve much of government and other actors as well. Many of these other capacities are far from adequate.[19] Thus, it is not enough for DOD to retain, and indeed improve further, its capacities. As the government agency with by far the most resources, it must remain sufficiently focused on these kinds of missions to play a successful prodding role in ensuring that the entirety of the U.S. government—as well as America's alliances, the UN system, and other actors—improve their capabilities for such operations. We are probably not done with them yet, if indeed we ever will be.

Preparing for complex missions is often a useful way to hone various types of combat skills, and indeed to promote military innovation and entrepreneurship. For example, the much more widespread and creative use of robotics on the battlefield has come largely out of the experiences in Iraq and Afghanistan (and Pakistan and Yemen and Libya) of the last fifteen years. The shortening of reaction time associated with generating tactical intelligence, acting promptly on that intelligence, and more generally linking intelligence units and combat forces together in what General Stan McChrystal calls a "team of teams" emphasizing rapid battlefield response came largely out of these wars as well.[20] To be sure, the United States should not fight ugly, sanguinary, and hugely costly wars just to have new ways of fostering innovation. The above lessons came at a very high price for the nation and its brave men- and women-at-arms. But in principle at least, if complex missions were taken seriously in the course of military education and training, some of these kinds of innovations could possibly take place even in peacetime in the future.

All that said, there is no denying that there is some inherent tension between broadening the skill set of the future soldier and preparing him or her for excellence in core expertise. If the peacetime Army becomes fixated on a laundry list of superficial preparations for a range of hypothetical missions, the excellence that has characterized the American army at war could be jeopardized.[21] The U.S. Marine Corps creed of "every Marine a rifleman" constitutes a useful reminder of how to prioritize and sequence the education and training of any trooper.[22] So while preparing for a broad set of tasks, the Army and Marine Corps need to retain focus and simplicity—they must not become slaves to regulation or to long checklists of preparation for myriad secondary tasks. A modest number of demanding exercises mimicking stability or counterinsurgency or other complex missions is better than a slew of "certifications."

Another corollary of the above discussion is that the excellence of today's American armed forces should not be jeopardized by a return to the draft. Even if the latter might be desirable on grounds of fairness and equity, it would almost surely be harmful for the military. This is not an argument against national service. But if there were to be any consideration of obligatory national service for the nation's youth, military service should be just one option among many, with the armed forces themselves having a major say on whom they would accept as future men- and women-at-arms.[23] Indeed, demographic considerations alone would require such a multifaceted approach, since nearly 5 million Americans reach the age of eighteen each year, but there are in total fewer than 1.5 million active duty personnel in the entire military. There are not enough military positions to absorb a wide-reaching conscript pool.

One final point that follows as well from the above is that there is no crisis in the balance of combat capabilities versus support skills in today's American military. Some argue that the "tooth-to-tail" ratio is too low, for example—that there are not enough trigger pullers relative to all the engineers and logisticians and other support personnel. This line of reasoning is wrong. The U.S. military is excellent, and unique, just as much because of the latter soldiers and Marines as because of its warriors. Without these support personnel, U.S. forces simply could not project and sustain power abroad. Nor could they handle the various tasks associated with stabilization or disaster relief or other important missions. Such functions cannot be outsourced principally to contractors either, given the importance of being able to respond rapidly to crises that may erupt. There is plenty of room for debate about how to modify U.S. Army, and Marine Corps, force structure, to be sure. But there is no powerful case at present for fundamentally reshaping either one.

FROM TWO MAJOR WARS TO A "1+2" FRAMEWORK

How many wars and other major operations do America's ground forces realistically need to handle at a time? Attempting an answer to this question requires an assessment of not only the plausibility of the kinds of scenarios I have discussed in this book but also of their likelihood. It also requires attention to the broader question of deterrence. If the United States does find itself involved in the future in a major operation, to what extent does it need the manifest capacity to handle another major crisis or conflict simultaneously, so as to avoid creating any temptations for would-be aggressors?

During the cold war, these latter considerations typically led to some form of a two-war capability as the objective for American military capacity. American defense posture varied between periods of major ambition—as with the "2½ war" framework of the 1960s, which envisioned simultaneous conflicts against the Soviet Union (probably in Europe), China in East Asia, and some smaller foe elsewhere—and somewhat more realistic approaches. Notably, President Nixon reduced the planning requirement to 1½ wars, while asking more of America's global allies as the principal response force and deterrent, particularly in Asia. Nixon's "1 war" would have been conflict in Europe against the Warsaw Pact countries; a regional conflict elsewhere provided the basis for his additional "½ war" capability.[24]

These military planning frameworks grew out of the cold war logic of containment, which identified key American strategic interests abroad in Western Europe and Japan, and eventually the Middle East as well. Since there was believed to be a single central adversarial entity orchestrating trouble around the world and looking for opportunities to exploit, it was considered especially important that the United States and its allies have the capacity to respond to more than one specific crisis or conflict at a time.[25]

Throughout the 1990s, U.S. ground forces were sized and shaped primarily to maintain a two-regional-war capability. This was true even though there was no longer a single calculating adversary with global ambition and the capacity to cause multiple, overlapping crises or wars. But the logic of being able to deter a second potential adversary while fighting a first was still considered powerful, especially since the United States wound up facing conflicts, or at least severe crises, in both Iraq and North Korea within a short period of time in the 1990s.

According to this post–cold war planning framework, the two possible wars were assumed to begin in fairly rapid succession (though not exactly simultaneously), and then overlap, lasting several months to perhaps a year or two. Three separate administrations—Bush 41, Clinton 42, and Bush 43—and a total of five defense secretaries—Cheney, Aspin, Perry, Cohen, and Rumsfeld—endorsed some variant of it. They formalized the logic in the first Bush administration's 1992 "Base Force" concept, the Clinton administration's 1993 "Bottom-Up Review," the first Quadrennial Defense Review in 1997, and then Secretary Rumsfeld's own 2001 Quadrennial Defense Review.[26] In these debates in the dozen years following the cold war and Desert Storm, most considered simultaneous combat in two places unlikely, but the deterrent logic was still seen as useful. In addition, the two-war construct (even if it eventually proved inadequate for the two wars the United States did fight, in Iraq and Afghanistan) provided a cushion in case a single war proved more difficult than expected. It also provided a capability for "lesser included cases"—military operations other than war—missions that were generally viewed as having much lower priority than main combat operations but were nonetheless recognized as not always avoidable.

In short, the history of all these efforts at determining national strategy and establishing reasonable goals and benchmarks for the nation's armed forces includes many judgment calls. There were no scientifically provable right answers. There probably were at least two clear wrong answers—the lack of preparation for the type of combat waged in Vietnam, and the failure to deter the Korean War. The latter resulted from the nation's general military unpreparedness at the time, combined with poor signaling about the importance of the peninsula to the United States—including not only Secretary of State Dean Acheson's infamous early 1950 speech but also the earlier decision to remove U.S. combat forces from South Korea in 1948.[27]

Similarly, there is no rigorous way to determine precisely how many major ground wars the United States must be able to wage at a time today. Predicting human behavior is too murky a business for us to know just how many conflicts might realistically occur in the future. Moreover, national security policymaking is about achieving very good security at reasonable cost, rather than absolute security at any cost. The latter standard would be a practical impossibility, and if pursued, the effort could easily so weaken the nation's economy as to sacrifice long-term national security in the process.

In my judgment, however, the bottom line for the United States today is the following: a two-land-war capability is no longer necessary. This conclusion is reinforced by the costs of aiming for a higher standard—and the likely damage that such an ambitious and onerous approach to national security could do to long-term U.S. economic and national power.

With the demise of Saddam's regime, the likelihood of a major overland threat by one crucial Middle Eastern state against another has declined, even if the likelihood of disorder in the region has on balance increased since 2003. Korea remains a significant threat, but South Korea's much greater military preparedness than in the past reduces the pressure on the United States at least modestly for near-term responsiveness—and for avoiding deterrence failure. Other missions of the type developed and analyzed in previous chapters, such as a counteroffensive against Russia after a Russian attack on a Baltic state or a notional invasion of Iran by the United States, are important enough to plan for, but not at all likely to be conducted.

It is far from implausible that two major conflicts could break out at once. But it is rather unlikely that both would require major U.S. ground force responses. Today's highest-likelihood scenarios are largely maritime or irregular in nature—a possible Iranian threat to the Persian Gulf region, a possible Chinese threat to Taiwan or to other neighbors in the East China Sea and South China Sea vicinities, a threat from ISIL or another al Qaeda-ist threat in the Middle East or South Asia. The United States does need the capacity for multiple responses at once. But the likelihood of needing two large, simultaneous ground operations is quite low.

As such, I would propose a "1+2" framework for sizing the future U.S. ground forces. The idea is to have enough capacity for a single, robust, large-scale operation—that is the "1" in the force-sizing construct. Several of the possible missions I explore in chapters 3 and 4 could become this single, main mission—especially those in chapter 3, as well as some variants of the scenarios analyzed in chapter 4. Simultaneously, however, the nation should have capacity to carry out two potentially difficult and lengthy, and presumably also multilateral, stabilization or deterrent or response missions. These would be more on the scale of the typical post–cold war U.S. mission in Somalia, Bosnia, Kosovo, or Afghanistan through 2008 (and in Afghanistan, again after 2014). Often, the nation has conducted two such mid-sized missions at a time, making that number a reasonable standard for sizing future forces. Future such missions could include a U.S. role in a UN peacekeeping or disaster response mission in Congo or Sudan or Nigeria; a U.S. role in backstopping a multilateral force to implement an Israeli-Palestinian peace accord; a U.S. reassurance and deterrence mission with ground forces in Gulf Cooperation Council states in the aftermath of an air strike campaign against Iran's nuclear facilities; or some more modest variants of the Syria and Central America and Pakistan scenarios considered in earlier chapters.

The 1+2 construct results in recommendations for an Army and Marine Corps of comparable size to those planned today by the Obama administration. A single high-intensity war could require up to some twenty brigades of combined Army and Marine Corps capability, based on past experience and past estimates.[28]

A smaller mission might require one to three brigades for a period of years, based on past cases, as in Bosnia and Kosovo. These numbers could certainly double for some of the possible missions considered in this book. So if two to six U.S. brigades were needed, that would imply a rotation base of six to eighteen active duty brigades.

This ratio of one deployed unit for every two stateside would reflect the lessons of Iraq and Afghanistan, where a higher pace of deployment caused huge problems for U.S. soldiers and Marines. The 1:2 ratio is still demanding, if sustained over a number of years, but it is more reasonable. According to the logic, units returning home would first go through a reset and rest phase, and then a more intensive training phase, before being available for deployment again. This cycle is now codified officially in what the Army calls ARFORGEN, the somewhat clumsy acronym simply standing for Army force generation.[29] It is a very reasonable logic, without all the Pentagonese and jargon associated with the formal concept, for the simple reason that it gives soldiers or Marines returning from deployment a significant period of recuperation time, with less intense training and travel, before entering into an intense training cycle. Given the distressingly high rates of suicide, divorce, and posttraumatic stress syndrome that afflicted America's Army and Marines in the wars of the twenty-first century, when recovery times were often much shorter than the ARFORGEN model intends, it is incumbent on the nation to take better care of its men- and women-at-arms in any future periods of comparable intensity.

The above estimates focus on active duty forces. If instead the forces were drawn from the National Guard, all the above figures would nearly double. That is based again on a simple concept of fairness about what a reservist expects when signing up for part-time soldiering. More specifically, in the Army's view, while an active duty brigade can deploy one in every three years, a Guard or Reserve unit should only deploy one in every five.[30] So one needs five Guard units to do the same thing as three active duty units, averaged over time.

Let's imagine that all these missions occurred simultaneously, the single large war and two smaller but protracted and prolonged multilateral operations. As noted, the single large war could require twenty brigades for the high-intensity phase. In light of what we learned in Iraq and Afghanistan, it would be prudent to assume that while the high-intensity phase might not last a long period, forces employed in that phase should not be considered available for other contingencies for some time. Collectively, they might need to sustain an ongoing if smaller stabilization mission or other postconflict operation in the location where they had previously waged high-end combat. This follow-on effort could itself last years. Certainly, it could be quite demanding into a second or third year, as noted in the discussion of Korea contingencies in chapter 3. For example, residual violence, land mines and other dangers, loose or missing weapons of mass destruction, and huge humanitarian relief requirements could make the going quite tough for an extended period. South Korean forces, focused on aiding their own countrymen south of the 38th parallel as well, might not be able to devote their full capacities to the stabilization mission north of the DMZ at first, and might well need substantial U.S. help (with a few other countries likely making modest contributions as well). Such considerations make it unwise to plan to resource the two smaller, simultaneous missions out of the same pool of forces initially deployed to the major war.

The two smaller operations could each, over time, require as many as eighteen active duty brigades, as noted. In theory, that implies a need for fifty-six active duty brigades between the Army and Marine Corps—twenty for the combat mission and its aftermath, up to eighteen each for the other two operations, including rotation bases.

If some of the forces were drawn from the Army Reserve component, the numbers would change. For example, begin with the assumption that thirty-nine active duty brigades could come from the active duty Army and Marine Corps combined, as called for by the Obama administration's current plan. That is seventeen less than what the above calculations would advise. Translating into National Guard units by the 5:3 ratio noted above implies a need for twenty-eight Guard brigades. Indeed, the administration plans to keep twenty-seven brigade combat teams in the National Guard.[31]

These numbers should not be taken too literally, of course. It is impossible to foresee the character or scale of future hypothetical missions. Requirements could be lower than forecast—though they could also be higher. For example, two simultaneous stabilization operations each fielding six brigades at a time would be quite large by comparison with recent experience. On the other hand, the force structure as derived above provides a potentially inadequate rotation base for the follow-on operations in the single large war. Thus, the 1+2 construct also presumes that, if a major operation does prove necessary, a fairly prompt and sustained increase in the size of the Army's end strength would probably have to be promptly initiated, if all three missions were expected to endure a number of years.

ALLIES AND PARTNERS

Central to any discussion of the future of the U.S. ground forces is the role of allies and security partners—of which the United States has more today than at any time in the past, and more than any country has ever enjoyed previously in the long history of warfare.

That is mostly a good thing, even if it risks dragging the United States into conflicts it might prefer to avoid. Caution and care are needed to avoid such entrapment at times. Washington has been relatively successful at this. While there have been some U.S. allies that have sometimes asserted themselves too much in one way or another—Taiwan in promoting steps towards independence in the 1990s and early 2000s, for example, or Israel in its settlement policies—these examples are fairly few and far between. Moreover, the two cases noted above do *not* involve treaty allies per se, and the United States has in fact deliberately created ambiguity about whether it would come to the direct defense of either, especially should they seem to have a hand in provoking their own conflicts.

Most important interstate wars since World War II—the North Korean invasion of South Korea, various Arab-Israeli wars, the Iran-Iraq War, the Iraqi invasion of Kuwait, Soviet and Chinese attacks on their neighbors at various junctures, the Tanzanian-led overthrow of Idi Amin in Uganda, the Vietnamese-led overthrow of the Khmer Rouge in Cambodia, conflicts in the Horn of Africa—were initiated by countries that were not U.S. allies. An exception has been the Indo-Pakistani wars—but it is hard to blame the United States for these conflicts, given that their genesis predated its role as anyone's ally in South Asia. Those who argue about entrapment seem more worried about the theoretical possibility than concerned with the empirical record to date. On balance, the U.S. alliance system would appear to have been a remarkably powerful stabilizing force in world politics, not only helping win the cold war but also helping produce the most stable period of interstate relations in modern world history.

This broad assessment of the value of alliances then leads to several other more specific observations. One is that the United States will virtually never have to go it alone in future military operations. Even in highly controversial cases, such as the 2003 Iraq War (in which several dozen countries offered at least modest help), the United States will have partners.[32]

Second, however, the nature of allied and coalition help will be a strong function of the character of the specific operation and the interests of the different potential partners. Generally, the contributions of most allies will be quite limited. The 2003 Iraq War is a good case in point. Only Britain provided initial invasion forces that were truly significant and proportionate in some way to America's contribution when adjusted for the respective size of the two countries' militaries and populations.

NATO's average military spending level now fails to equal even 1.5 percent of GDP, well below the modest alliance goal of 2 percent. For all the talk of an East Asian arms race, most major American security partners there continue to spend modest fractions of their total national wealth on their armed forces—just under 2 percent for Taiwan, 2 percent for Australia, still only 1 percent for Japan, 2.5 percent for South Korea.

The United States is blessed by having the strongest coalition of security partners in world history, together constituting some 70 percent of world GDP and world military spending (see table 5-3). Yet it is also constrained severely by the deep-rooted limitations of what these sixty or so nations are willing to do to provide for broader regional and global security in addition to their own security.

On balance, the future will probably closely resemble the past. Allied troop contributions could range from the 20 to 30 percent that characterized much of the Iraq War (excluding the Iraqi forces themselves) to the levels of 70 percent or more that have typified some prolonged peace implementation missions. It is regrettable, to be sure, that in some operations allies would likely not be able to do more. But the United States must also bear in mind that if the glass is half empty, it is also half full, and the strength of the nation's broader security coalition is among its most important strategic assets. Moreover, that coalition endures largely because it is flexible, and Washington does not generally try to strong-arm other nations into participating in operations they do not believe serve their own security interests.

Beyond warfighting, the United States will surely wish to continue helping train overseas allies and other partners.[33] On a planet with 20 million full-time military personnel, nearly 15 million of them soldiers, it is

Table 5-3. Global Distribution of Military Spending, 2014

Country	Defense expenditure (US$millions)	Global total (percent)	Cumulative percentage
United States	581,000	36.4	36
NATO			
Canada	15,925	1.0	37
France	53,080	3.3	41
Germany	43,934	2.8	44
Italy	24,274	1.5	45
Spain	15,070	0.9	46
Turkey	10,047	0.6	47
United Kingdom	61,818	3.9	51
Rest of NATO[a]	56,783	3.6	54
Total NATO, excluding U.S.	280,931	17.6	
Total NATO	861,931	54.1	
Rio Pact[b]	49,621	3.1	57
Key Asia-Pacific allies			
Japan	47,685	3.0	60
South Korea	34,438	2.2	62
Australia	22,512	1.4	64
New Zealand	3,186	0.2	64
Thailand	5,685	0.4	64
Philippines	2,035	0.1	64
Total key Asia-Pacific allies	115,541	7.2	
Informal U.S. allies			
Israel	20,139	1.3	66
Egypt	5,449	0.3	66
Iraq	18,868	1.2	67
Pakistan	6,006	0.4	68
Gulf Cooperation Council[c]*	113,722	7.1	75
Jordan	1,268	0.1	75
Morocco	3,859	0.2	75
Mexico	6,548	0.4	75
Taiwan	10,126	0.6	76
Total informal allies	185,985	11.7	

Country	Defense expenditure (US$millions)	Global total (percent)	Cumulative percentage
Other nations			
Non-NATO Europe	21,857	1.4	78
Other Middle East and North Africa[d]*	20,745	1.3	79
Other Central and South Asia[e]*	11,647	0.7	80
Other East Asia and Pacific[f]	23,092	1.4	81
Other Caribbean and Latin America[g]*	284	0.0	81
Sub-Saharan Africa	24,184	1.5	83
Total other nations	101,809	6.4	
Major neutral nations			
China	129,408	8.1	91
Russia	70,048	4.4	95
India	45,212	2.8	98
Indonesia	7,076	0.4	98
Total major neutral nations	251,744	15.8	
Nemeses and adversaries			
Iran	15,705	1.0	99
North Korea[h]	5,000	0.3	100
Syria*	2,300	0.1	100
Venezuela	4,655	0.3	100
Total nemeses and adversaries	27,760	1.7	
TOTAL	1,594,391	100.0	

Source: International Institute for Strategic Studies, *The Military Balance 2015* (New York: Routledge Press, 2015), pp. 484–90.

a. Albania, Belgium, Bulgaria, Croatia, Czech Republic, Denmark, Estonia, Greece, Hungary, Iceland, Latvia, Lithuania, Luxembourg, Netherlands, Norway, Poland, Portugal, Romania, Slovakia, Slovenia.

b. Argentina, Bahamas, Bolivia, Brazil, Chile, Colombia, Costa Rica, Dominican Republic, Ecuador, El Salvador, Guatemala, Haiti, Honduras, Nicaragua, Panama, Paraguay, Peru, Trinidad and Tobago, Uruguay.

c. Bahrain, Kuwait, Oman, Qatar, Saudi Arabia, United Arab Emirates.

d. Algeria, Lebanon, Libya, Mauritania, Tunisia, Yemen.

e. Afghanistan, Bangladesh, Kazakhstan, Kyrgyzstan, Nepal, Sri Lanka, Tajikistan, Turkmenistan, Uzbekistan.

f. Brunei, Cambodia, Fiji, Laos, Malaysia, Mongolia, Myanmar, Papua New Guinea, Singapore, Timor-Leste, Vietnam.

g. Antigua and Barbuda, Barbados, Belize, Guyana, Jamaica, Suriname.

h. North Korea value is an author estimate.

* At least a portion of the total cited here is from earlier years because 2014 data are not available.

the U.S. Army (as well as the Marine Corps) that must do much of the work with other countries that helps prepare them to provide front-line defenses and response capabilities for their own nations. Other countries can and do contribute to such engagements, to be sure.[34] But the excellence of American ground forces, and their widely recognized capability as the world's best, makes the United States the natural leader in such efforts—a role that should not be undervalued in future discussions of the proper size and capacities of the U.S. Army.

Sometimes American engagement with foreign partners will be done with the stationing of ground forces in key places—as in Korea, Kuwait, and Western Europe. That is especially true when the possibility of acute nearby threats gives added impetus to sustaining such forward presence for the sake of deterrence. A modest standing capability in the Baltic states may be warranted as well, depending most importantly on the future behavior of Vladimir Putin. For example, a brigade of light forces, dispersed into battalion-size units in each of the three NATO member-states there, would allow patroling tasks to be carried out multilaterally.[35] This may wind up being prudent in the years ahead.

As noted, the costs of U.S. forward presence in places such as Korea and Germany are generally not high relative to other defense expenses. Typical additional annual costs are usually in the low tens of thousands of dollars per person—meaning about $1 billion a year for every 30,000 to 40,000 personnel abroad, roughly—in such situations. (By contrast, in active war zones like Iraq and Afghanistan, costs have been closer to $1 billion for every 1,000 U.S. uniformed personnel.)[36] Some might still argue against a forward presence on the grounds that it reduces allies' incentives to provide for their own defense. But empirically, the evidence for this claim is unpersuasive. Indeed, NATO allies reduced their military spending considerably, and at a faster pace than the United States, even as U.S. Army forces in Europe were reduced in recent decades from cold war norms averaging some 225,000 to well under 100,000 in the 1990s and now to well under 50,000 in the Obama years.[37] South Korea remains among the most stalwart of American allies, spending a considerably higher fraction of its GDP on armed forces than the average, despite a strong ongoing U.S. troop presence on the peninsula. Taiwan's spending has sagged even as the U.S. military commitment has been deliberately muddied by Washington. There is no clear correlation in general between the United States doing more and its allies doing less to help themselves, or vice versa. Even if there were such a correlation, there would also be dangers in scaling back the U.S. role—more allies might seek nuclear weapons or launch preemptive attacks against possible adversaries. Such a world would probably not be more peaceful than today's, which, as noted, despite its challenges, is easily the most stable in modern history.

A final observation is in order about General Raymond Odierno's regionally aligned forces initiative. The concept was developed and promoted during his tenure as Army Chief of Staff from 2011 through 2015.[38] The general idea is to link more forces to specific overseas theaters, not as their sole responsibility but as a way of facilitating long-term relationships with foreign partners. An additional purpose is to increase expertise about key parts of the world within the U.S. armed forces.[39] The concept is very good but needs further fleshing out. It is difficult to understand from official army documents how many units and command headquarters at various echelons are now regionally aligned, what percentage of their time is spent in preparation for activities or operations in a given part of the world, or what change has resulted in their operational deployment patterns as a result of the new policy.[40] This lack of information makes it hard to know how the Army's force structure requirements are affected by this new approach to preparing and employing forces around the world.

Nonetheless, the bottom line is clear. The case for ongoing U.S. Army engagement in a world of land-force-dominated militaries is powerful. Also, allies, for all their limits, are a clear strategic asset for the United States.

THE ARMY RESERVE AND THE ARMY NATIONAL GUARD

Looking down the road, what should the mix of active duty, National Guard, and Army Reserve forces be in the U.S. Army? This question about the Total Force is particularly salient for the Army, since among U.S. ground forces, the Marine Corps has always been principally an active duty and responsive force. There is little reason for that to change. But today's Army has slightly more than half its soldiers in the reserve component. That is typical for the modern era (see table 5-4). However, historically, especially before the world wars, it had a much larger aggregate militia than a standing active duty force. If and when most of

Table 5-4. Recent Trends in the Total Army Force Mix
Number of soldiers

Year	Active duty force	Total army	Active duty as percent of total army
1989	770,000	1,546,000	49.1
2001	480,000	1,035,000	46.4
2010	570,000	1,134,000	50.3
2015 (request)	490,000	1,042,000	47.0
2017 (plan)	450,000	980,000	45.0

Source: Andrew Feickert and Lawrence Kapp, "Army Active Component (AC)/Reserve Component (RC) Force Mix: Considerations and Options for Congress" (Washington: Congressional Research Service, December 2014), p. 8 (www.fas.org/sgp/crs/natsec/R43808.pdf).

the nation's urgent threats such as Korea are largely resolved, some will surely argue that the Army should go back to its roots and revert to such a "citizen-soldier" militia-based force. Given America's favorable geography, which makes it safe from foreign invasion, and given its traditions and its culture, some may argue that such an army is the natural state for America.

Relations between the active duty Army and the Army National Guard have been complex in the modern era. In Operation Desert Storm, even after activating them and training them, the Army chose not to deploy three mobilized National Guard "roundout" brigades that were intended to constitute parts of several active duty divisions. This decision was seen as a mark of disrespect by many in the Guard. It came after a complex history between these army components dating back to Vietnam, a war in which the Guard was largely kept home, despite having had a much more collaborative and forward role in earlier conflicts, notably World War II, and a major role in war plans for a possible showdown against the Warsaw Pact in Europe.[41] There was much less debate about whether support units, largely from the Army Reserve, were up to snuff; their wartime performance was widely respected.[42]

Several factors need to be kept in mind when considering the right blend of active, Guard, and Army Reserve forces. On balance, they lead me toward a cautious view about any major shift in the relative proportion of each. There is room for creative thinking, and perhaps even a testing of certain modified types of units that blend active and reserve personnel, or keep certain reserve component units at a higher level of readiness than others. But on balance, part-time soldiers are still part-time soldiers, meaning that whatever their abilities, they will need time to be deployable. Saying this is no insult to reservists, of the Army National Guard or Army Reserve. Nor is it an argument that reservists are unimportant strategically. But one needs to bear in mind at the same time the rapidity with which crises or conflicts can erupt, and the duration of time over which they can continue.

First, as noted above, today's active duty Army is already slightly smaller than the reserve component. For the other U.S. military services, reservists are much less numerous than active duty personnel.

Second, and relatedly, it is worth bearing in mind that as a function of its overall defense budget, its overall military strength, its role in the world, and historical standards of the last hundred years, today's active duty Army is already quite small. The U.S. Army is only the world's fourth largest, and indeed is not far from sinking to seventh or eighth place among global powers. While size is not the best metric of capability, the old Bolshevik saw that quantity has a quality all its own is nonetheless worth bearing in mind. This is especially true in light of the facts that most of the world's militaries are army-centric, with nearly three-fourths of all men- and women-at-arms globally being soldiers, and that 100 percent of the world's population lives on land—an observation that General Ray Odierno liked to underscore when Army Chief of Staff. Even if one adds in the U.S. Marine Corps and counts it as part of the nation's ground forces—an assumption that is partly justifiable, even if the Marine Corps also needs to be viewed as both a naval force (being part of the Department of the Navy) and an expeditionary force—U.S. active duty ground forces are still only the fourth largest in the world, and still only about half of the U.S. armed forces in aggregate.

Third, while the Army Reserve and National Guard are crucial elements of the Army that have performed in a brave and stalwart fashion in the nation's wars, their limitations as well as their strengths need to be remembered.[43] Specifically, while the Army Reserve has many supporting capabilities that it provides in greater numbers than the active force, and quite often with as great or arguably even greater excellence in some cases, the combat formations of the Army National Guard are not likely to be the equal of those in the active force, now or in the future. This should make American planners particularly wary of assuming that Guard units can "own" large sectors of a future battlefield.

Brigade combat teams in the Army National Guard can do a great deal, to be sure. And they constitute an important strategic reserve for the nation as well. Already they are nearly as numerous in the Total Force as are active duty brigade combat teams. But the notion that, even with a few months of full-time training, they can reliably be expected to perform as well as active duty units in the early going of a future military operation is suspect.

Army National Guard and Army Reserve personnel served very impressively in Iraq and Afghanistan.[44] For example, at the start of 2005 there were 60,000 U.S. reservists in Iraq, out of a Total Force then of 150,000.[45] Many hundreds gave their lives in Iraq and Afghanistan as well. That said, when Guard units were asked to control sectors of the battlespace in Iraq and Afghanistan, they had challenges. More research is needed on this issue, and the nation is overdue in commissioning a major study that would attempt to capture the lessons of recent wars for the reserve component.[46] But as an interim measure, for the purposes of this study, we surveyed a number of active duty Army officers about their impressions of the performance of the Guard and Reserve in recent wars. Out of forty-nine respondents, admittedly a small sample, a plurality believed that smaller reserve component units performed quite effectively in their missions. But when considering larger units, roughly three-fourths felt that National Guard brigade combat teams were not as effective as their active duty counterparts. On balance, it is right to be wary of claims that the National Guard was the full equal of the Active Army when asked to shoulder complete responsibility for a given geographic sector in Iraq or Afghanistan.

This is not surprising. Modern-day soldiering is inherently difficult. It is not simply a matter of being able to aim a rifle correctly, drive a tank safely, or even fly an aircraft with care. All of these skills can be, and are, maintained well by many units of the American military's reserve component. But larger-unit coordinated maneuvers require intense and frequent practice, after-action assessments, and frequent teamwork so as to improve. Moreover, the much broader set of skills rightly included and emphasized in the Army's Operating Concept requires full-time work as well.[47]

The challenge of maintaining excellence in a spectrum of skills can be mitigated by the presence of a significant number of former active duty soldiers within the National Guard. But the availability of such soldiers is constrained by the size of the active duty force, obviously, and therefore a substantial reduction in the absolute and relative size of the active duty Army would naturally tend to reduce the percentage of Guard personnel who had previously been full-time soldiers. Indeed, the stresses of the wars of the 2000s already slowed this recruiting pipeline for the Army's reserve component, reducing the number of prior-service recruits to just 37 percent of the Army National Guard and 45 percent of the Reserve in 2007 (relative to 1997 levels of 61 and 59 percent, respectively). For the Marine Corps, the drop was similar, from 50 percent in 1997 to 34 percent in 2007.[48]

The above is not an argument against the reserve component. Nor is it meant to dismiss new ideas in building the total force—such as another version of the 1980s roundout brigade or the cadre division concept.[49] Some such ideas may be worth exploring. But there should also be considerable caution in considering any radical change.[50]

READINESS AND MOBILIZATION

What readiness for rapid responsiveness do the majority of U.S. ground forces need to retain? And on the flip side, in the event of major war, how can the United States prepare for a more general mobilization, to increase the Army's size as might be needed?

Regarding readiness, in its past wars, the United States has often had the luxury of losing early battles, only to build up large forces, improve its performance, and prevail down the road. But even in the past, this approach to national military strategy cost huge numbers of dollars and lives, as the United States suffered severe setbacks in combat and failed to deter some conflicts that were perhaps preventable.

In the future, such a luxury may not be available to us, as many of my scenarios would suggest.[51] Allies could be overrun, nuclear conflicts unleashed, fragile peace accords in key regions of the world shattered, or huge natural catastrophes affecting tens of millions unmitigated by any response unless ample forces were available quickly.

All that said, it is important not simply to worship at the readiness altar. It is quite feasible, given the political debates often associated with even modest signs of limited unpreparedness in the nation's armed forces, to overdo it. The consequences can be a force run ragged with excessive preparations for near-term battles that never happen quite as expected in any event, a misallocation of resources away from longer-term preparedness in favor of short-term vigilance, and thus an unbalanced force.[52]

Something akin to a U.S. Navy (or Marine Corps) readiness model is probably best for the Army too, with roughly a quarter to a third of the force quickly employable and deployable and other elements available within some one to three months. That smaller fraction is about as much of the force as could be quickly deployed anyway, given the constraints of available strategic transport assets—roughly three divisions of fast sealift, another two brigades of amphibious lift, and roughly a division of prepositioned supplies in key theaters that can be joined by personnel to operate the equipment on short order.[53] (It would also be consistent with the constraints of infrastructure in most possible battle zones.) And rapid deployment of a force of such size is also, innately, a reasonable way to prepare an initial defense perimeter in preparation for more conclusive operations down the road.

On the subject of mobilization, how should the United States prepare for a much larger armed conflict than most of the scenarios considered in this book? The scenarios involving China hint at the scale of the possible. The most important question here is probably not how to envision the mass mobilization of some 20 million to 30 million Americans (the equivalent, relative to population size, of World War II's burden on the nation) but instead to imagine a prolonged operation at the outer edge of my scenarios that takes longer or encounters more unexpected setbacks than presently anticipated. This is a question not only about military manpower but also about technological preparedness, research and development, prototyping strategies, and industrial capacity.[54]

In thinking about mobilization strategies, it is important to begin by recalling that the force-sizing paradigm proposed here is rather modest for the possible requirements that U.S. ground forces could face in the years ahead. In particular, my approach envisions only a single major war at a time. This planning assumption strikes me as a reasonable way to avoid overinvesting in near-term military readiness at the expense of longer-term preparedness—and also at the expense of retaining the fiscal and scientific and human resources to keep America's economy strong as the crucial element in long-term national power. But this framework also implies that, in the event of a major war, the nation should immediately grow its active duty ground forces as a precautionary measure, since the active duty force will have little slack within it.

The United States knows from the experience of the 2000s that increasing the size of the Army by roughly 15 percent over half a decade is well within the institutional capacity of the armed forces and well within the demographic and economic capacity of the nation. But the country also waited too long to make the decision, wondering along the way if the wars in Iraq and Afghanistan would really prove protracted—and if they were really so important to the nation's security as to require an increase in the "permanent" strength of the Army. In fact, that very phrase is oxymoronic. There never has been and never could be a permanent strength for a force that needs to receive a new budget from Congress each and every year.

Next time, if there is a next time, the United States needs to flip the logic. The strong presumption should be that the Army *will* grow, temporarily at least, for as long as that war continues. The price to be paid by such a temporary growth of the Army should be seen as a bargain compared with the alternative of maintaining a conservatively sized force at all times. The initial response to such a conflict should be a temporary activation of a proportionate percentage of the National Guard, followed quickly by a change in the targeted "end strength" of the active duty force. Given the likely requirements of many of the scenarios sketched out here, an increase of 15 to 30 percent—achievable certainly within a decade, based on what we have learned in the 2000s, and perhaps substantially more quickly—should be initiated, if and when such a major contingency develops.

EFFICIENCIES AND ECONOMIES

This book is focused less on an Army budget plan for any given period than on a broader determination of likely ground force requirements for the United States in the decades to come. Nonetheless, several broad arguments are in order about the way in which the Army in particular can seek to make its force as efficient as possible.

First is the matter of military compensation. At one level, the nation can never fully compensate its men- and women-at-arms for the service they provide the country, and the risks they incur in doing so. But it is nonetheless important to understand that regular military compensation (or RMC)—including basic pay, housing and living allowances, and tax advantages, but not even including various incentives and bonuses or health care benefits or accrual for retirement—compares very favorably with direct pay in the private sector. Specifically, for enlisted personnel of a given age, education, and experience, average RMC equals the 90th percentile in the nonmilitary workforce, and for officers, the 83rd percentile, according to the most recent official Pentagon review.[55] In other words, enlisted personnel of a given age and experience tend to make more than 90 percent of all civilian employees with comparable characteristics. Were health care and retirement factored in, the percentages would actually grow even higher (without counting Veterans Affairs health benefits for the disabled).[56] Not all of this compensation is necessarily provided in ways that are efficient and fair across the all-volunteer force.[57] But overall levels of compensation are reasonably robust.

Just over 250,000 civilians work for the Department of the Army as well. In other words, there is slightly more than one such employee for every two full-time soldiers. Specifically, in 2015, the official figure will be 53 civilians for every 100 full-time soldiers—up modestly from 50 percent in the 1980s, to take one recent point of reference, and up rather more considerably from the 45 to 100 ratio at the end of the Clinton administration and beginning of the George W. Bush years.[58]

What kinds of savings might be achieved in some of these areas? If the size of the civilian workforce could decline to 45 or 48 percent the size of the active duty uniformed Army, the number of individuals affected could be 30,000 to 40,000, and the annual savings for the Army budget once the changes were achieved could near $5 billion if the jobs could truly be eliminated.[59]

Changes to military pensions and to cost sharing in military health care are worth considering, even beyond the levels that the Pentagon has advocated in recent times. They could quite plausibly save the Army another $5 billion a year once in place.[60]

Further savings are possible, too. They could result from the Army's share of another round of base closures (up to $1 billion a year), the streamlining of military commissaries to where they are truly needed (perhaps another $500 million annually), the widespread use of so-called strategic sourcing for supplies, and the use of performance-based logistics that give companies incentives to make equipment maintenance as efficient as possible (some $1 billion a year from each).[61]

Taken together, these reforms could possibly save $10 billion a year once fully enacted. That could approach 6 to 8 percent of expected Army resources in the years ahead, and is very important therefore to attempt to achieve. But it is not so great as to permit the Army a pain-free way of absorbing massive cuts to its budget in the years ahead either.

TECHNOLOGY AND TRANSFORMATION

A key premise of this study is that the implications of technological change for American ground forces will continue to be significant—but they will tend to be evolutionary rather than revolutionary. Some would agree with this assessment but attribute it to bureaucratic inertia and traditional views of combat within the nation's armed forces that impede more rapid and radical change.[62] However, there is also a strong case that it is inherent in the nature of warfare and the true potential of technology to effect radical change.

To be sure, some areas of technology are indeed making revolutionary headway. Robotics, including drones, and computer technologies, including those enabling cyberwar capabilities, lead the way in this regard.[63] It is entirely possible that autonomous vehicles on land, for example, will complement the unmanned aerial vehicle/drone advances of the last fifteen years or so. It is not yet clear if what P. W. Singer calls "warbots," possibly in humanoid form, will wind up holding weapons and making decisions themselves on whom to shoot and whom not to shoot in the time frame of this study. But it does seem quite likely that robotic devices of one type or another will gather various kinds of intelligence, move supplies about the battlefield, and go beyond the limited uses such as removal of dangerous ordnance that they already carry out today.[64]

Impediments often slow the Pentagon's responsiveness to new threats, and reducing them can make an important difference. The experience with developing and purchasing technologies such as mine-resistant ambush-protected vehicles in the wars of the twenty-first century to date is a case in point.[65]

Yet in all likelihood, technological innovation will not fundamentally change ground warfare in the decades ahead, especially in the close fight, and in complex environments. When enemy forces are intermixed with civilian populations similar in appearance to friendly forces, or otherwise hard to identify through reliable algorithms that a machine could be charged with following, it will be very hard to replace soldiers with machines in going after them.[66] (It is also is an open question whether it would even be desirable, of course.)[67] Among other causes, this is because of limitations on the ability of sensors based on light or other parts of the electromagnetic spectrum, sound, or chemical or radioactive signatures to find militarily significant objects from long range.[68]

Some historical perspective is in order, as well. Often when the Army has tried to innovate rapidly in the past, it has failed—as with the creation of the Pentomic division in the 1950s or the Future Combat Systems in the 2000s.[69] It turned out that many of the technology options purported to be radical in their implications—the speed of vehicles, the resilience of those vehicles to enemy attack, the sensor capabilities of the vehicles, and so forth—proved far less transformative than predicted.

In some cases, technological change will be impressive, but will partly cancel itself out by helping both sides in a given type of war. A case in point is social media, which can help insurgents or terrorists recruit and mobilize followers, to be sure, but can also help Western intelligence agencies track the enemy, and help America's allies counter an extremist message.[70]

A key consequence of my argument that technological change will be significant and important but not revolutionary is the prescription that the Army need not radically reform or restructure itself. The Army has imposed many significant changes on itself already over the past two decades, including the creation of Stryker brigades, of brigade combat teams, of modular brigades, and most recently of more muscular brigade combat teams.[71] If anything, it is generating ideas for restructuring and reform too quickly, given the intellectual and bureaucratic bandwidth required to manage such change. My perspective would tend to suggest a period of calm and stability in the basic elements of the Army's force structure.

CONCLUSION

Building on earlier parts of the book, this chapter has developed a number of conclusions about the future of the U.S. Army in particular, where the questions loom largest about its future size and central characteristics.

Future American ground forces will need to avoid false choices about which kinds of major operations will dominate their future portfolio. Instead, they should prepare for a wide range of missions including even the currently unpopular counterinsurgency and stabilization variety. The most plausible future threats to American security include a number of such scenarios. As such, future soldiers and Marines will need a wide range of skills—including the capacity to work with non-military and foreign partners in various types of complex operations.

American ground forces will need the capacity to carry out more than one significant mission at once. It may now be reasonable for the first time since World War II for the nation to have the capacity for only one large ground war at a time. However, it may have to carry out that large war at the same time it quite plausibly conducts one or two large, multilateral, prolonged missions of other types. As such, a 1+2 paradigm for sizing the ground forces makes the most sense—even in the aftermath of a possible defusing of the Korean standoff as it exists today in Northeast Asia. To be sure, this 1+2 construct is somewhat stylized; there may be a blurring of the lines between what is a major operation (the 1 war) and what is a different type of mission (the 2 simultaneous operations). But as a shorthand, this is a useful framing.

The mix of active and reserve component forces needed to sustain such a capability should not vary too much from the current mix. Particularly if the Korean contingency becomes less worrisome and less demanding over time, there will surely be voices in the United States calling for radical cuts in the size of the active duty Army and a return to something like the roots of the American ground forces during the first half of the republic's existence. Indeed, such voices are already discernible in today's debate. But in fact, today's Active Army is already only a modest fraction of the Total Force. Even when the Marine Corps is added to the ledger, U.S. active duty ground forces are quite modest in size compared with any relevant benchmark—their own recent historical sizes, the sizes of the ground forces of other major powers, the sizes of the populations of overseas countries where one type of stabilization mission or another could become necessary, the requirements of various plausible missions.

Deterrence remains a preferable, and time-tested, form of strategic posture for the United States—and deterrents are more credible when they are quickly available as well as deployable. And the degree to which the standards of excellence that have characterized the American armed forces can be sustained in a reserve-dominant Army is open to doubt. This line of reasoning is also an argument for having most active duty Army personnel sufficiently ready that it can deploy quickly at most times—though it does not require all to be immediately deployable.

America's allies are on balance a very considerable blessing for the United States. Never before in human history has two-thirds of world GDP and world military spending been organized, even loosely, within one alliance community. Geostrategically, this structural feature of the current international system is a tremendous advantage for the United States and correlates with one of the most peaceful periods between states in all of human history. But militarily and operationally, allies and other security partners of the United States provide a less compelling advantage because of their their limited capacities—and their collective disinclination to change this reality through greater burden sharing. This is not a reason to discard alliances or denigrate those contributions that are made to a given mission, and U.S. forces should continue to prioritize engagement with them, which will remain a demanding task for the Army. But it is a strong argument for caution in assuming large allied contributions in any future military operation.

And finally, in terms of the highlights of this chapter, technology remains a very potent instrument for the U.S. armed forces, including the Army and Marine Corps. It also continues to move ahead quickly and to provide great new opportunities for the United States—as well as its potential adversaries. But nothing about trends in technology, or in warfare, suggests a radical change in how forces are sized and structured for most ground combat missions. Nor is the basic character of warfare likely to change, especially for the close-in fight in urban or other complex terrain. Contemporary changes in technology, and the associated changes in tactics and operational methods they facilitate, are rapid but evolutionary more than revolutionary. Many new capabilities have a mixed character in that they can help the enemy as much as the United States and its allies. Robotics and advanced computing, perhaps the two most impressive areas of technology development at present, offer a number of important capabilities and opportunities. But they have shown no sign yet of replacing soldiers with machines on the battlefield, or of making the ground combat environment transparent to American sensors, or of otherwise redefining warfare in a radical way. It is notable that the Amos-Petraeus criteria for sizing ground forces during the surge in Iraq (and later in Afghanistan), based on historical data from earlier decades, proved roughly correct for sizing forces in the twenty-first century as well.

These observations about trends in technology are a good way to sum up the overall strategic picture. A thorough examination of the future of land warfare suggests strongly that it may not be so radically different in future decades from what it has been in the past. To the extent it does change, moreover, it could get messier and harder rather than easier, simpler, or somehow less central to human security.

CHAPTER SIX

The Case for a
Million-Soldier U.S. Army

ALL THE CONSIDERATIONS OF this book point ultimately toward the importance of maintaining relative stability in the size, structure, posture, and capabilities of the U.S. Army in the years and decades to come. These conclusions remain true even if the war on terror gradually winds down in the years ahead and even if the Korean conflict, today the most significant military contingency undergirding U.S. Army force planning, is defused or resolved. Similar arguments pertain to the Marine Corps, though that service is less likely to suffer from the wide swings in strategic thought that often affect how the United States builds its Army.

My conclusion can be summarized simply: the United States should maintain roughly a million-soldier Total Army. That is very similar to where the U.S. Army is today, in total size, counting some 500,000 active duty soldiers and 550,000 reservists. It is almost identical to the 975,000-strong force that is envisioned for later in the decade under the 2015 Obama administration's budget plan—though those numbers could decline to perhaps 900,000 under a possible return to sequestration-like levels of funding. The calculations in this book are not precise enough to lead me to object to the 975,000-strong force, but a Total Army of less than 950,000 would be smaller than I would recommend based on the analyses developed in this book.

The 1+2 mission set that I propose here requires a significant active duty Army. The U.S. Marine Corps is the nation's expeditionary service, and it has a remarkable military capability. But it is focused on maritime environments and on missions of moderate size and scale, involving at most a few brigades in most cases (say, 20,000 to 30,000 armed personnel). Army airborne and special forces similarly are extraordinarily impressive, and geographically flexible. But they too are modest in size and, for the most part, in armament as well. The National Guard is crucial to the nation's security posture and plays a central role in the strategy I propose here. But the Army reserve component already represents more than half the nation's soldiers (and draws quite considerably on the active duty force for its recruiting pool, which raises questions of where the competent soldiers would come from, if the ratio of reservists and Guardsmen to active duty soldiers were to be notably changed). Many of the plausible missions the 1+2 posture is designed to handle could arise quickly or require continuous attentiveness and preparation. They also place a premium on deterrence. It is best to reduce the odds further that any will happen in the first place, which necessitates preparation, so that would-be adversaries realize that the United States has the capacity—and, quite likely, the will—to oppose possible aggressions promptly, before potential invasions abroad create faits accomplis. An active duty U.S. force, consisting in part of forward-deployed units large enough at least to constitute a trip-wire force, and ideally an initial holding force in key theaters, is the most prudent way to be ready for missions that may arise quickly. These U.S. military capabilities, of course, should be developed in association with U.S. allies. But the allies will often not be able to handle the full burden absent American help.

Because of my view that much of this American ground capability should remain in the active duty forces, the implication is that not only the aggregate size but also the individual components of the U.S. Army should remain roughly as they are today as well. In addition, the force structure should remain capable of high-end maneuver warfare in distant regions. In other words, it will still require armor, significant numbers of brigade combat teams and aviation brigades, supporting logistics, and many other existing capabilities. The Army of the future should not be radically different from the Army of today—though of course technological modernizations should be continued and other innovations pursued as well. There is, to be sure, enough uncertainty in these analyses, and enough room for reasonable debate, that my book cannot definitively disprove the viability of, say, the 420,000-soldier active force that today's Army says would result from sequestration. I do not favor such a force, largely because it falls towards the lower end of the range of what my calculations would say is acceptable. But it is not fundamentally different from the Army that seems advisable. That said, Active Army postures that dropped below 400,000 would most likely lack adequate capacity for the missions that history and current geopolitics suggest it prudent to prepare for.

Under my overall proposal, Army civilians would number in the ballpark of 225,000, modestly fewer than today. Some reforms and efficiencies would result in a smaller workforce, but the basic responsibilities of the federal civilian workforce would not change radically either.

Two hundred pages later, I have found my way back to defending the status quo in respect to the Army's size and composition—and suggesting that it be largely sustained well into the future. The force-sizing construct for the Army would shift, however. It would no longer derive from a modified and reduced form of a two-war capability, as it is under the 2014 Quadrennial Defense Review. Instead, it would be founded on what I call a 1+2 posture, that is, having the capability to wage one major all-out regional battle while contributing substantially to two multiyear, multilateral operations of different possible character.

Still, there would be more continuity than change in my proposal. There is good reason for that. While the precise level of forces cannot be confidently computed for an Army of 2020 or 2030, broad-brush considerations point to the case for strategic conservatism.

There is a strong case for keeping an Army, and a Marine Corps, with a broad range of capabilities and the overall size and responsiveness needed to undergird a 1+2 force-sizing paradigm. The former missions could include the more demanding of those considered here—not only highly unlikely contingencies involving Russia or China but also possible fights in Korea and the Middle East. The larger operations could also include complex missions; not all would necessarily be wars in the classic sense. But they could be long and dangerous and occur in austere conditions. They would likely involve the participation of American allies and other security partners and international actors. Some such missions could be carried out primarily by non-American personnel. They could well be important enough to U.S. security that American decisionmakers would find it essential that the United States play a considerable role under certain circumstances.

My specific arguments about the size and capabilities of the U.S. Army flow out of detailed analyses of various scenarios:

—Deterring Russia from even contemplating attacks on the Baltic states or China from considering an unfriendly future role on the Korean Peninsula,

—Handling an asymmetric threat in the South China Sea by constructing and protecting a number of bases in the Philippines and elsewhere,

—Helping South Asia cope with a shaky cease-fire after a potentially nuclear war between India and Pakistan or handle the aftermath of a major and complex humanitarian disaster superimposed on a security crisis,

—Deterring Iran from use of weapons of mass destruction, with the implied prospect of an in extremis ground invasion capability,

—Restoring order in a place like Saudi Arabia or Syria,

—Coping with a severe Ebola outbreak or the equivalent not in the small states of West Africa but in Nigeria at the same time that that country falls further into violence, or

—Handling a further meltdown in law and order in Central America that could result in much more direct threats to the American people— these are the scenarios I have considered in this book. By way of reference to the 1+2 posture, some operations would be closer to the "1" larger war, others closer to the "2" multilateral missions of a different sort. They are, one hopes, all individually unlikely, but they are meant to be plausible, and stressful tests of any proposed American military force posture. They strike me as likely to be representative of the kinds of threats that the next decades of the twenty-first century could present.

The logic behind the individual scenarios grows out of a broader perspective on the character of today's world, and America's role within it. The planet today is far more peaceful and stable than in most of human history, and while nuclear deterrence and globalization and other such factors probably play a role in achieving that, the U.S.-led international order undoubtedly does as well. Yet it is a fragile peace in places—in Central Europe as well as in the western Pacific. It is a world in open conflict in other places, most notably the broader Middle East, including some of South Asia, and much of northern and Central Africa. Serious criminality is found in many of these places too, as well as in large parts of Latin America, an otherwise promising region but one still very much weighed down by widespread violence. Nuclear proliferation remains an acute worry in regard to Iran, North Korea, and Pakistan.

New twenty-first-century dangers abound as well. They include advanced biological pathogens, changes in weather and climate (and with them, changed rainfall patterns and storms, as well as drought), and the sheer demands on the planet's environment and infrastructure brought on by a human population that could reach 10 billion sometime this century. While the major industrial nations do not appear on the verge of running out of key raw materials anytime soon, there are enough resources under stress, especially the ocean fisheries and tropical forests, and enough valuable resources that could entice greedy actors into conflict in places like Central Asia, the broader Middle East, and southern Africa, that natural resource issues could contribute to conflict as well. In some cases, conflicts could have an aura of "back to the future." In others, they could produce a uniquely modern witches' brew of multiple causes exacerbated by the demographic, economic, technological, and meteorological trends of the twenty-first century.

On balance, the world is moving in a direction compatible with American interests and indeed with universal values of human rights and dignity and freedom and greater prosperity. Never has there been so much progress in such a short space of time than in recent decades. Because far larger populations exist on the planet today than ever before, this reality translates into enormous improvement in the human condition. But the rate of change is inherently destabilizing too, in many places, and the progress is quite fragile in much of the world.

America's grand strategy is working. The Army and Marine Corps are crucial elements in that strategy, for deterring conflict, partnering with allies and others abroad, resolving conflicts when necessary, and helping keep the peace in general. But their work, and that of the nation, is far from done. We would be tempting fate and playing with danger if we were to remove or significantly weaken some of the key linchpins in the successful strategy of the last seventy years out of a conviction that warfare, or the world, or the nature of man had dramatically changed.

Resources and War

WHAT ROLE MIGHT RESOURCES play in sparking or exacerbating future global conflict? Will China be tempted by Siberia's water and open spaces and other resources? Will India and Pakistan find a new reason to fight, this time over water? Will Middle Eastern and northern African states do the same? Will rich diamond deposits and mineral wealth near borders that were drawn arbitrarily by colonial powers decades ago tempt leaders in Africa to contest certain territories in the interest of redrawing national frontiers? With maritime disputes over resources and waterways intensifying in parts of the world, will states be tempted to seize certain land formations near those prized waters so as to enhance their legal and political claims—and their access—to the riches in the waters and in the seabed beneath? This appendix seeks to provide a context for answering such questions by creating, in broad strokes, mental maps of where the world's most crucial resources may be found in the decades ahead.

The analysis in this appendix is not limited to a simple recitation of where the most strategically or economically vital natural resources are now found. It also considers man-made infrastructure as well. Here, much of my interest is in examining the potential for future, massive humanitarian disasters that could either precipitate or greatly complicate ongoing security problems, or be of such a huge scale as to necessitate the employment of military capabilities to mitigate them and save lives. For example, could a nuclear reactor accident in a region upwind of several major Asian cities create an urgent need to evacuate those cities? Could destruction of electrical infrastructure, whether from natural or man-made causes, put tens of millions in the dark for months and create a comparably urgent humanitarian dilemma?

We should not assume just because the world has experienced major catastrophes already—the Southeast Asian tsunami of 2004, several major Pakistani earthquakes, the Haiti earthquake of 2010, the Fukushima nuclear reactor disaster of 2011, the Philippines typhoon of 2013, and Nepal's terrible 2015 earthquake—that we know how to handle such problems. As a result of the growing density of human populations, the possibility exists of a class of disasters at least tenfold as destructive and threatening to future human life.

The following examination of what might be called global geoeconomics is organized into two main parts. The first examines the distribution of natural resources, where the resources under consideration include people and populations; water and arable land; strategic metals, precious gems, other valuable natural resources, some more important for their military implications and others simply for their commercial value; and energy. The second part considers places where man-made infrastructure is potentially most fragile. The signal issue here is nuclear power plants, but major cities, particularly those near earthquake fault lines or coastal regions, rank high as well.

VALUABLE AND STRATEGIC RESOURCES

An examination of where on the planet scarce resources are found, particularly when these resource sites are mapped in relation to locales where populations are largest or powerful countries are proximate, can greatly help in determining where future conflicts might be of greatest strategic salience.

The implicit assumption in this analysis is that interstate conflict at a strategically significant scale is more likely when populous and powerful states disagree over who owns valuable resources to which more than one can lay claim, or when states vulnerable to internal chaos are of such a size and character that their internal dissolution could have major ramifications for the international community. States with nuclear weapons capabilities pose an additional concern.

This framework admittedly has limitations. It likely would not have identified Afghanistan before 2001 as an area of strategic import, for example. Nor might it help us identify a future country that harbors a terrorist group or develops advanced biological pathogens or emits extremely hazardous pollutants into the global commons or winds up possessing most of the world's supply of what proves to be a future strategically crucial commodity. As such, if anything, the analysis provided in this chapter understates those places on land where the United States could witness the development of major challenges to its security in the years ahead.

Population

Human beings are both the greatest asset of governments and the greatest challenge to governments. And they have never been more numerous. The Earth's population tops 7 billion now and will likely exceed 10 billion in the course of the twenty-first century, even as growth rates slow (the world's population increase in the twentieth century was greater in proportional terms, though comparable in likely overall magnitude).[1]

The world's population is concentrated first and foremost along the Eurasian littoral. But there are also substantial populations in the Americas (also largely along the coasts). Africa is increasingly densely populated in places such as Nigeria. Middle Eastern populations are large, especially when measured relative to their scarce water resources and paucity of arable land, particularly in countries such as Egypt. Indonesia has the world's fourth largest population, and the Philippine archipelago holds a large number of people as well. But it is from Western Europe through Turkey and Iran, and then particularly through South Asia, Southeast Asia, and the East Asian coastal regions, where most of the world's people are found.

Just as significant, in terms of trying to foresee trends in conflict, is to note where populations are still growing fast. An examination of such trends suggests where competition for resources could intensify and where large human populations could develop the greatest new dependencies on fragile or inadequate infrastructure. Viewed through this prism, Africa has the greatest percentage growth rates overall, with Afghanistan, Oman, Yemen, and parts of Central America also experiencing rapid relative growth. With their large population bases, countries in South Asia, as well as Indonesia, Egypt, and Mexico, have noteworthy growth rates too, even if below most of those in Africa in annual percentage terms.[2] Many traditional American allies have shrinking populations, though the United States enjoys a modestly upward demographic trajectory.[3]

Water, Farmland, Forests, and Fisheries

Water and farmland are clearly fundamental to human life. With growing global populations, improving living standards, and changing climactic conditions, they are also under severe stress in many places. The same is true of forests and fisheries.

Logically speaking, after human populations themselves, water should be next on the list of crucial commodities. It is essential for human life and crucial for large-scale industry. And it is needed in such large amounts that normal trade mechanisms do not work particularly well for this commodity. Apart from the occasional visionary plan to tow an iceberg to a parched nation of the Middle East, water scarcity issues almost always involve immediate neighbors or, at most, several states sharing a single river system. Groups of states sharing a single aquifer or depending on a given river system may wind up in strategically significant competition for water.[4]

In this regard, the world's regions of greatest water scarcity are fairly easy to identify. They include the broad swath of northern Africa known as the Sahel and extending to the Horn of Africa; the Middle East into part of South Asia; much of China, particularly in the north; virtually all of Australia; southern Africa; parts of west-central South America; and a swath of North America, including most of the western United States and much of Mexico as well.

The situation is more complicated when one examines the situation country by country. Among those populous and otherwise strategically important nations with particular water challenges in terms of renewable resources are Algeria, Bangladesh (despite the monsoons), China, Egypt, Ethiopia, Hungary, India, Iran, Iraq, Israel, Jordan, Kenya, Lebanon, Nigeria, Pakistan, Poland, Saudi Arabia, South Africa, Sudan, Syria, Ukraine, and Yemen.

Naturally, the severity of the water shortages varies by country, and by year within each country. Moreover, the same amount of water may represent a shortage for one country and a surplus for another, depending on industrial and agricultural uses and on the efficiency of consumption. But this is definitely an area of significant concern, on balance, for trends in international order and governance. A British Ministry of Defense study estimated in 2014 that nearly 4 billion people could suffer water shortages by mid-century if current trends continued.[5]

With respect to farmland, the world's zones of greatest agricultural potential correlate closely with those receiving ample rain, though climate and soil also play important roles. In broad terms, there is much to be happy about when examining farmland worldwide. Every continent has large territories that are arable. Nearly every populous state, with the exception of several in the broader Middle East region in particular, has considerable amounts of land it can devote to producing its own food. In addition, there is a great deal of marginal land around the world that could if necessary, though at somewhat lower rates of production, be brought into cultivation. The economics of agriculture mean that, sadly, not every part of the world is well fed, but this does not seem to be in the first instance a consequence of the lack of available land. Indeed, the world has more than three times as much land that is usable for agriculture as is actually cultivated, the figures being 38 percent of the planet's entire land area versus 11 percent, respectively.[6]

Not all the news is good, of course. Several large and strategically crucial states have very limited arable land per capita. Egypt, Bangladesh, and China top this particular list.[7]

Equally significant to today's breakdown of key farming regions is a prognostication as to what is likely to change in the decades ahead, as a result particularly of climate change. Not surprisingly, most of the world's dry regions are expected to get worse. But most of Central Africa, central South America, and the southern half of the United States are expected to lose productivity as well. This is a foreboding map, even if it offers some relatively good news for Canada, Russia, and, perhaps surprisingly, China.

Meanwhile, two more trends bear mentioning in regard to farmland. First, more is being demanded from it, as world population growth, together with improving living standards, is naturally creating far more requirement for output. Indeed, the UN Food and Agricultural Organization forecasts that need will grow by 70 percent globally by 2050. Second, and relatedly, this trend will likely reinforce the ongoing pressures to generate more food yield per acre of farmland or ranchland, which in turn will reinforce the ongoing dependence on high-yield seed, fertilizer, and other elements of modern agriculture. This trend creates a certain fragility in the food production chain owing to dependence on properly functioning infrastructure to bring these raw materials to farmers and then to get farm products to market.[8]

Similarly, an examination of trends in forest coverage around the world yields both good news and bad. Forests are widely dispersed around the world and stable in many places. They are most abundant in northern Eurasia, Southeast Asia and Indonesia, the Congo basin of Africa and much of the southern parts of West Africa, the broader Amazon basin, large swaths of Central America into Mexico, the eastern coast of the United States, and Canada. But the rate of tropical deforestation is quite worrisome—for its implications for global climate, and for the sustainability of forest products, including timber, as well. Looked at differently, the potential of forests to mitigate global warming could be quite important as a future policy tool, if deforestation can be halted or reversed.[9]

Food from fishing presents another set of potential challenges. Many ocean fisheries are being depleted. The challenge of developing common approaches to managing the rates of exploitation of these resources is considerable. The UN Food and Agriculture Organization estimates that 85 percent of the world's fisheries are already fully exploited, overexploited, depleted, or recovering from depletion.[10] With global populations growing and human standards of living improving, the pressures are only likely to grow.[11]

Energy—Oil and Gas

Today's oil and gas production worldwide is reasonably well diversified, and the North American energy revolution is improving the situation further. But the concentration of reserves still favors certain parts of the world disproportionately, potentially increasing their strategic significance and making the world highly dependent on them in the future, to the extent that the global economy continues to run largely on hydrocarbons (see table A-1).

The Middle East still leads the world in oil production, with Russia/Eurasia in second place regionally. Still, every other major region save Western Europe accounts for a significant share of the world total. In regard to natural gas, Russia and Eurasia lead the way, followed closely by North America, with the Middle East and the Asia Pacific region

Table A-1. Recoverable Oil, Gas, and Liquid Natural Gas (LNG) for Provinces of the World by Region, 2012

Units as indicated

| | | Oil (million barrels) | | | | Total undiscovered resources | | | | | | | |
| | | | | | | Gas (billion cubic feet) | | | | LNG (million barrels) | | | |
Regions	Field type	F95	F50	F5	Mean	F95	F50	F5	Mean	F95	F50	F5	Mean
Arctic Ocean	Oil	15,984	45,559	177,175	66,211	54,892	178,640	606,787	237,485	2,083	6,487	19,754	8,193
Former Soviet Union	Gas					343,396	1,058,432	3,448,972	1,385,046	8,009	25,058	76,955	31,786
Middle East and North Africa	Oil	43,316	101,406	212,678	111,201	49,194	124,226	308,443	144,797	1,578	4,026	10,389	4,764
	Gas					334,063	729,200	1,490,538	796,513	10,363	23,220	50,605	25,912
Asia and Pacific	Oil	20,950	43,607	87,744	47,544	52,579	117,354	253,416	130,483	1,173	2,742	6,346	3,125
	Gas					269,523	562,461	1,110,663	607,845	7,517	16,340	33,736	17,917
Europe	Oil	4,344	8,561	19,417	9,868	6,605	16,422	50,460	21,171	245	570	1,616	710
	Gas					54,072	109,589	249,678	127,454	912	1,924	4,401	2,219
North America	Oil	25,500	62,618	208,032	83,386	42,498	112,675	398,902	152,847	897	2,685	11,923	4,103
	Gas					117,885	300,810	111,423	420,890	2,910	10,489	43,785	15,164
South America and Caribbean	Oil	44,556	108,098	261,862	125,900	99,532	246,922	637,661	295,475	2,909	7,570	20,048	9,119
	Gas					130,015	324,762	838,345	383,062	3,941	9,937	26,532	11,882
Sub-Saharan Africa	Oil	40,777	102,961	232,090	115,333	40,553	104,711	262,898	122,188	1,237	3,394	9,237	4,089
	Gas					278,230	557,579	1,190,770	621,341	9,425	20,584	49,935	23,879
South Asia	Oil	3,323	5,575	9,339	5,855	8,404	14,648	25,087	15,419	189	337	586	356
	Gas					68,651	134,622	250,144	143,620	1,623	3,197	6,155	3,450
Total conventional resources					565,298				5,605,626				166,668

Source: World Petroleum Resources Project, "An Estimate of Undiscovered Conventional Oil and Gas Resources of the World, 2012," United States Geological Survey. April 2012 (http://pubs.usgs.gov/fs/2012/3042/fs2012-3042.pdf).

a. Numbers are fully risked estimates. Liquid gases are included as LNG. F95 indicates a 95 percent chance of at least the amount shown; other fractiles are the same. If shaded gray, not applicable.

following. On balance, current hydrocarbon production does show a significant ongoing focus on the broader Middle East and Russia, especially under and immediately around the Persian Gulf, as well as near the Caspian Sea and in western Siberia. But there is still considerable diversity in worldwide production.

In the future the situation may not remain quite so favorable (if indeed it can be said to be favorable now). The Middle East and Russia/Eurasia between them hold an estimated 80 percent of the world's known natural gas reserves, though the shale gas revolution improves North America's position somewhat. The Middle East alone has two-thirds of the world's proven oil reserves, though fortunately, the remainder is distributed throughout Africa and Latin America (and to a very limited extent North America) rather than being just in the Russia/Eurasia region.[12] To be sure, these figures for proven reserves may change. The world may well hold 5 trillion barrels of oil, for example, and not simply the 1.5 trillion now considered to be proven reserves (on top of the 1 trillion already consumed). There could be another 8 trillion barrels in oil sands (three-fourths in the United States). The United States also has about 200 trillion cubic meters of gas by the latest official estimates, roughly comparable to world oil reserves in collective energy content, with perhaps much more in shale. There are large amounts of coal as well, and in many different parts of the world, with little sign that this type of fuel will become less important, despite its generally undesirable climactic and environmental effects.[13] The world's dependence on hydrocarbons probably will not change dramatically in the coming decades, in light of the various constraints and challenges associated with most renewables and nuclear power. Those forms of energy likely will provide substantially more power than they do today. But when growing demand is taken into account, hydrocarbons are likely to still provide 75 to 80 percent of global energy supply in 2030, according to Daniel Yergin and other experts.[14]

Strategic Metals

A number of minerals and metals are of considerable interest when one tries to anticipate where future conflict might occur. Some, such as uranium or tungsten or rare earth metals, have very specialized military purposes. Control of large fractions of such resources by hostile powers could, under certain circumstances, be strategically worrisome for the

United States. Others, such as diamonds, are of interest commercially, making areas rich in such resources potentially attractive to would-be aggressors because of their simple monetary value.

There are a number of metals that can be deemed critical or strategic for the United States. Generally, these are defined based on their critical importance in key industrial and military applications, juxtaposed with their potential scarcity.

Based on various U.S. government surveys and other criteria, a list of the most strategically critical metals would include aluminum, beryllium, chromium, cobalt, manganese, niobium (a.k.a. columbium), platinum, tantalum, tin, titanium, tungsten, yttrium (and other rare earth metals), and zinc.[15] I have added a few others in the discussion below as well.

Many countries are known to have significant reserves of uranium. Australia is the best endowed, followed by Kazakhstan. Russia and Canada follow, with the United States, Brazil, South Africa, Namibia, Mali, and China following next. India and Mongolia also have modest estimated deposits.

The world's top gold deposits are in Indonesia, South Africa, Papua New Guinea, Uzbekistan, Russia, Mongolia, the Dominican Republic, Australia, and Ghana.[16] Rubies and sapphires are found largely in Myanmar, Sri Lanka, Tajikistan, Pakistan, Afghanistan, Laos, Vietnam, Kenya, Tanzania, Madagascar, Malawi, Colombia, and Australia.[17]

Rare earth metals are used to produce a number of important technologies, including magnets, metallurgical alloys, and catalysts for the creation of other industrial products. As was witnessed in recent years when China cut off supplies to Japan, current rare earth metals production is concentrated in China, with 90 percent of global output in 2012 and 2013 coming from that one country. However, overall economic reserves are somewhat more evenly distributed, with China holding about half the world's total and a number of nations, including the United States, Brazil, India, and Australia, having considerable holdings. Moreover, over the last couple of years, the substitution of different materials for rare earth metals and the development of new sources of materials and refining have reduced China's stranglehold on the market.[18]

Aluminum is used in various vehicles, packaging, machinery, consumer durables, and buildings. The preeminent producer of aluminum, in terms of smelting the final product, is far and away China, which accounts for nearly half of the global production, with Russia, Canada, the United States, Brazil, India, the United Arab Emirates, and Australia all following. The global production of bauxite, from which aluminum is made, is greatest in Australia, accounting for almost a third of the global total, followed by China, Brazil, Indonesia, and India. Global reserves are greatest in Guinea, Australia, Brazil, Vietnam, Jamaica, and Indonesia.[19]

Beryllium, used in various electronics and in structural metals in sectors such as aerospace, is currently produced mainly in the United States. The United States also possesses about two-thirds of the estimated world reserves.[20] Chromium is important in superalloys. It is mined, and its reserves are concentrated overwhelmingly in two places, Kazakhstan and South Africa. India and the United States also have limited supplies.[21] Cobalt has similar types of applications in superalloys in devices such as aircraft engines; cobalt reserves are concentrated in Congo and Australia, with current production dominated by Congo.[22]

Industrial diamonds are mined and found in southern Africa— Botswana, South Africa, Congo—as well as China and Australia. China is a major manufacturer of synthetic diamonds. Gem-quality diamond production is greatest in Botswana, Russia, Canada, Angola, and Congo, followed by South Africa and Namibia.[23]

Manganese, used in steel production, is mined in South Africa, Australia, China, Gabon, Brazil, and elsewhere. The largest reserves are in South Africa, Ukraine, and Brazil, with India and China also holding significant amounts.[24] Niobium, also known as columbium, is used in steels and superalloys and is mined primarily in Brazil, where most reserves are located as well.[25] For platinum and palladium, used in catalytic converters and some chemical processes, production is greatest in South Africa, followed by Russia and then Canada and the United States. Reserves are overwhelmingly located in South Africa.[26] Tantalum, used largely in electronics, is mined in Brazil, Congo, Rwanda, Mozambique, Nigeria, and Canada, with reserves believed to be largest in Australia and Brazil.[27] Tin is mined in many places, beginning with China, Indonesia, and Peru; reserves are greatest in China, Indonesia, Brazil, and Bolivia.[28]

Titanium, important because of its high strength relative to weight, is refined from mined materials found in a wide range of countries (though only modest amounts are found in the United States). Key producers include South Africa and Australia, as well as Canada, China, India, Madagascar, Mozambique, Norway, Ukraine, and Vietnam, among others. There is no predominant supplier. Estimated reserves are greatest in

China and Australia, but again, a number of other countries have considerable holdings, too.[29] Tungsten, used in various tools and other applications where high-density materials are required, is produced mostly in China. It is there that most global reserves (more than 50 percent of the total) are found as well.[30] Zinc, used in galvanizing and other work with metals, is mined mainly in China, Peru, and Australia. These are also the countries that rank first, second, and third in estimated reserves.[31]

To synthesize and summarize the above, the world's greatest concentrations of strategic minerals and metals tend to be in Africa from Congo southward, Australia, Brazil, Canada, China, Kazakhstan, and the United States. India, Indonesia, Russia, and Ukraine account for considerable production or hold substantial reserves as well. Most of northern Africa, most of the broader Middle East, Western and Central Europe writ large, Japan and Korea, most of Southeast Asia, and large swaths of Spanish-speaking Latin America are less well endowed, on balance. But no such short list can truly do the subject justice, as there may be, for a given particular resource at a given moment in time, a deposit somewhere else that proves enticing or strategic. On balance, however, the overall message of this analysis is generally reassuring: most strategic minerals and metals are found in many parts of the world, with few cases where a hostile power or major disruptive event could bring the world's economy to its knees with a cutoff of supply.

THE GEOGRAPHY OF HUMAN FRAGILITY: ANTICIPATING CATASTROPHES

Arguably, on a strategic scale, the world has not witnessed a true catastrophe since World War II. That may sound like a heartless comment from a comfortable American sitting in the nation's capital, generally far removed from the devastation of various droughts, diseases, earthquakes, tsunamis, and, most of all, civil wars in recent decades. My point, however, is not to downplay in the slightest the humanitarian importance of those kinds of afflictions—which, on balance, the world community could have and should have done a better job of addressing. Far too many lives have been directly lost, and far too many countries have been held back from achieving their people's potential, by such tragedies. The point rather is that there has not been an epochal event the sheer magnitude of which has affected the basic functioning of the world economy

or political system in any significant and lasting way. There have arguably been silent and slow catastrophes, such as the prevalence of malaria
throughout much of the developing world, but these are of a different
character in terms of the crisis management implications. From the point
of view of military planning, any responses to these types of disasters
have, in the words of defense reviews of the 1990s in particular, been
"lesser included cases" for force planning—with traditional combat missions dominating the Pentagon's list of most important scenarios driving
the nation's force structure and global posture.

This could change. It is possible to imagine a category of disasters,
either purely natural or some combination of natural and man-made,
that dwarf our experiences to date. One reason for this concern is the
possibility that pure chance could produce far worse devastation than
that witnessed so far. One need not posit the highly improbable, such
as a large asteroid strike, to see the dangers. Only a little imagination
extrapolating from past tragedies already experienced, and allowing for
the possibility of a cascading series of unlucky events that create a snowballing effect, is required.

The earthquake in Pakistan in 2005 that killed nearly 100,000 could
have struck a city rather than a relatively remote area. The tsunami of
2004 could likewise have hit large cities, not only killing hundreds of
thousands but leaving tens of millions without functioning infrastructure
or reliable access to food and water and health care. The Japanese earthquake and tsunami of 2011 could have destroyed a nuclear power plant
far closer to Tokyo.

The growing concentrations of large numbers of humans, many of
them poor and dependent on fragile infrastructure, near coastal regions
or earthquake-prone zones make for unsettling possibilities. These demographic and developmental trends, when juxtaposed with the possible
effects of global climate change and rising sea levels, increase the risks
even further.[32] And should a tragedy of major magnitude affect a country already at risk from civil conflict, widespread terrorism, or a major
dispute with a neighbor, the situation could become far worse still, as
malevolent actors sought to take advantage of the chaos.

Where are civilization's greatest Achilles' heels, its most acute vulnerabilities, in the twenty-first century? The discussion below is far from comprehensive, of course. Its purpose, rather, is to establish a sense of scale.

The Physical Backdrop: Old-Fashioned Storms,
Droughts, and Earthquakes

While much of the discussion about twenty-first-century natural calamities centers on global warming, it is important to establish a baseline that predates any such trends. The world has had plenty of terrible storms and earthquakes and environmental stresses, a number exacerbating internal or interstate conflict, long before anthropogenic climate change posed additional concerns.[33]

Tropical storms have been and are most likely to affect South and East Asia extending through Southeast Asia and to the Philippine archipelago, western Mexico and Central America, the Caribbean, and the eastern United States. Europe, the Middle East, Africa, and South America, as well as the heart of Eurasia, are generally spared this particular affliction, though they suffer from others.[34] The United States and Canada are the most vulnerable parts of the Earth to tornadoes because of the large North American land mass, which is for the most part uninterrupted by mountain ranges in the eastern and central zones of the continent (meaning that cold and warm air masses can more easily mix, producing conditions conducive to tornado formation). Bangladesh and certain other parts of Asia are vulnerable as well.[35]

As noted briefly before, droughts of long duration are most notable in the Sahara and Sahel regions of Africa, as well as in the northern, Arab parts of the African continent; in much of the Arabian Peninsula and Levant region of the Middle East; in southwestern Africa; throughout most of Australia; along the western coasts and mountainous regions of the Americas; in parts of Central Asia and South Asia; and in parts of China and eastern Siberia. They tend to be less problematic throughout the eastern two-thirds of the Americas, Europe (including European Russia), the central part of Africa, and most of South and Southeast Asia.[36] Many countries have learned more efficient ways of using water, and desalination technologies offer promise as well.[37] But these hopeful indicators must compete with growing populations and, in some places, gradually worsening drought conditions.

Earthquake patterns are quite different. Earthquakes are most likely to occur along the entire western rim of the Americas (north and south), Turkey and Iran and the Caucasus, the broad Himalayan region (including northern Pakistan and India, and extending into western China as well as Burma), Japan, New Zealand, and parts of Indonesia. Virtually all the rest of the Americas and Europe, northern Eurasia, the Arabian Peninsula, Africa, and Australia are generally safe.[38]

Patterns for tsunamis are somewhat similar to those for earthquakes. The regions with greatest risk for mass casualty events are in Japan, Southeast Asia, and to an extent western South America.[39]

The Physical Backdrop:
Rising Sea Levels and Climate Change

It is too soon to know how terrible global warming may turn out to be in the broad sweep of human history. It could wind up less severe than some forecasts predict. It could actually improve net agricultural production globally, even if it damages it considerably in some places. It is not clear that storms are becoming radically more powerful owing to global warming to date, either. Current projections suggest that the intensity of global hurricanes by century's end may increase by roughly 2 to 20 percent as a result of anthropogenic global warming—nontrivial, to be sure, but not transformative, either.[40] The fact that damage has grown in some storms may have more to do with growing populations and enlarging (if often rickety) infrastructure than with the intensity of the weather patterns per se.[41] And rising ocean levels may not inundate as many islands and low-lying coastal regions as was first assumed, because deposits of sediment from those rising oceans may help some land formations themselves rise, along with the sea waters.[42]

Even if climate change proves significant in magnitude, as seems likely, its effects could be mitigated if they arrive gradually enough. If the scale of change is measured in many decades—the time period over which many buildings are razed or reconstructed, infrastructure is overhauled, and population shifts are likely to happen anyway, based on past precedent—the economic as well as the security implications could be tolerable. Relatedly, it is entirely possible that climate engineering will prove safer and more controllable than many now fear. Injecting aerosols or water droplets into the upper atmosphere and seeding the oceans with iron to induce the growth of carbon-absorbing plankton are among the more plausible notions.

Moreover, even if it occurs at a relatively rapid pace and is unmitigated by climate engineering measures, global warming may not prove the driving concern in terms of civilization's vulnerability to natural catastrophe. The combination of growing populations, many concentrated in dense megalopolises in poorer countries dependent on vulnerable infrastructure, and sheer probability and statistics—that is, the possibility of extreme bad luck in where or how a storm or earthquake strikes—may prove the far greater worry.

That said, the potential dangers from global warming cannot be ignored.[43] Hundreds of billions of dollars worth of property is at extreme risk of severe damage—to itself and its inhabitants—from storms that, once they occur, could leave at least that much property in urgent need of repair. A significant fraction of this danger could arise as a result of climate change. As a point of reference, even if their linkages to climate trends remain unclear, the Katrina and Sandy hurricane experiences in 2005 and 2012 in the United States cost roughly $125 billion and $65 billion, respectively, and indicate the potential for even worse events.[44] One recent estimate, if anything cautious, suggested an average annual increase in likely damage in the range of $10 billion owing to greater storm activity.[45]

Tens of millions, and perhaps even hundreds of millions, of people could be displaced by rising sea levels. Even if population displacement from this cause occurred relatively gradually, in principle allowing time for adjustment, the scale of the challenge could be enormous. Some of the world's most densely populated areas and most economically vibrant—but in some cases also economically quite fragile—regions could be significantly affected. Eastern China is one such area. Large swaths of the Middle East and North Africa are another. Bangladesh and India represent a third zone. Stronger preparation of coastal defenses, such as dikes, can help in some areas, but doing so is expensive, and such methods are more difficult to apply around rivers and marshes. Moreover, the effects of declining water tables and increasing populations could serve to exacerbate the effects of rising sea levels by making lowlands descend in some cases. Some lands could move downward, even as waters around them rose one to several meters.[46]

Farmland yields could be affected dramatically too, with estimates of a loss of 50 percent to 70 percent productivity in such places as parts of the lower Great Plains in the United States.[47] Again, this may seem like a slow-motion economic effect rather than a reason for an acute disaster response. Perhaps that will be the case in the United States. But comparable effects in regions of the world already supporting populations living on the brink could produce a gradually worsening chronic food shortage, which could then be punctuated, in any given year, by a disastrous drought or other such event. The potential for mass famine would be real.

Global climate change could influence the future prospects for conflict or other types of violence. It is possible, for example, that one country or a group of countries, severely affected by climate change, could decide to take measures that mitigated the incidence of solar radiation on the entire planet. Injecting aerosols or particulate matter into the upper reaches of the atmosphere via aircraft, seeding clouds with additional water to increase their reflectivity, or adding iron to the oceans to increase their absorptive capacity for carbon could seem reasonable steps to a country or group of states that had suffered acute damage from storms, rising sea levels, and other possible effects from climate change. If that country or group of countries felt the rest of the world was the main cause of the crisis yet also inattentive to addressing the problem (for example, in financing steps that reduced global warming or helped relocate affected populations), it might take action. But any steps to mitigate warming might overshoot their targeted effects, disrupt rainfall in regions that needed it, lead to the creation of dead zones in the ocean (as a result of excessive plankton growth), or otherwise produce harmful consequences that would make the measures controversial globally.[48] That could lead to threats, perhaps even military threats, to make the country in question cease its climate engineering activities.

Nuclear Power Plants and Related Dangers

Concerns about global warming are also likely to sustain the case for nuclear power, despite the risks of proliferation and accident. It is worth noting the blunt words of the Intergovernmental Panel on Climate Change on this subject: "decarbonizing electricity generation is a key component of cost-effective mitigation strategies."[49] Of course, renewables can and will contribute too, but it is hard to see them absorbing the full burden of the shift in fuels for electricity generation that might seem imperative quite soon.

Nuclear power plants may be the single most dangerous category of technology prevalent around the world today. To be sure, some types of toxic chemical plants could cause severe damage and loss of life, as the

Bhopal, India, tragedy of 1984 that killed several thousand showed. And in theory, an attack with an advanced biological pathogen, while perhaps not directly disruptive to property, could kill millions (while also conceivably necessitating the quarantining of large population groups, perhaps even through the use of force in an extreme scenario).[50] Catastrophic damage to a large dam with major populations downriver of the dam or otherwise vulnerable to its potential floodwaters could also constitute a serious danger; the worst to date, a dam failure on the Yellow River in China in 1975, killed nearly 100,000.[51] A similar catastrophe in today's more populous world might kill multiples of that figure and displace hundreds of thousands or millions more.

But on balance, nuclear power plants are in a class by themselves, especially among technologies that are fairly numerous around the world. This is particularly true in regard to the affected area, which could require the mass evacuation of human populations for sustained periods of time, thereby placing enormous demands on first responders, and on governments more generally, in the event of a future accident or other tragedy.

Of course, nuclear power plants and associated infrastructure for making fuel and separating waste can also provide the wherewithal for nuclear weapons.[52] The world's operational nuclear power plants numbered roughly 435 as of 2014 (see table A-2). The total tally includes about 120 in North America, 4 in South America, 48 in Russia and Ukraine, 136 in Western and Central Europe, 1 in the broader Middle East, 2 in Africa, 24 in India and Pakistan, 48 in Japan, 21 in China, 6 in Taiwan, and 23 in South Korea.[53] States with weapons-usable nuclear materials of some type, such as fuel or waste associated with research reactors, and at least some issues with their nuclear safety and security policies (at a minimum, failure to join certain nuclear security accords) include Argentina, Belarus, Ghana, India, Iran, Israel, Italy, Japan, North Korea, Norway, Pakistan, Russia, South Africa, Sweden, Syria, the United States, and Vietnam.[54]

All of these reactors, if to varying degrees, could be sources of enormous trouble as a result of accident, terrorist attack, extreme weather or other natural events, or breakdowns in the infrastructure, such as electricity systems, necessary for the proper functioning of the reactors.

Most notable on the list of worries are probably those reactors in South and East Asia that are closest to major population centers and also, in some cases, near earthquake fault lines or proximate to potential

Table A-2. Operational Nuclear Power Plants by Country, as of Early 2015

United States	99	Germany	9	Pakistan	3
France	58	Spain	8	Brazil	2
Japan	48	Belgium	7	Bulgaria	2
Russia	34	Czech Republic	6	Mexico	2
China, mainland	27	Taiwan	6	Romania	2
South Korea	24	Switzerland	5	South Africa	2
India	21	Finland	4	Armenia	1
Canada	19	Hungary	4	Iran	1
United Kingdom	16	Slovak Republic	4	Netherlands	1
Ukraine	15	Argentina	3	Slovenia	1
Sweden	10				

Source: World Nuclear Association database (www.world-nuclear.org/nucleardatabase/Default. aspx?id=27232).

conflict zones. Reactors in or near developing countries with weak infrastructure or other limitations on their response capabilities, in the event of accident, also warrant special attention.

The 1986 Chernobyl, Ukraine, tragedy provides a sense of the scale of what can happen in a major nuclear accident. That accident, the result largely of design flaws and operator error, was horrible—but it could have been far worse, as it occurred in a relatively sparsely populated part of the then Soviet Union. Within a 30-kilometer radius, somewhat more than 300,000 people were ultimately resettled (in Belarus as well) after the fire and explosion at Reactor 4. The size of a region deemed unsafe for permanent human habitation after another reactor accident would naturally be a function of the severity of the accident, together with weather conditions and water drainage patterns in the vicinity. But the fact that some 3,000 to 4,000 square kilometers of land were deemed unfit for human life after the accident is sobering when one imagines a region of similar size in one of the world's more densely populated zones. Of course, the 2011 Fukushima tragedy did occur in such a zone, in the nation of Japan—but luckily, it was in a relatively less densely populated part of Honshu island, and prevailing wind patterns blew fallout out toward the sea, which is also where contaminated water used for cooling was able to escape.[55] A brief word on biological technologies is in order. In principle, they could lead to the development of extremely potent agents, with contagious qualities not unlike those of the flu and lethal effects on an infected organism not unlike those of smallpox (or, for that matter, the Ebola virus). Or dangerous pathogens could evolve naturally. It is difficult to pinpoint the regions of the world where the threat might be greatest. Certainly, the combination of scientific talent, an economic system with important elements of microbiology research and production, and a lack of political transparency could represent the witches' brew of dangers. But while it is not easy to concoct advanced pathogens, there are so many parts of the world where they could in principle be fabricated that it is difficult to develop a cartographical picture of this hypothetical threat.[56]

A SURVEY OF RESPONSES TO PAST DISASTERS

Establishing a sense of the scale of major global disasters to date, and of the associated scale of the responses to them, can provide useful context as one considers the possibility of potentially larger catastrophes—as populations grow and as certain types of dangers from climate, nuclear power, toxic chemical facilities, or other causes expand as well. The cases discussed below are meant to be illustrative, and to create a notional rather than precise sense of what the necessary level of response may be in the future.

The world's worst tragedies of the twenty-first century have been terrible, but they have not been as bad as could easily have been imagined. For one thing, they tended to affect relatively limited populations, usually not more than 1 million to 4 million. (That was generally true as well in the 1990s.)[57] That is admittedly a lot, in terms of how many of our fellow human souls suffered some form of catastrophe. But in terms of the demand imposed on response systems, things could have been far worse—and might be worse in the future.

The 2004–05 American response to the tsunami in the Indian Ocean, which killed about 300,000 and displaced another 1.1 million, was most notable for its airlift and naval operations. The U.S. airlift effort averaged more than 250 tons a day of supplies—the equivalent of perhaps half a dozen flights of large transport aircraft with full loads—though it involved in various ways some thirty-five C-17 airlifters, twenty-four C-5s, twenty-one C-130 tactical airlifters, and a number of other planes. Nearly twenty Navy ships were also employed.[58]

The Kashmir earthquake of October 2005 killed nearly 100,000 people, destroyed some 30,000 buildings, and left about 4 million homeless, most in the country of Pakistan.[59] One component of the relief effort in ensuing months, by the Pakistani Red Crescent Society as well as related international Red Cross and Red Crescent associations, delivered nearly 1,000 tons of supplies to help slightly more than 100,000 of those displaced (by nearly 300 truck trips and more than 50 helicopter sorties). Scaling these figures, one might estimate that as many as 30,000 tons of supplies were provided to cover the entire displaced population.[60]

Hurricane Katrina in and around New Orleans in 2005 led to the deployment of some 45,000 National Guard personnel for response in Louisiana and Mississippi, and nearly 20,000 active duty personnel.[61] Despite the scale of the response, the overall government effort, led by FEMA, was marred by many difficulties and proved extremely controversial in American politics. The storm intensively affected a region including something in the range of 5 million people, with the city of New Orleans itself having a population somewhat shy of 1 million. Clearly, as this tragedy occurred on U.S. soil, there was no intercontinental or "strategic" dimension to the logistics operation; it was effectively a tactical effort to get relief and help and supplies to specific afflicted areas. That said, some of the assets involved in the operation came from hundreds or thousands of miles away within the United States, so there were significant longer-range transportation challenges involved, even if nothing like what was required to deal with several overseas tragedies.

The terrible earthquake in Haiti in 2010 killed more than 200,000, injured more than 300,000, and left some 2 million homeless and destitute, many in the capital city of Port-au-Prince, with a population of nearly 1 million. Again, by comparison with other tragedies, this was more of a tactical challenge than a long-range one for the United States. There was no shortage of assets to get materials to staging bases in southern Florida, where they could be offloaded and then airlifted or sealifted to their destination. Some 20,000 U.S. military personnel were involved in the effort, perhaps roughly half on land. Among the major efforts were providing temporary shelter to more than 1 million individuals, including the construction of more than 30,000 temporary structures; flying 3.5 million tons of supplies to the country, with peak airlift rates reaching some 150 flights a day; and delivering some 10 million tons of supplies by cargo ship. Medical treatment was provided for nearly

10,000 patients, and a good deal of damaged infrastructure and housing was removed or repaired.[62]

The earthquake near Japan in March 2011, which was followed by the terrible tsunami and resulting Fukushima nuclear reactor disaster, killed some 20,000 and devastated the homes, workplaces, and surrounding lands for hundreds of thousands more. The resulting American response, largely from the U.S. Navy, involved nearly 20,000 personnel and up to 24 naval vessels and 174 aircraft over a period of nearly two months. Thousands were rescued, nearly 50,000 tons of supplies were delivered, and considerable specialized gear for dealing with a radioactive environment to help in restoring airport and seaport facilities and other infrastructure was provided as well.[63]

CONCLUSION: CURSES, BLESSINGS, AND OTHER VULNERABILITIES

Trying to look two to three decades into the future and ascertain where the world's resources and valuable commodities, as well as weaknesses and shortfalls in global supply, could most plausibly lead to conflict or catastrophe is of course very difficult. There are too many possibilities, and some seemingly remote or improbable scenarios could become all too real in the future.

That said, planning must begin somewhere. It is helpful to try to summarize, region by region, the world's blessings and curses as well as its vulnerabilities, with a particular emphasis on parts of the world besides the established and (apparently) rather stable Organization for Economic Cooperation and Development nations.

In Latin America, the greatest resources are found on balance in Brazil, including minerals and metals, water, farmland, and forests. But there is also considerable oil in Mexico and Venezuela, and strategic metals and minerals are distributed among several Andean states. Parts of the region are vulnerable to earthquakes and tsunamis, but in broad perspective, this continent is perhaps somewhat less likely than others to be hit hard by natural tragedy.

Africa is rich in various strategic minerals and metals, particularly in its southern third (roughly from the Democratic Republic of Congo southward). The continent possesses large swaths of the world's most arid land—making for vulnerability to droughts, which could well be intensified by climate change—but also boasts large zones of underdeveloped farmland and forests. Certain parts of its western coast are rich in oil resources as well.

The broader Persian Gulf region is notable both for its abundance of oil and gas and for its general dearth of water, and so of farmland. Central Eurasia, including the Caucasus and former Soviet republics, ranging from Kazakhstan to Kyrgyzstan, is rich in hydrocarbons in places, and in a number of key strategic minerals and metals in other places. Some parts of this region are especially vulnerable to drought, others to earthquakes.

Russia has a similar set of attributes and assets, but on a larger scale. It also has a good deal of farmland and a great deal of forested land, and climate trends may make these regions, many in Siberia, even more appealing and accessible as the century progresses. Ukraine is notable for its farmland, too. Both these nations, of course, also possess nuclear power plants, making them vulnerable to accidents. Their overall vulnerability to natural catastrophe is modest, and indeed, global climate trends could help them.

The Indian subcontinent is famous for its extreme population densities. It is moderately well endowed in minerals and metals and quite well endowed in water—though the latter is somewhat unevenly spread throughout the region and highly dependent on replenishment by monsoons, which can be fickle and may be altered by global climate change. So will the Himalayan glaciers that feed the subcontinent's rivers, providing water not only for India but for Pakistan and other nations as well. Farmland is a mixed bag—reasonably productive in many areas, but dependent on water, and threatened in Bangladesh in particular by a combination of overpopulation, salinization of land, rising sea levels, and depletion of water tables. The region also has its fair share of nuclear power plants and other potentially dangerous industrial facilities and often fragile infrastructure.

Roughly similar conclusions can be drawn about Indonesia and certain other parts of Southeast Asia. On the assets side of the ledger, a good deal of forest is also found in these areas. This general part of the world, beginning with India, and then moving eastward through the Association of Southeast Asian Nations (ASEAN) region and extending to the Philippines, is quite vulnerable to extreme weather events, particularly in the form of monsoons, typhoons, earthquakes, and tsunamis.

The vulnerability to extreme weather and other natural disasters extends upward to coastal China (and of course Japan). Here the confluence of people, factories, nuclear power plants, earthquake fault lines, and extreme weather events makes one of the most economically dynamic parts of the world also one of the most fragile. Water and farmland scarcity, exacerbated by severe population, intensify the problem. Risks of pandemics are also highest, it would appear, in this part of the world (as well as in parts of Africa and South Asia). China is also very well endowed with often scarce strategic minerals and metals. This concentration of resources, while a boon to China, could become a worry for the rest of the world if China chooses to engage again in economic strong-arm tactics and withhold supply.

Finally, an added dimension to the political topography of global resources and global dangers arises when one considers disputed maritime resources. Ownership or control of a given piece of land may turn out to be less important for what that land directly holds than for the adjacent waters that may be claimed, under the Law of the Sea Treaty and international traditions, by whoever has sovereign control of key land masses. This consideration is clearly relevant in the Black Sea, the South China Sea, parts of the Mediterranean, and parts of the Indian Ocean.

The world is an interesting place. With populations growing, dependence on infrastructure and on a somewhat fragile globalized economic system expanding, and the availability of resources limited, it will not become any less interesting in the decades ahead. Superimposing international and internal political-military issues on this map of the world's natural and man-made resources provides a basis for predicting where the world's most important future zones of contestation for control of land and of people may occur in the early decades of the twenty-first century.

Breakdown of the U.S. Army
by Function, 2014

Function	Numbers of soldiers[a]	
	Total	Active
Maneuver	252,791	140,358
Aviation	58,021	30,106
Bands	4,444	1,702
Chemical	12,446	2,370
Engineer	67,093	9,280
Fires	14,640	5,178
Medical	26,989	6,914
Ordnance	7,092	3,759
Quartermaster	24,813	4,879
Signal	19,786	10,862
Adjutant general	4,726	1,321
Finance	3,213	1,260
Chaplain	130	n.a.
Military police	51,370	15,180
Military history	119	5
Legal	2,024	90
Military intelligence	14,632	6,890
Special operations	40,261	22,503
Maneuver support	3,981	240
Space	1,235	608
Maintenance	12,708	1,984
Air defense artillery	14,634	11,368
Public affairs	1,697	230
Battlefield surveillance brigade	3,500	0
Operational headquarters	22,781	13,979
Information operations	1,529	175
Transportation	52,574	10,276
Sustainment headquarters	51,803	17,638
Acquisition, logistics, technology	1,469	1,049
Total	772,501	320,204

Source: Department of the Army, "America's Army: The Strength of the Nation" (November 21, 2014).

a. Soldiers not accounted for above may be in the education or training systems or otherwise unassigned.

U.S. Army and Marine Corps Personnel by Region and Country, 2014

Region	Country	Army	Marine Corps
United States and Territories	Continental United States	406,000	153,140
	Alaska	11,942	7
	Guam	72	15
	Hawaii	22,246	7,677
	Puerto Rico	106	8
	Regional total	440,366	160,847
Europe	Albania	1	0
	Austria	5	0
	Belgium	685	10
	Bosnia and Herzegovina	1	0
	Bulgaria	2	0
	Croatia	3	0
	Cyprus	3	0
	Czech Republic	5	0
	Denmark	2	0
	Estonia	1	0
	Finland	2	0
	France	20	3
	Germany	23,682	962
	Greece	7	0
	Hungary	5	0
	Ireland	2	0
	Italy	3,943	21
	Latvia	0	1
	Lithuania	2	0
	Macedonia	4	0
	Netherlands	143	7
	Norway	29	4
	Poland	23	1
	Portugal	2	6
	Romania	3	0

Region	Country	Army	Marine Corps
Europe (*continued*)	Slovakia	1	0
	Spain	27	24
	Sweden	1	0
	Switzerland	1	0
	Turkey	115	2
	United Kingdom	215	19
	Regional total	28,935	1,060
Former Soviet Union	Armenia	2	0
	Azerbaijan	3	1
	Georgia	12	1
	Kazakhstan	6	0
	Kyrgyzstan	1	0
	Russia	9	1
	Tajikistan	2	0
	Ukraine	5	0
	Uzbekistan	3	0
	Regional total	43	3
East Asia and Pacific	Australia	32	12
	Burma (Myanmar)	3	0
	Cambodia	4	0
	China, Communist	6	2
	Hong Kong	2	0
	Indonesia	10	1
	Japan	2,403	15,870
	Korea[a]	20,000	100
	Laos	2	0
	Malaysia	3	0
	Marshall Islands	17	0
	Mongolia	3	0
	New Zealand	1	1
	Philippines	10	2
	Singapore	9	2
	Taiwan	0	1
	Thailand	38	215
	Vietnam	6	1
	Regional total	22,549	16,207
North Africa, Near East, and South Asia	Algeria	1	0
	Bahrain	22	168
	Bangladesh	5	0
	Egypt	237	1
	India	5	0

a. Numbers are estimates based on reporting.

Region	Country	Army	Marine Corps
North Africa, Near East, and South Asia (*continued*)	Israel	7	2
	Jordan	11	1
	Lebanon	4	0
	Morocco	2	0
	Nepal	3	0
	Oman	3	1
	Pakistan	2	1
	Qatar	365	0
	Saudi Arabia	212	0
	Sri Lanka	2	0
	Syria	1	0
	Tunisia	4	0
	United Arab Emirates	23	196
	Yemen	7	0
	Regional total	916	370
Sub-Saharan Africa	Angola	2	0
	Botswana	4	0
	Burkina	0	1
	Burundi	1	0
	Cameroon	3	0
	Chad	3	0
	Congo, Democratic Republic of the	5	0
	Djibouti	1	0
	Ethiopia	6	0
	Gabon	2	0
	Ghana	5	1
	Guinea	4	0
	Ivory Coast	3	0
	Kenya	16	2
	Liberia	3	0
	Mali	3	0
	Namibia	1	0
	Niger	6	0
	Nigeria	3	0
	Rwanda	2	0
	Senegal	4	1
	Sierra Leone	1	0
	South Africa	3	214
	Sudan	3	0
	Tanzania	3	0
	Uganda	4	0
	Zambia	1	0
	Zimbabwe	4	0
	Regional total	96	219

Region	Country	Army	Marine Corps
Western Hemisphere	Argentina	2	1
	Bahamas, The	1	0
	Barbados	2	0
	Belize	4	0
	Bolivia	5	0
	Brazil	7	2
	Canada	8	1
	Chile	6	0
	Colombia	30	3
	Costa Rica	1	0
	Cuba	173	21
	Dominican Republic	6	2
	Ecuador	3	0
	El Salvador	7	1
	Guatemala	17	0
	Guyana	1	0
	Haiti	5	0
	Honduras	225	0
	Jamaica	1	0
	Mexico	9	0
	Nicaragua	10	0
	Panama	14	0
	Paraguay	5	0
	Peru	14	2
	St. Christopher and Nevis	1	0
	Suriname	2	0
	Uruguay	2	0
	Venezuela	1	0
	Regional total	562	33
Contingencies	Afghanistan	9,405	3,209
	Iraq	990	68
	Kuwait	9,631	154
	Kyrgyz Republic	14	199
	Germany	28	0
	Turkey	0	3
	Other/unknown	8,484	389
	Regional total	28,552	4,022
	Non-U.S. total	81,653	21,914
	Overall total	522,019	182,761

Source: Department of Defense, Defense Manpower Data Center (February 4, 2015) (https://www.dmdc.osd.mil/appj/dwp/dwp_reports.jsp).

Key World Indicators: Competitiveness and Vehicle and Steel Production

Table D-1. Top Twenty Countries on Global Competitiveness Report, 2014–15

Out of a measure of 1 to 7

Switzerland	5.70	Norway	5.35
Singapore	5.65	United Arab Emirates	5.33
United States	5.54	Denmark	5.29
Finland	5.50	Taiwan	5.25
Germany	5.49	Canada	5.24
Japan	5.47	Qatar	5.24
Hong Kong SAR	5.46	New Zealand	5.20
Netherlands	5.45	Belgium	5.18
United Kingdom	5.41	Luxembourg	5.17
Sweden	5.41	Malaysia	5.16

Source: World Economic Forum, *The Global Competitiveness Report 2014–2015*, p. 13 (http://reports.weforum.org/global-competitiveness-report-2014-2015/rankings/).

Table D-2. Top Countries for Vehicle Production, Private and Commercial, 2014

Number of vehicles

China	23,722,890	Russia	1,886,646
United States	11,660,699	Thailand	1,880,007
Japan	9,774,558	France	1,817,000
Germany	5,907,548	United Kingdom	1,598,879
South Korea	4,524,932	Indonesia	1,298,523
India	3,840,160	Czech Republic	1,251,220
Mexico	3,365,306	Turkey	1,170,445
Brazil	3,146,118	Iran	1,090,846
Spain	2,402,978	Slovakia	993,000
Canada	2,393,890	Italy	697,864

Source: International Organization of Motor Vehicle Manufacturers (www.oica.net/category/production-statistics/).

Table D-3. Twenty Biggest Producers of Steel, 2014
Thousands of tons

China	822,700	Italy	23,735
Japan	110,665	Taiwan	23,250
United States	88,347	Mexico	18,977
India	83,208	Iran	16,331
South Korea	71,036	France	16,143
Russia	70,651	Spain	14,163
Germany	42,946	Canada	12,595
Turkey	34,035	United Kingdom	12,065
Brazil	33,912	Poland	8,620
Ukraine	27,170	Austria	7,859

Source: World Steel Association (www.worldsteel.org/statistics/statistics-archive.html).

Notes

CHAPTER 1

1. For good treatments of the capacities of special forces that at the same time do not overstate their realistic roles or falsely imply the obsolescence of major combat units, see Phillip Lohaus, *A Precarious Balance: Preserving the Right Mix of Conventional and Special Operations Forces* (Washington: American Enterprise Institute, 2015); and Brian S. Petit, *Going Big by Getting Small: The Application of Operational Art by Special Operations in Phase Zero* (Denver, Colo.: Outskirts Press, 2013).

2. Department of Defense, *Sustaining U.S. Global Leadership: Priorities for 21st Century Defense* (January 2012), available at http://www.defense.gov/news/Defense_Strategic_Guidance.pdf.

3. Michael E. O'Hanlon, "Sizing U.S. Ground Forces: From '2 Wars' to '1 War Plus 2 Missions,'" *Washington Quarterly* 37, no. 1 (Spring 2014): 151–64, available at https://twq.elliott.gwu.edu/sites/twq.elliott.gwu.edu/files/downloads/O'Hanlon_PDF.pdf.

4. Department of Defense, *Quadrennial Defense Review* (March 2014), p. vii, available at defense.gov/pubs/2014_Quadrennial_Defense_Review.pdf.

5. International Institute for Strategic Studies, *The Military Balance 2014* (Oxfordshire, UK: Routledge, 2014).

6. Secretary of Defense Chuck Hagel, *Quadrennial Defense Review 2014* (Department of Defense, 2014), p. 22, available at defense.gov/pub s/2014_Quadrennial_Defense_Review.pdf.

7. Peter D. Feaver, "Eight Myths about American Grand Strategy," in *Forging an American Grand Strategy: Securing a Path through a Complex Future*, edited by Sheila R. Ronis (Carlisle, Pa.: Strategic Studies Institute, U.S. Army War College, 2013), p. 37.

8. Richard N. Haass, *War of Necessity, War of Choice: A Memoir of Two Iraq Wars* (New York: Simon and Schuster, 2009).

9. Stephen Brumwell, *George Washington: Gentleman Warrior* (New York: Quercus, 2012), p. 421.

10. John Quincy Adams, address to the U.S. House of Representatives, July 4, 1821.

11. Farewell Address of George Washington, 1796, available at http://avalon.law.yale.edu/18th_century/washing.asp.

12. Henry Adams, *The War of 1812* (New York: Cooper Square Press, 1999), p. 3.

13. Paul Kennedy, *The Rise and Fall of the Great Powers* (New York: Random House, 1987), p. 154.

14. Ulysses S. Grant, *The Complete Personal Memoirs of Ulysses S. Grant*, reprint (Boston, Mass.: Seven Treasures Publications, 2010), pp. 32–52.

15. Adam Goodheart, *1861: The Civil War Awakening* (New York: Alfred A. Knopf, 2011), pp. 159–60.

16. Nathaniel Philbrick, *The Last Stand: Custer, Sitting Bull, and the Battle of the Little Bighorn* (New York: Viking, 2010), p. 41.

17. Edward M. Coffman, *The Regulars: The American Army, 1898–1941* (Harvard University Press, 2004), pp. 3–4.

18. Kennedy, *The Rise and Fall of the Great Powers*, pp. 199–203.

19. Russell F. Weigley, *The American Way of War* (Indiana University Press, 1973), pp. 167–91.

20. Coffman, *The Regulars*, pp. 203–35.

21. Colonel Cole Kingseed, "Army Blues to Olive Drab: A Modern Fighting Force Takes the Field," in *The Army*, edited by Brigadier General Harold W. Nelson (Arlington, Va.: Army Historical Foundation, 2001), pp. 212–13.

22. Weigley, *The American Way of War*, pp. 223–41.

23. Michael D. Doubler, *I Am the Guard: A History of the Army National Guard, 1636–2000* (Department of the Army, 2001), pp. 65–75.

24. Graham A. Cosmas, *An Army for Empire: The United States Army in the Spanish-American War* (Texas A&M University Press, 1971), pp. 4–9.

25. Doubler, *I Am the Guard*, pp. 136–45.

26. U.S. Marine Corps, "Timeline" (Washington, 2014), available at http://www.marines.com/history-heritage/timeline; and "U.S. Marine Corps," Encyclopedia.com, 2000, available at http://www.encyclopedia.com/topic/United_States_Marine_Corps.aspx.

27. Barry R. Posen, *Restraint: A New Foundation for U.S. Grand Strategy* (Cornell University Press, 2014), pp. 135–75.

28. See, for example, Michael E. O'Hanlon, *Healing the Wounded Giant: Maintaining Military Preeminence While Cutting the Defense Budget* (Brookings, 2012), p. 11; and Office of Management and Budget, *Budget of the U.S. Government, Fiscal Year 2015: Historical Tables* (Government Printing Office, 2014), p. 156.

29. Aaron L. Friedberg, "Why Didn't the United States Become a Garrison State?," *International Security* 16, no. 4 (Spring 1992): 109–42.

30. For perspective on how much of the force planning behind these numbers was conducted, see Robert P. Haffa Jr., *The Half War: Planning U.S. Rapid Deployment Forces to Meet a Limited Contingency, 1960–1983* (Boulder, Colo.: Westview Press, 1984); Alain C. Enthoven and K. Wayne Smith, *How Much Is Enough? Shaping the Defense Program 1961–1969* (Santa Monica, Calif.: RAND, 1971); and William W. Kaufmann, *Planning Conventional Forces, 1950–1980* (Brookings, 1982).

31. Kingseed, "Army Blues to Olive Drab," in *The Army*, edited by Brigadier General Harold W. Nelson, p. 239.

32. Weigley, *The American Way of War*, p. xxii; and Carl H. Builder, *The Masks of War: American Military Styles in Strategy and Analysis* (Santa Monica, Calif.: RAND, 1989).

33. James M. McPherson, *Battle Cry of Freedom: The Civil War Era* (New York: Ballantine Books, 1988), pp. 306–07.

34. Brumwell, *George Washington: Gentleman Warrior*, pp. 249, 380; Kennedy, *The Rise and Fall of the Great Powers*, p. 99.

35. Robert Kagan, *Dangerous Nation: America's Foreign Policy from Its Earliest Days to the Dawn of the Twentieth Century* (New York: Vintage Books, 2006).

36. See Barton Gellman, *Contending with Kennan: Toward a Philosophy of American Power* (New York: Praeger, 1984), pp. 38, 121.

37. Donald Kagan, *On the Origins of War* (New York: Doubleday/Anchor Books, 1995), pp. 354–417.

38. John Keegan, *The Second World War* (New York: Penguin, 1989), pp. 253–54.

39. For the seminal discussion of both concepts, see Robert Jervis, *Perception and Misperception in International Politics* (Princeton University Press, 1976), pp. 58–83.

40. Raymond L. Garthoff, *A Journey through the Cold War: A Memoir of Containment and Coexistence* (Brookings, 2001), pp. 1–8.

41. See John Lewis Gaddis, *Strategies of Containment: A Critical Appraisal of Postwar American National Security Policy* (Oxford University Press, 1982); and Barry M. Blechman and Stephen S. Kaplan, *Force without War: U.S. Armed Forces as a Political Instrument* (Brookings, 1978).

42. See Micah Zenko, *Between Threats and War: U.S. Discrete Military Operations in the Post–Cold War World* (Stanford University Press, 2010); and Derek

Chollet and James Goldgeier, *America between the Wars: The Misunderstood Years between the Fall of the Berlin Wall and the Start of the War on Terror* (New York: Public Affairs, 2008).

43. See Andrew Krepinevich Jr., "From Cavalry to Computer The Pattern of Military Revolutions," *National Interest* 37 (Fall 1994): 31–33; Max Boot, *War Made New: Technology, Warfare, and the Course of History, 1500 to Today* (New York: Gotham Books, 2006); and Jared Diamond, *Guns, Germs, and Steel: The Fates of Human Societies* (New York: W. W. Norton, 1997).

44. See, for example, Christopher Bowie, Fred Frostic, Kevin Lewis, John Lund, David Ochmanek, and Philip Propper, *The New Calculus: Analyzing Airpower's Changing Role in Joint Theater Operations* (Santa Monica, Calif.: RAND, 1993).

45. Trevor N. Dupuy, *Attrition: Forecasting Battle Casualties and Equipment Losses in Modern War* (Fairfax, Va.: HERO Books, 1990), p. 28.

46. For two very good treatments of this subject, see Krepinevich, "From Cavalry to Computer"; and Boot, *War Made New.*

47. Michael O'Hanlon, *Technological Change and the Future of Warfare* (Brookings, 2000), pp. 11–18.

48. See, for example, National Defense Panel, *Transforming Defense: National Security in the 21st Century. Report of the National Defense Panel, December 1997* (Arlington, Va., 1997), pp. 2, 23, 49, 59, 79–86, available at http://www.dod.gov/pubs/foi/administration_and_Management/other/902.pdf; and David A. Ochmanek, Edward R. Harshberger, David E. Thaler, and Glenn A. Kent, *To Find, and Not to Yield: How Advances in Information and Firepower Can Transform Theater Warfare* (Santa Monica, Calif.: RAND, 1998).

49. For skeptics of these theories in regard to various earlier eras, see Robert A. Pape, *Bombing to Win: Air Power and Coercion in War* (Cornell University Press, 1996); and Tami Davis Biddle, *Rhetoric and Reality in Air Warfare: The Evolution of British and American Ideas about Strategic Bombing, 1914–1945* (Princeton University Press, 2002).

50. Robert H. Scales Jr., "Cycles of War: Speed of Maneuver Will Be the Essential Ingredient of an Information-Age Army," *Armed Forces Journal International* 137 (July 1997): 38; National Defense Panel, *Transforming Defense,* pp. 7–8; Andrew J. Bacevich, *The Pentomic Era: The U.S. Army between Korea and Vietnam* (National Defense University Press, 1986); John Keegan, *A History of Warfare* (New York: Alfred A. Knopf, 1993); O'Hanlon, *Technological Change and the Future of Warfare,* pp. 17–29; Marc V. Schanz, "Space Launch Renaissance," *Air Force Magazine,* June 2014, pp. 20–25; and John R. Galvin, *Fighting the Cold War: A Soldier's Memoir* (University Press of Kentucky, 2015).

51. O'Hanlon, *Technological Change and the Future of Warfare,* p. 65.

52. For a similar view, see David W. Barno and Nora Bensahel, "New Challenges for the U.S. Army," in *American Grand Strategy and the Future of U.S.*

Landpower, edited by Joseph Da Silva, Hugh Liebert, and Isaiah Wilson III (Carlisle, Pa.: Strategic Studies Institute, U.S. Army War College, 2014), p. 235.

53. See, for example, General Stanley McChrystal, *My Share of the Task: A Memoir* (New York: Penguin, 2013), pp. 237–53.

54. See, for example, Daniel Byman, *A High Price: The Triumphs and Failures of Israeli Counterterrorism* (Oxford University Press, 2011), pp. 190–205, 251–65.

55. Posen, *Restraint,* pp. 135–75.

56. Stephen Biddle, *Military Power: Explaining Victory and Defeat in Modern Battle* (Princeton University Press, 2004).

57. See, for example, Chollet and Goldgeier, *America between the Wars,* pp. 7–8.

58. See, for example, Stephen John Stedman, Donald Rothchild, and Elizabeth M. Cousens, *Ending Civil Wars: The Implementation of Peace Agreements* (Boulder, Colo.: Lynne Rienner, 2002); and Adekeye Adebajo, *U.N. Peacekeeping in Africa: From the Suez Crisis to the Sudan Conflicts* (Boulder, Colo.: Lynne Rienner, 2011).

59. Gareth Evans, *The Responsibility to Protect: Ending Mass Atrocity Crimes Once and for All* (Brookings, 2008), pp. 3–12, 99.

60. Kennedy made the comment in his third presidential debate against Richard Nixon. See Carnegie Endowment for International Peace, "JFK on Nuclear Weapons and Nuclear Proliferation" (Washington, November 2003), available at http://carnegieendowment.org/2003/11/17/jfk-on-nuclear-weapons-and-non-proliferation.

61. Don Oberdorfer, *The Two Koreas: A Contemporary History* (Reading, Mass.: Addison-Wesley, 1997), pp. 306–29.

62. Robert Einhorn, "Deterring an Iranian Nuclear Breakout," *International Herald Tribune,* February 27, 2015, available at http://www.nytimes.com/2015/02/27/opinion/deterring-an-iranian-nuclear-breakout.html.

63. George Tenet, *At the Center of the Storm: My Years at the CIA* (New York: HarperCollins, 2007), pp. 268–69.

64. On the general trends, see Steven Pinker, *The Better Angels of Our Nature: Why Violence Has Declined* (New York: Penguin Books, 2011), pp. 189–294.

65. On some of these possibilities, see Robert Jervis, *Perception and Misperception in International Politics* (Princeton University Press, 1976).

66. Lotta Themnar and Peter Wallensteen, "Armed Conflict, 1946–2013," *Journal of Peace Research* 51, no. 4 (2014), available at pcr.uu.se/research/ucdp/charts_and_graphs; and Pinker, *The Better Angels of Our Nature,* pp. 303–04.

67. See "The Long and Short of the Problem," *The Economist,* November 9, 2013, available at http://www.economist.com/news/briefing/21589431-bringing-end-conflicts-within-states-vexatious-history-provides-guide.

68. Roland Paris, *At War's End: Building Peace after Civil Conflict* (Cambridge University Press, 2004); and Stephen John Stedman, Donald Rothchild,

and Elizabeth M. Cousens, eds., *Ending Civil Wars: The Implementation of Peace Agreements* (Boulder, Colo.: Lynne Rienner, 2002).

69. Center on International Cooperation, *Annual Review of Global Peace Operations 2013* (New York: Lynne Rienner, 2013), p. 9.

70. See United Nations High Commissioner for Refugees, "Global Trends 2013: War's Human Cost" (New York, 2014), available at http://reliefweb.int/report/world/unhcr-global-trends-2013-wars-human-cost.

71. RAND National Defense Research Institute Project, "Total Number of Terrorist Incidents" and "RAND Database of Worldwide Terrorism Incidents" (Santa Monica, Calif.: RAND, 2012), available at http://smapp.rand.org/rwtid/search.php.

72. Philip Bobbitt, *The Shield of Achilles: War, Peace, and the Course of History* (New York: Penguin, 2002), p. 806.

73. David Kilcullen, *Out of the Mountains: The Coming Age of the Urban Guerrilla* (Oxford University Press, 2013); see also, on a related subject, Thomas P. M. Barnett, *The Pentagon's New Map: War and Peace in the Twenty-First Century* (New York: G. P. Putnam's Sons, 2004).

74. Stephanie Condon, "Al Qaeda Is 'Morphing,' Not on the Run, Intel Chiefs Say," *CBS News,* February 11, 2014, available at http://www.cbsnews.com/news/al-qaeda-is-morphing-not-on-the-run-intel-chiefs-say.

75. See Response of Director of National Intelligence James Clapper to Question by Senator Dianne Feinstein, in "Transcript: Senate Intelligence Hearing on National Security Threats," *Washington Post,* January 29, 2014, available at http://www.washingtonpost.com/world/national-security/transcript-senate-intelligence-hearing-on-national-security-threats/2014/01/29/b5913184-8912-11e3-833c-33098f9e5267_story.html.

76. See, for example, Herve Ladsous, Under Secretary General of the United Nations for Peacekeeping Operations, "New Challenges and Priorities for U.N. Peacekeeping," speech delivered at the Brookings Institution, Washington, June 17, 2014; Seth G. Jones, *A Persistent Threat: The Evolution of al Qaeda and Other Salafi Jihadists* (Santa Monica, Calif.: RAND, 2014), pp. x, 64–65; Katherine Zimmerman, Critical Threats Project, American Enterprise Institute, "Al Qaeda Renewed," *National Review,* December 26, 2013; and International Institute for Strategic Studies, *The Military Balance 2014* (London: Routledge, 2014), pp. 476–85.

77. L. E. Cederman, "Back to Kant: Reinterpreting the Democratic Peace as a Macrohistorical Learning Process," *American Political Science Review* 95, no. 1 (March 2001): 15–31, cited in Pinker, *The Better Angels of Our Nature,* p. 294; and Michael W. Doyle, "Kant, Liberal Legacies, and Foreign Affairs," *Philosophy and Public Affairs* 12, no. 3 (Summer 1983): 213–15.

78. See, for example, John M. Owen IV, *Liberal Peace, Liberal War: American Politics and International Security* (Cornell University Press, 1997); Shadi Hamid, *Temptations of Power: Islamists and Illiberal Democracy in a New*

Middle East (Oxford University Press, 2014); Stephen R. Grand, *Understanding Tahrir Square: What Transitions Elsewhere Can Teach Us about the Prospects for Arab Democracy* (Brookings, 2014), p. 15; Freedom House, "The Democratic Leadership Gap" (Washington, 2014), available at http://freedomhouse.org/sites/default/files/Overview%20Fact%20Sheet.pdf; and John J. Mearsheimer, *The Tragedy of Great Power Relations* (New York: W. W. Norton, 2001).

79. See, for example, Lawrence Freedman, *The Evolution of Nuclear Strategy* (New York: St. Martin's Press, 1981); Thomas C. Schelling, *The Strategy of Conflict* (Harvard University Press, 1960); Thomas C. Schelling, *Arms and Influence* (Yale University Press, 1966); Barry R. Posen, *Inadvertent Escalation: Conventional War and Nuclear Risks* (Cornell University Press, 1991); Bruce G. Blair, *Strategic Command and Control: Redefining the Nuclear Threat* (Brookings, 1985); Michael Dobbs, *One Minute to Midnight: Kennedy, Khrushchev, and Castro on the Brink of Nuclear War* (New York: Alfred A. Knopf, 2008); McGeorge Bundy, *Danger and Survival: Choices about the Bomb in the First Fifty Years* (New York: Vintage Books, 1988); Robert Jervis, *The Illogic of American Nuclear Strategy* (Cornell University Press, 1984); Frederick Kempe, *Berlin 1961: Kennedy, Khrushchev, and the Most Dangerous Place on Earth* (New York: G. P. Putnam's Sons, 2011); and Richard K. Betts, *Nuclear Blackmail and Nuclear Balance* (Brookings, 1987).

80. See, for example, Francois Heisbourg, "Nuclear Proliferation—Looking Back, Thinking Ahead: How Bad Would the Further Spread of Nuclear Weapons Be?," in *Moving Beyond Pretense: Nuclear Power and Nonproliferation*, edited by Henry Sokolski (Carlisle, Pa.: Strategic Studies Institute, U.S. Army War College, 2014), pp. 17–43.

81. See, for example, Geoffrey Blainey, *The Causes of War* (New York: Free Press, 1973), pp. 247–49; and John Keegan, *The First World War* (New York: Alfred A. Knopf, 1999).

82. Jeff D. Colgan, "Fueling the Fire: Pathways from Oil to War," *International Security* 38, no. 2 (Fall 2013): 147–80.

83. See, for example, Stephen Biddle, *Military Power: Explaining Victory and Defeat in Modern Battle* (Princeton University Press, 2004); P. W. Singer, *Wired for War: The Robotics Revolution and Conflict in the 21st Century* (New York: Penguin Press, 2009); and O'Hanlon, *Technological Change and the Future of Warfare*. On this general subject, see also Martin van Creveld, *Technology and War: From 2000 B.C. to the Present*, rev. ed. (New York: Free Press, 1991); George Friedman and Meredith Friedman, *The Future of War: Power, Technology and American World Dominance in the Twenty-First Century* (New York: Crown, 1996); and Boot, *War Made New*.

84. John Mueller, *Atomic Obsession: Nuclear Alarmism from Hiroshima to Al-Qaeda* (Oxford University Press, 2010), pp. 29–42.

85. On these issues, see, for example John D. Steinbruner, *Principles of Global Security* (Brookings, 2000); Bruce Jones, Carlos Pascual, and Stephen

John Stedman, *Power and Responsibility: Building International Order in an Era of Transnational Threats* (Brookings, 2009); Anthony Lake, *Six Nightmares: Real Threats in a Dangerous World and How America Can Meet Them* (Boston: Little, Brown, 2000); Graham Allison, *Nuclear Terrorism: The Ultimate Preventable Catastrophe* (New York: Henry Holt, 2004); and Matthew Bunn, Martin B. Malin, Nickolas Roth, and William H. Tobey, *Advancing Nuclear Security: Evaluating Progress and Setting New Goals* (Harvard University Press, 2014).

86. For example, Richard Betts of Columbia (and a number of others) argued strongly against NATO expansion in the 1990s on the ground that it could isolate, embitter, and provoke Russia—though few if any of those scholars have gone so far as to assert that the U.S./NATO decisions of that era provided a legitimate rationale for Vladimir Putin to act as he did in Georgia in 2008 and in Ukraine in 2014. See Richard K. Betts, *American Force: Dangers, Delusions, and Dilemmas in National Security* (Columbia University Press, 2012), pp. 189–98. More recently, Barry Posen has argued that U.S. alliance commitments, generally viewed as stabilizing because they help reassure many countries that might otherwise build up large militaries or acquire nuclear weapons to ensure their security, may embolden some of these countries to behave more assertively and thus more dangerously than they otherwise would. But his main concern is that the United States pays excessive costs because of primacy, not that the world has become fundamentally more dangerous as a result of U.S. actions. See Posen, *Restraint*. See also Campbell Craig, Benjamin H. Friedman, Brendan Rittenhouse Green, and Justin Logan, as well as Stephen G. Brooks, G. John Ikenberry, and William C. Wohlforth, "Correspondence—Debating American Engagement: The Future of U.S. Grand Strategy," *International Security* 38, no. 2 (Fall 2013): 181–99.

87. Michael Mastanduno, "Preserving the Unipolar Moment: Realist Theories and U.S. Grand Strategy after the Cold War," *International Security* 21, no. 4 (Spring 1997): 49–88.

88. On these trends, see Fareed Zakaria, *The Post-American World* (New York: W. W. Norton, 2008); Charles A. Kupchan, *No One's World: The West, the Rising Rest, and the Coming Global Turn* (Oxford University Press, 2012); and Ian Bremmer, *The End of the Free Market: Who Wins the War between States and Corporations?* (New York: Portfolio, 2010).

89. Woosang Kim and James D. Morrow, "When Do Power Shifts Lead to War?," *American Journal of Political Science* 36, no. 4 (November 1992): 896–922.

90. See Bruce Jones, *Still Ours to Lead: America, Rising Powers, and the Tension between Rivalry and Restraint* (Brookings, 2014); Robert Kagan, *The World America Made* (New York: Alfred A. Knopf, 2012); Michael O'Hanlon, *The Wounded Giant: America's Armed Forces in an Age of Austerity* (New York: Penguin, 2011); G. John Ikenberry, *After Victory: Institutions, Strategic Restraint, and the Rebuilding of Order after Major War* (Princeton University Press, 2001); and G. John Ikenberry, *Liberal Leviathan: The Origins, Crisis, and Transformation of the American World Order* (Princeton University Press, 2011).

91. Joseph S. Nye Jr., *The Paradox of American Power: Why the World's Only Superpower Can't Go It Alone* (Oxford University Press, 2002).

92. Stephen M. Walt, *The Origins of Alliance* (Cornell University Press, 1990); Kennedy, *The Rise and Fall of the Great Powers*; Robert Gilpin, *War and Change in World Politics* (Cambridge University Press, 1981); Kenneth N. Waltz, *Theory of International Politics* (New York: Random House, 1979); and O'Hanlon, *The Wounded Giant*, pp. 130–31.

CHAPTER 2

1. Sam Jones, "'Masterly' Russian Operations in Ukraine Leave NATO One Step Behind," *Financial Times*, June 8, 2014; Andrew Higgins, Michael R. Gordon, and Andrew E. Kramer, "Photos Link Masked Men in East Ukraine to Russia," *New York Times*, April 20, 2014, available at http://www.nytimes.com/2014/04/21/world/europe/photos-link-masked-men-in-east-ukraine-to-russia.html.

2. On Chechnya, see, for example, Carlotta Gall and Thomas de Waal, *Chechnya: Calamity in the Caucasus* (New York University Press, 1998).

3. On this fear, then and now, see Ariel Cohen, *Russia's Counterinsurgency in North Caucasus: Performance and Consequences* (Carlisle, Pa.: Strategic Studies Institute, U.S. Army War College, 2014); and Richard J. Krickus, *Russia after Putin* (Carlisle, Pa.: Strategic Studies Institute, U.S. Army War College, 2014).

4. Angela E. Stent, *The Limits of Partnership: U.S.-Russian Relations in the Twenty-First Century* (Princeton University Press, 2014), pp. 272–73.

5. See, for example, James Sherr, *Hard Diplomacy and Soft Coercion: Russia's Influence Abroad* (London: Royal Institute of International Affairs, 2013), pp. 54–64; and Alexander Lukin, "What the Kremlin Is Thinking," *Foreign Affairs* 93, no. 4 (July/August 2014): 85–93.

6. For a similar argument about the importance of the passage of time in Russia, though one written before the crises of 2014, see Jeffrey Mankoff, "Russia, the Post-Soviet Space, and Challenges to U.S. Policy," in *The Policy World Meets Academia: Designing U.S. Policy toward Russia*, edited by Timothy Colton, Timothy Frye, and Robert Legvold (Cambridge, Mass.: American Academy of Arts and Sciences, 2010), p. 49.

7. Gudrun Persson, "Security Policy and Military Strategic Thinking," in *Russian Military Capability in a Ten-Year Perspective—2013*, edited by Jakob Hedenskog and Carolina Vendil Pallin (Stockholm: FOI, 2013), p. 72.

8. See Sherr, *Hard Diplomacy and Soft Coercion*, p. 57.

9. Dmitry Adamsky, "Defense Innovation in Russia: The Current State and Prospects for Revival," IGCC Defense Innovation Brief (Berkeley: University of California Institute on Global Conflict and Cooperation, January 2014).

10. Robert Legvold, "Russian Foreign Policy During Periods of Great State Transformation," in *Russian Foreign Policy in the Twenty-First Century and the*

Shadow of the Past, edited by Robert Levgold (Columbia University Press, 2007), pp. 109–21.

11. For one view that Putin himself subscribes largely to this worldview, see Timothy Garten Ash, "Putin's Deadly Doctrine," *New York Times,* July 18, 2014, available at http://www.nytimes.com/2014/07/20/opinion/sunday/protecting-russians-in-ukraine-has-deadly-consequences.html. See also Clifford G. Gaddy and Fiona Hill, *Mr. Putin: Operative in the Kremlin* (Brookings, 2013), pp. 54–71.

12. John E. Herbst, William B. Taylor, and Steven Pifer, "When Sanctions Aren't Enough," Foreignpolicy.com, March 31, 2014.

13. Stephen J. Blank, "Enter Asia: The Arctic Heats Up," *World Affairs,* March/April 2014, p. 23.

14. Stephen J. Blank, "Introduction," in *Politics and Economics in Putin's Russia,* edited by Stephen J. Blank (Carlisle, Pa.: Strategic Studies Institute, U.S. Army War College, 2013), pp. 1–34; and James R. Clapper, Director of National Intelligence, "Statement for the Record: Worldwide Threat Assessment of the U.S. Intelligence Community" (Senate Select Committee on Intelligence, January 29, 2014), p. 23, available at www.intelligence.senate.gov/140129/clapper.pdf.

15. On the Arctic, see Christian Le Miere and Jeffrey Mazo, *Arctic Opening: Insecurity and Opportunity* (London: International Institute for Strategic Studies, 2013); and Department of Defense, *Arctic Strategy* (2013), available at www.defense.gov/pubs/2013_Arctic_Strategy.pdf.

16. See, for example, International Crisis Group, "The Philippines: Dismantling Rebel Groups" (Brussels, June 2013), available at http://www.crisisgroup.org/en/regions/asia/south-east-asia/philippines/248-the-philippines-dismantling-rebel-groups.aspx; Elizabeth Pisani, "Indonesia in Pieces: The Downside of Decentralization," *Foreign Affairs* 93, no. 4 (July/August 2014): 142–52; and International Crisis Group, "How Indonesian Extremists Regroup" (Brussels, July 2012), available at http://www.crisisgroup.org/en/regions/asia/south-east-asia/indonesia/228-how-indonesian-extremists-regroup.aspx.

17. For a good depiction of how Communist threats influenced U.S. policy toward the Philippines during the cold war, see Stephen J. Solarz, *Journeys to War and Peace: A Congressional Memoir* (Brandeis University Press, 2011), pp. 112–29.

18. Central Intelligence Agency, *CIA World Factbook* (2014), available at https://www.cia.gov/library/publications/the-world-factbook/geos/id.html and https://www.cia.gov/library/publications/the-world-factbook/geos/rp.html.

19. See John K. Fairbank, "Introduction," in *Chinese Ways in Warfare,* edited by Frank A. Kierman Jr. and John K. Fairbank (Harvard University Press, 1974), pp. 25–26; and Huiyun Feng, *Chinese Strategic Culture and Foreign Policy Decisionmaking* (London: Routledge, 2007), pp. 26–27.

20. Geoff Wade, "The Zheng He Voyages: A Reassessment," *Journal of the Malaysian Branch of the Royal Asiatic Society* 77, pt. 1 (2005): 27–58, cited in

Yuan-kang Wang, *Harmony and War: Confucian Culture and Chinese Power Politics* (Columbia University Press, 2010), p. 256. Wang disputes the "peaceful" character of Zheng He's voyages (*Harmony and War*, pp. 157–64).

21. Cited in Wang, *Harmony and War*, p. 2. See also the remarks of Prime Minister Wen Jiabao, "China tomorrow will continue to be a major country that loves peace and has a great deal to look forward. Peace loving has been a time-honored quality of the Chinese nation." Wen Jiabao, "Turning Your Eyes to China," *Harvard Gazette*, December 10, 2003, available at http://www.news.harvard.edu/gazette/2003/12.11/10-wenspeech.html.

22. See Information Office of the State Council, "Defense White Paper 2013: The Diversified Employment of China's Armed Forces" (Beijing, April 2013), available at http://news.xinhuanet.com/english/china/2013-04/16/c_132312681_2.htm.

23. Dai Bingguo, "Adhere to the Path of 'Peaceful Development,'" Xinhua News Agency, December 6, 2010, available at http://china.usc.edu/ShowArticle.aspx?articleID=2325.

24. It is noteworthy that one of the earlier contemporary references to the "China Dream" came in a speech by the most prominent exponent of the "peaceful rise" approach. See Zheng Bijan, "China's Rise Is a Peaceful Rise," in Zheng Bijan, *China's Road to Peaceful Rise: Observations on Its Cause, Basis, Connotation, and Prospect* (New York: Routledge, 2011), pp. 264–68.

25. Donald Gross, *The China Fallacy: How the U.S. Can Benefit from China's Rise and Avoid Another Cold War* (New York: Bloomsbury, 2013).

26. A number of these more hawkish voices are active duty flag officers, including, among others, General Zhang Zhaozhong, Rear Admiral Yang Yi, Major General Han Xudong, and Major General Luo Yuan. See Willy Lam, "China's Hawks in Command," *Wall Street Journal*, July 1, 2012, available at http://online.wsj.com/article/SB10001424052702304211804577500521756902802.html. See also David Lai, "The Coming of Chinese Hawks" (Carlisle, Pa.: Strategic Studies Institute, U.S. Army War College, October 2010), available at http://www.strategicstudiesinstitute.army.mil/Pubs/display.cfm?pubid=1028; Aaron L. Friedberg, *A Contest for Supremacy: China, America, and the Struggle for Mastery in Asia* (New York: W. W. Norton, 2012), pp. 1–10; and Avery Goldstein, *Rising to the Challenge: China's Grand Strategy and International Security* (Stanford University Press, 2005), p. 38.

27. See the Chinese sources discussed in Alastair Iain Johnston, "How New and Assertive Is China's New Assertiveness?," *International Security* 37, no. 4 (Spring 2013): 7–48, at 43–45, available at http://belfercenter.ksg.harvard.edu/publication/22951/how_new_and_assertive_is_chinas_new_assertiveness.html.

28. See Wen Jiabao's speech to the United Nations, September 2010, cited in Johnston, "How New and Assertive Is China's New Assertiveness?," p. 19.

29. For a discussion of the ambiguity of the territorial scope of China's core national interest, see Chris Buckley, "China Affirms Policy on Islands," *New York Times*, January 29, 2013; for a history of the Chinese usage of "core

national interests," see Michael D. Swaine, "China's Assertive Behavior: Part One—On 'Core Interests,'" *China Leadership Monitor* 34 (Washington: Hoover Institute, February 2011), available at http://www.hoover.org/publications/ china-leadership-monitor/article/67966.

30. Swaine indicates that as a matter of official policy, the scope of "core interests" as applied to territory has been limited. A close examination of the historical record, along with personal conversations with knowledgeable senior U.S. officials, confirms that at least through the time of Swaine's writing, the Chinese government has officially, and repeatedly, identified only three closely related issues as specific core interests: the defense of China's sovereignty claims regarding Taiwan, Tibet, and Xinjiang. See Swaine, "China's Assertive Behavior." See also Dingding Chen and Jianwei Wang, "Lying Low No More? China's New Thinking on the Tao Guang Yang Hui Strategy," *China: An International Journal* 9, no. 2 (September 2011), available at http://muse.jhu.edu/ login?auth=0&type=summary&url=/journals/china/v009/9.2.chen.html; Andrew Scobell, *China and Strategic Culture* (Carlisle, Pa.: Strategic Studies Institute, U.S. Army War College, 2002), p. 11; Kenneth D. Johnson, *China's Strategic Culture: A Perspective for the United States* (Carlisle, Pa.: Strategic Studies Institute, U.S. Army War College, 2009), p. 10; and Thomas J. Christensen, "Chinese Realpolitik," *Foreign Affairs* 75, no. 5 (September/October 1996), available at http://www.foreignaffairs.com/articles/52434/thomas-j-christensen/ chinese-realpolitik-reading-beijings-world-view.

31. George J. Gilboy and Eric Heginbotham, *Chinese and Indian Strategic Behavior: Growing Power and Alarm* (Cambridge University Press, 2012), p. 78.

32. See Li Jinming and Li Dexia, "The Dotted Line on the Chinese Map of the South China Sea: A Note" (Xiamen, China: School of Southeast Asian Studies, Xiamen University), reprinted in *Ocean Development and International Law* 34, nos. 3–4 (2003): 287–95, available at http://cat.middlebury.edu/~scs/docs/Li%20 and%20Li-The%20Dotted%20Line%20on%20the%20Map.pdf.

33. For the Chinese argument, see, for example, Han-yi Shaw, "The Inconvenient Truth behind the Diaoyu/Senkaku Islands," *New York Times*, September 19, 2012, available at http://kristof.blogs.nytimes.com/2012/09/19/the-inconvenient-truth-behind-the-diaoyusenkaku islands/.

34. Keith Bradsher, "Okinawa Piques Chinese Papers," *New York Times*, May 8, 2013, available at www.nytimes.com/2013/05/09/world/asia/okinawa-piques-chinese-papers. See also statements by deputy chief of the PLA General Staff, Lt. Gen. Qi Jianguo, at Shangri-La Forum in June 2013, "Shangri-La Dialogue: China Not Disputing Japan Sovereignty Over Okinawa," *Straits Times*, June 2, 2013, available at http://www.straitstimes.com/breaking-news/asia/story/ shangri-la-dialogue-china-not-disputing-japan-sovereignty-over-okinawa-2013.

35. Harry Harding, *China's Second Revolution: Reform after Mao* (Brookings, 1987), p. 260.

36. Ray Kamphausen and Andrew Scobell, eds., *Right Sizing the People's Liberation Army: Exploring the Contours of China's Military* (Carlisle, Pa.: Strategic Studies Institute, U.S. Army War College, 2007), p. 31.

37. Evan S. Medeiros, *China's International Behavior: Activism, Opportunism, and Diversification* (Santa Monica, Calif.: RAND, 2009), p. 109; National Institute for Defense Studies, *East Asian Strategic Review 2014* (Tokyo: Japan Times, 2014), pp. 231–32; and Jonathan Holslag, *Trapped Giant: China's Military Rise* (London: International Institute for Strategic Studies, 2010), pp. 92–93.

38. Robert D. Kaplan, *Asia's Cauldron: The South China Sea and the End of a Stable Pacific* (New York: Random House, 2014), pp. 56–57.

39. Larry M. Wortzel, *The Dragon Extends Its Reach: Chinese Military Power Goes Global* (Washington: Potomac Books, 2013), p. 97.

40. Shen Dingli, "The Changing Security Environment in Northeast Asia and the Dynamic Role of Regional Relationships," *Aspen Institute Congressional Program—America's Rebalance toward Asia: Trade, Security and Resource Interests in the Pacific* 29, no. 2 (April 2014): 87

41. On the regional implications of the Democratic People's Republic of Korea bomb program, see Jonathan D. Pollack, *No Exit: North Korea, Nuclear Weapons and International Security* (London: International Institute for Strategic Studies, 2011); Nuclear Threat Initiative, "Country Profiles: North Korea" (Washington, 2014), available at http://www.nti.org/country-profiles/north-korea; Yoichi Funabashi, *The Peninsula Question: A Chronicle of the Second Korean Nuclear Crisis* (Brookings, 2007), p. 475; and Michael J. Green, *Japan's Reluctant Realism: Foreign Policy Challenges in an Era of Uncertain Power* (New York: Palgrave, 2001), pp. 111–44.

42. Victor D. Cha, "Weak but Still Threatening," in *Nuclear North Korea: A Debate on Engagement Strategies,* edited by Victor D. Cha and David C. Kang (Columbia University Press, 2003), p. 40.

43. Chico Harlan, "China May Block Korean Unification, Says U.S. Report," *The Guardian,* January 22, 2013, available at www.theguardian.com/world/2013/jan/22/china-block-korean-unification-us; and David Scofield, "China Puts Korean Spat on the Map," *Asia Times Online,* August 19, 2004, available at atimes.com/atimes/Korea/FH19Dg01.html.

44. Tanvi Madan, "Premier Li Keqiang of China Goes to India," *Up Front* (blog), Brookings Institution, May 18, 2013, available at http://www.brookings.edu/blogs/up-front/posts/2013/05/18-li-keqiang-china-india-madan.

45. Gilboy and Heginbotham, *Chinese and Indian Strategic Behavior,* pp. 56–57.

46. Henry Kissinger, *On China* (New York: Penguin Press, 2011), pp. 184–92.

47. Holslag, *Trapped Giant,* pp. 86–87.

48. Office of the Secretary of Defense, *Annual Report to Congress: Military and Security Developments Involving the People's Republic of China, 2014*

(Department of Defense, 2014), p. 21, available at http://www.defense.gov/pubs/2014_DoD_China_Report.pdf.

49. David M. Malone, *Does the Elephant Dance? Contemporary Indian Foreign Policy* (Oxford University Press, 2011), pp. 146–48.

50. In his last speech as Communist Party secretary on November 8, 2012, Hu Jintao stated, "We should enhance our capacity for exploiting marine resources, resolutely safeguard China's maritime rights and interests, and build China into a maritime power," "Excerpts of Hu Jintao's Speech to China Party Congress," Reuters, November 8, 2012, available at http://www.reuters.com/article/2012/11/08/china-congress-hu-idUSL5E8M77P620121108.

51. See Nan Li, "Evolution of Strategy from 'Near Coasts' to 'Far Seas,'" in *The Chinese Navy: Expanding Capabilities, Evolving Roles*, edited by Phillip Saunders (National Defense University Press, 2011), p. 129.

52. Stephen P. Cohen and Sunil Dasgupta, *Arming without Aiming: India's Military Modernization* (Brookings, 2010).

53. See, for example, Jaswant Singh, *Jinnah: India-Partition, Independence* (New Delhi: Rupa, 2009).

54. Arvin Bahl, *From Jinnah to Jihad: Pakistan's Kashmir Quest and the Limits of Realism* (New Delhi: Atlantic, 2007), quotation from jacket cover.

55. Daniel Byman, *Deadly Connections: States That Sponsor Terrorism* (Cambridge University Press, 2005), pp. 155–85.

56. Henry A. Crumpton, *The Art of Intelligence: Lessons from a Life in the CIA's Clandestine Service* (New York: Penguin Press, 2012), p. 280.

57. See, for example, C. Christine Fair, *The Madrassah Challenge: Militancy and Religious Education in Pakistan* (Washington: U.S. Institute of Peace, 2008).

58. Stephen P. Cohen, *The Idea of Pakistan* (Brookings, 2004), pp. 236, 248.

59. United Nations Development Program, *Human Development Report 2013—The Rise of the South: Human Progress in a Diverse World* (New York, 2013), available at http://hdr.undp.org/sites/default/files/Country-Profiles/PAK.pdf.

60. Pervaiz Iqbal Cheema, "The Kashmir Dispute: Key to South Asian Peace," *IPRI Journal* 14, no. 1 (Winter 2014): 18–20; and Stephen P. Cohen, *Shooting for a Century: The India-Pakistan Conundrum* (Brookings, 2013), pp. 160–63.

61. Bruce Riedel, *Deadly Embrace: Pakistan, America, and the Future of the Global Jihad* (Brookings, 2011), pp. 130–31.

62. Ibid., p. 116.

63. Cohen and Dasgupta, *Arming without Aiming*, pp. 53–70.

64. Fitzpatrick, *Overcoming Pakistan's Nuclear Dangers* (Oxfordshire, UK: Routledge, 2014), pp. 80–82.

65. Adil Sultan, "South Asian Stability-Instability Paradox: Another Perspective," *IPRI Journal* 14, no. 1 (Winter 2014): 34–37; and Fitzpatrick, *Overcoming Pakistan's Nuclear Dangers*, pp. 80–84.

66. See, for example, Herman Kahn, *On Thermonuclear War* (Princeton University Press, 1961); and Barry R. Posen, *Inadvertent Escalation: Conventional War and Nuclear Risks* (Cornell University Press, 1991).

67. Ira Helfand, "Nuclear Famine: Two Billion People at Risk? Global Impacts of Limited Nuclear War on Agriculture, Food Supplies and Human Nutrition" (Washington: International Physicians for the Prevention of Nuclear War, Physicians for Social Responsibility, November 2013), available at www.psr.org/assets/pdfs/two-billion-at-risk.pdf.

68. J. J. Messner, Nate Haken, Krista Hendry, Patricia Taft, Kendall Lawrence, Laura Brisard, and Felipe Umaña, *Fragile States Index 2014* (Washington: Fund for Peace, 2014), available at http://ffp.statesindex.org.

69. Bruce Riedel, *Avoiding Armageddon: America, India, and Pakistan to the Brink and Back* (Brookings, 2013), pp. 184–88.

70. Raj Mehta, "Re-Plumbing China: Leading to the World's First Water War?," *CLAWS Journal* (Summer 2010): 123.

71. Cohen and Dasgupta, *Arming without Aiming*, pp. 123–42.

72. Vijay Sakhuja, "China-Bangladesh Relations and Potential for Regional Tensions," *China Brief* 9, no. 15 (July 23, 2009), available at http://www.jamestown.org/single/?tx_ttnews%5Btt_news%5D=35310&tx_ttnews%5BbackPid%5D=7.

73. International Crisis Group, "The Threat from Jamaat ul-Mujahideen Bangladesh," March 2010, available at http://www.crisisgroup.org/en/regions/asia/south-asia/bangladesh/187-the-threat-from-jamaat-ul-mujahideen-bangladesh.aspx.

74. Gurmeet Kanwal and N. Manoharan, "Conclusion: Beginning of an End," in *India's War on Terror*, edited by Gurmeet Kanwal and N. Manoharan (New Delhi: Center for Land Warfare Studies, 2010), p. 265.

75. Stephen Philip Cohen, *India: Emerging Power* (Brookings, 2001), pp. 232–41.

76. See Pranab Kumar Panday and Ishtiaq Jamil, "Conflict in the Chittagong Hill Tracts of Bangladesh: An Unimplemented Accord and Continued Violence," *Asian Survey* 49, no. 6 (November/December 2009): 1070; and Asian Indigenous Peoples Pact, "A Brief Account of Human Rights Situation of the Indigenous Peoples in Bangladesh" (Chiang Mai, Thailand, August 2007), available at http://www.medipeace.org/eng/sites/default/files/Bangladesh%20-%20indigenious%20people.pdf.

77. Sumit Ganguly, "The Rise of Islamist Militancy in Bangladesh" (Washington: U.S. Institute of Peace, August 2006), p. 9, available at http://www.usip.org/publications/the-rise-of-islamist-militancy-in-bangladesh.

78. See Bruce Riedel, *The Search for al Qaeda: Its Leadership, Ideology, and Future* (Brookings, 2008); Robin Wright, *Sacred Rage: The Wrath of Militant Islam* (New York: Simon and Schuster, 1985); Daniel Benjamin and Steven Simon, *The Age of Sacred Terror* (New York: Random House, 2002); Jessica

Stern, *Terror in the Name of God: Why Religious Militants Kill* (New York: HarperCollins, 2003); Steve Coll, *Ghost Wars: The Secret History of the CIA, Afghanistan, and Bin Laden, from the Soviet Invasion to September 10, 2001* (New York: Penguin Books, 2004); and Lawrence Wright, *The Looming Tower: Al-Qaeda and the Road to 9/11* (New York: Vintage Books, 2006).

79. See, for example, Vali Nasr, *The Shia Revival: How Conflicts within Islam Will Shape the Future* (New York: W. W. Norton, 2007).

80. Yahya Sadowski, *The Myth of Global Chaos* (Brookings, 1998).

81. See, for example, Don Eberly, *Liberate and Leave: Fatal Flaws in the Early Strategy for Postwar Iraq* (Minneapolis, Minn.: Zenith Press, 2009); Larry Diamond, *Squandered Victory: The American Occupation and the Bungled Effort to Bring Democracy to Iraq* (New York: Times Books, 2005); George Packer, *The Assassins' Gate: America in Iraq* (New York: Farrar, Straus and Giroux, 2005); and Kurt M. Campbell and Michael E. O'Hanlon, *Hard Power: The New Politics of National Security* (New York: Basic Books, 2006), pp. 47–74.

82. For arguments largely consistent with this view, see Nir Rosen, *In the Belly of the Green Bird: The Triumph of the Martyrs in Iraq* (New York: Free Press, 2006); Toby Dodge, *Iraq: From War to a New Authoritarianism* (London: International Institute for Strategic Studies, 2012); and Bernard Lewis, *What Went Wrong? Western Impact and Middle Eastern Response* (Oxford University Press, 2002).

83. Kanan Makiya, *Republic of Fear: The Politics of Modern Iraq*, updated ed. (University of California Press, 1998), pp. 66–70, 99–104.

84. Packer, *Assassins' Gate*, pp. 96–97.

85. On this issue, see Juan Cole, *Engaging the Muslim World* (New York: Palgrave Macmillan, 2009); Robert A. Pape and James K. Feldman, *Cutting the Fuse: The Explosion of Global Suicide Terrorism and How to Stop It* (University of Chicago Press, 2010).

86. David Kilcullen, *The Accidental Guerrilla: Fighting Small Wars in the Midst of a Big One* (Oxford University Press, 2009).

87. Shadi Hamid, *Temptations of Power: Islamists and Illiberal Democracy in a New Middle East* (Oxford University Press, 2014); and Stephen R. Grand, *Understanding Tahrir Square: What Transitions Elsewhere Can Teach Us about the Prospects for Arab Democracy* (Brookings, 2014).

88. See Olivier Roy, *The Failure of Political Islam* (Harvard University Press, 1994); Bernard Lewis, *The Crisis of Islam: Holy War and Unholy Terror* (New York: Modern Library, 2003); and Marc Sageman, *Understanding Terror Networks* (University of Pennsylvania Press, 2004).

89. Shibley Telhami, *The Stakes: America and the Middle East* (Boulder, Colo.: Westview Press, 2002); and King Abdullah II, *Our Last Best Chance: The Pursuit of Peace in a Time of Peril* (New York: Viking, 2011).

90. Kenneth M. Pollack, *A Path out of the Desert: A Grand Strategy for America in the Middle East* (New York: Random House, 2008); and Rachel

Bronson, *Thicker Than Oil: America's Uneasy Partnership with Saudi Arabia* (Oxford University Press, 2006), pp. 140–203, 248–62; see also Barry Rubin, *The Long War for Freedom: The Arab Struggle for Democracy in the Middle East* (Hoboken, N.J.: John Wiley and Sons, 2006); and Tamara Cofman Wittes, *Freedom's Unsteady March: America's Role in Building Arab Democracy* (Brookings, 2008).

91. Marwan Muasher, *The Arab Center: The Promise of Moderation* (Yale University Press, 2008).

92. See Kenneth M. Pollack, *Unthinkable: Iran, the Bomb, and American Strategy* (New York: Simon and Schuster, 2013), pp. 370–91.

93. For one account of al Qaeda proper's goals, see Robert O. Marlin IV, ed., *What Does Al-Qaeda Want? Unedited Communiques* (Berkeley, Calif.: North Atlantic Books, 2004).

94. See, for example, Gregory D. Johnsen, *The Last Refuge: Yemen, al-Qaeda, and America's War in Arabia* (New York: W. W. Norton, 2013); Emile Hokayem, *Syria's Uprising and the Fracturing of the Levant* (London: International Institute for Strategic Studies, 2013); and Jessica D. Lewis, "Al-Qaeda in Iraq Resurgent," Middle East Security Report 14 (Washington: Institute for the Study of War, 2013).

95. Steve Simon, "Egypt's Sorrow and America's Limits," *Survival* 55, no. 5 (October/November 2013): 79–83.

96. "Transcript: Senate Intelligence Hearing on National Security Threats," *Washington Post*, January 29, 2014, available at http://www.washingtonpost.com/world/national-security/transcript-senate-intelligence-hearing-on-national-security-threats/2014/01/29/b5913184-8912-11e3-833c-33098f9e5267_story.html.

97. For a landmark discussion of some of the key features of African politics in that early era, see Henry Bienen, *Armies and Parties in Africa* (New York: Africana Publishing Co., 1978).

98. Department of Economic and Social Affairs, United Nations, "World Population Prospects: The 2012 Revision" (New York: United Nations, 2013), pp. 56–59, available at http://esa.un.org/unpd/wpp/Documentation/pdf/WPP2012_HIGHLIGHTS.pdf.

99. See, for example, David Kilcullen, *Out of the Mountains: The Coming Age of the Urban Guerrilla* (Oxford University Press, 2013); and Moises Naim, *Illicit: How Smugglers, Traffickers, and Copycats Are Hijacking the Global Economy* (New York: Doubleday, 2005), pp. 1–7.

100. John Campbell, *Nigeria: Dancing on the Brink*, updated ed. (Lanham, Md.: Rowman and Littlefield, 2013), pp. x–10; and Gerald McLoughlin and Clarence J. Bouchat, *Nigerian Unity: In the Balance* (Carlisle, Pa.: Strategic Studies Institute, U.S. Army War College, 2013), pp. 5–49.

101. Terrence Lyons, *Voting for Peace: Postconflict Elections in Liberia* (Brookings, 1999), pp. 18–54; 'Funmi Olonisakin, *Peacekeeping in Sierra Leone: The Story of UNAMSIL* (Boulder, Colo.: Lynne Rienner, 2008), pp. 42–46; and

Adekeye Adebajo, *Liberia's Civil War: Nigeria, ECOMOG, and Regional Security in West Africa* (Boulder, Colo.: Lynne Rienner, 2002), p. 50.

102. See, for example, International Crisis Group, "Curbing Violence in Nigeria (II): The Boko Haram Insurgency" (Brussels, April 2014), available at http://www.crisisgroup.org/en/publication-type/media-releases/2014/africa/curbing-violence-in-nigeria-the-boko-haram-insurgency.aspx; Conway Waddington, "Boko Haram: Nigeria's Transnational Insurgency?," *African Defence Review*, February 2014, available at www.africandefence.net/boko-haram-nigerias-transnational-insurgency; and Benjamin S. Eveslage, "Clarifying Boko Haram's Transnational Intentions, Using Content Analysis of Public Statements in 2012," *Perspectives on Terrorism* 7, no. 5 (2013), available at www.terrorismanalysts.com/pt/index.php/pot/article/view/291.

103. International Monetary Fund, "Nigeria: Real GDP Growth" (Washington, 2014), available at http://knoema.com/atlas/Nigeria/GDP-growth.

104. Pew Research Center, "Ten Projections for the Global Population in 2050" (Washington, 2014), available at http://www.pewresearch.org/fact-tank/2014/02/03/10-projections-for-the-global-population-in-2050.

105. See Messner and others, *Fragile States Index 2014*.

106. Crawford Young, *The Politics of Cultural Pluralism* (University of Wisconsin Press, 1976).

107. Jason K. Stearns, *Dancing in the Glory of Monsters: The Collapse of the Congo and the Great War of Africa* (New York: Public Affairs, 2011); and Anthony W. Gambino, *Congo: Securing Peace, Sustaining Progress* (New York: Council on Foreign Relations, 2008), pp. 1–13.

108. Daniel Flynn and John Irish, "France Agrees to Help African Nations Set Up Military Force," Reuters, December 6, 2013, available at http://www.reuters.com/article/2013/12/06/us-africa-france-summit-idUSBRE9B50RN20131206.

109. Gambino, *Congo*, pp. 15–25.

110. On Africa's positive trends, see Steven Radelet, *Emerging Africa: How 17 Countries Are Leading the Way* (Washington: Center for Global Development, 2010).

111. Elizabeth G. Ferris, *The Politics of Protection: The Limits of Humanitarian Action* (Brookings, 2011), pp. 133–40.

112. See Gareth Evans, *The Responsibility to Protect: Ending Mass Atrocity Crimes Once and for All* (Brookings, 2008); and Office of the Special Advisor on the Prevention of Genocide, "The Responsibility to Protect" (New York: United Nations, 2014), available at http://www.un.org/en/preventgenocide/adviser/responsibility.shtml.

113. On these matters, see John D. Steinbruner, *Principles of Global Security* (Brookings, 2000), pp. 133–93; and Bruce Jones, Carlos Pascual, and Stephen John Stedman, *Power and Responsibility: Building International Order in an Era of Transnational Threats* (Brookings, 2009), pp. 139–203.

114. On this history, see, for example, Hilde F. Johnson, *Waging Peace in Sudan: The Inside Story of the Negotiations That Ended Africa's Longest Civil War* (Portland, Ore.: Sussex Academic Press, 2011).

115. Getahun Seifu, "Ethiopian-Eritrean Conflict: Options for African Union Intervention," in *Managing Peace and Security in Africa: Essays on Approaches to Intervention in African Conflicts* (Addis Ababa: Institute for Peace and Security Studies, December 2012), available at dspace.africaportal.org/jspui/bitstream/123456789/33888/1/MPSA_Anthology?Final?(3)%5b1%5d.pdf?1.

116. Goitom Gebreluel, "Ethiopia's Grand Renaissance Dam: Ending Africa's Oldest Geopolitical Rivalry?," *Washington Quarterly* 37, no. 2 (Summer 2014): 25–37.

117. International Crisis Group, "Ethiopia: Prospects for Peace in Ogaden" (Brussels, August 2013), available at http://www.crisisgroup.org/~/media/Files/africa/horn-of-africa/ethiopia-eritrea/207-ethiopia-prospects-for-peace-in-ogaden.pdf; and Colonel Goitom Farus Belay, "A Review of Ethiopia's Security Challenges in the Horn of Africa" (Carlisle, Pa.: Strategic Studies Institute, U.S. Army War College, March 2013), available at www.dtic.mil/cgi-bin/GetTRDoc?Location=U2&doc+GetTRDoc.pdf&AD=ADA588599.

118. United Nations Office on Drugs and Crime, *Global Study on Homicide, 2013* (New York, 2014), pp. 122–33; Nicolas Cook, "South Africa: Politics, Economy, and U.S. Relations" (Washington: Congressional Research Service, December 19, 2013), pp. 10–13; and Charles Goredema and Khalil Goga, "Crime Networks and Governance in Cape Town," Institute for Security Studies Paper 262 (Pretoria, S.A.: Institute for Security Studies, 2014), available at www.issafrica.org.

119. Grand, *Understanding Tahrir Square*, pp. 120–45.

120. Beth A. Simmons, "Territorial Disputes and Their Resolution: The Case of Ecuador and Peru," (Washington: U.S. Institute of Peace, 1999), available at http://www.usip.org/sites/default/files/pwks27.pdf.

121. Kevin Casas-Zamora, *The Besieged Polis: Citizen Insecurity and Democracy in Latin America* (Brookings, 2013), pp. 16–17, 34.

122. Federico Andreu-Guzmán, "Criminal Justice and Forced Displacement in Colombia," Brookings Project on Internal Displacement (Brookings, July 2012), available at http://www.ictj.org/sites/default/files/ICTJ-Brookings-Displacement-Criminal-Justice-Colombia-CaseStudy-2012-English.pdf.

123. See Vanda Felbab-Brown, *Shooting Up: Counterinsurgency and the War on Drugs* (Brookings, 2010), pp. 69–111; and Michael E. O'Hanlon and David Petraeus, "The Success Story in Colombia," *Politico*, September 24, 2013, available at http://www.brookings.edu/research/opinions/2013/09/24-colombia-success-ohanlon-petraeus.

124. See Ted Piccone and Harold Trinkunas, "The Cuba-Venezuela Alliance: The Beginning of the End?" (Brookings, Latin America Initiative, June

2014), available at http://www.brookings.edu/research/papers/2014/06/16-cuba-venezuela-alliance-piccone-trinkunas.

125. José R. Cárdenas, "A Nation Divided: Venezuela's Uncertain Future," *World Affairs,* March/April 2014, pp. 47–54.

126. Diana Villiers Negroponte, *Seeking Peace in El Salvador: The Struggle to Reconstruct a Nation at the End of the Cold War* (New York: Palgrave Macmillan, 2012).

127. Peter J. Meyer and Clare Ribando Seelke, "Central America Regional Security Initiative: Background and Policy Issues for Congress" (Washington: Congressional Research Service, May 2014), available at http://fas.org/sgp/crs/row/R41731.pdf.

128. See, for example, Diana Villiers Negroponte, ed., *The End of Nostalgia: Mexico Confronts the Challenges of Global Competition* (Brookings, 2013).

129. International Crisis Group, "Peña Nieto's Challenge: Criminal Cartels and Rule of Law in Mexico" (Brussels, 2013), available at http://www.crisis-group.org/en/regions/latin-america-caribbean/mexico/048-pena-nietos-challenge-criminal-cartels-and-rule-of-law-in-mexico.aspx; Vanda Felbab-Brown, "Changing the Game or Dropping the Ball?: Mexico's Security and Anti-Crime Strategy under President Enrique Peña Nieto" (Brookings, Latin America Initiative, November 2014); and Kimberly Heinle, Octavio Rodriguez Ferreira, and David A. Shirk, "Drug Violence in Mexico: Data and Analysis through 2013" (University of San Diego, April 2014), available at http://justiceinmexico.files.wordpress.com/2014/04/140415-dvm-2014-releasered1.pdf.

130. See, for example, Paul Griffith Garland, *A Businessman's Introduction to Brazilian Law and Practice* (New York: Chase Manhattan, 1966).

131. Lincoln Gordon, *Brazil's Second Chance: En Route toward the First World* (Brookings, 2001).

132. Riordan Roett, *The New Brazil* (Brookings, 2010).

CHAPTER 3

1. On what intelligence can and cannot realistically be expected to accomplish, see Paul R. Pillar, *Intelligence and U.S. Foreign Policy: Iraq, 9/11, and Misguided Reform* (Columbia University Press, 2011); and Richard K. Betts, *Enemies of Intelligence: Knowledge and Power in American National Security* (Columbia University Press, 2007).

2. Richard N. Haass, *War of Necessity, War of Choice: A Memoir of Two Iraq Wars* (New York: Simon and Schuster, 2009).

3. See, for example, Barry R. Posen, *Inadvertent Escalation: Conventional War and Nuclear Risks* (Cornell University Press, 1991); and Bruce G. Blair, *The Logic of Accidental Nuclear War* (Brookings, 1993).

4. See, for example, Michael O'Hanlon and Jeremy Shapiro, "Crafting a Win-Win-Win for Russia, Ukraine, and the West," *Washington Post,* December

7, 2014, available at http://www.washingtonpost.com/opinions/crafting-a-win-win-win-for-russia-ukraine-and-the-west/2014/12/05/727d6c92-7be1-11e4-9a27-6fdbc612bff8_story.html.

5. For intriguing thinking along these lines, see Richard H. Ullman, *Securing Europe* (Princeton University Press, 1991).

6. For a related discussion of the difficulty of using nuclear threats or attacks to roll back aggression, this time in a cold war context, see Richard K. Betts, *Surprise Attack* (Brookings, 1982), pp. 244–45.

7. See, for example, McGeorge Bundy, *Danger and Survival: Choices about the Bomb in the First Fifty Years* (New York: Vintage Books, 1988), pp. 236–70.

8. North Atlantic Treaty Organization, "The North Atlantic Treaty" (Washington, April 4, 1949), available at http://www.nato.int/cps/en/natolive/official_texts_17120.htm.

9. Treaty commitments themselves have been shown to have a powerful deterrent effect, but forces permanently stationed on land contribute significantly as well. See, for example, Barry M. Blechman and Stephen S. Kaplan, *Force without War: U.S. Armed Forces as a Political Instrument* (Brookings, 1978), pp. 525–30.

10. George Friedman, *The Next 100 Years: A Forecast for the 21st Century* (New York: Doubleday/Anchor Books, 2009), pp. 102–04.

11. William P. Mako, *U.S. Ground Forces and the Defense of Central Europe* (Brookings, 1983), pp. 46–47; Joshua M. Epstein, *Conventional Force Reductions: A Dynamic Assessment* (Brookings, 1990), p. 9.

12. See International Institute for Strategic Studies, *The Military Balance 1982–1983* (London, 1982), pp. 13–18.

13. Steven Erlanger, Julie Hirschfeld Davis, and Stephen Castle, "NATO Plans a Special Force to Reassure Eastern Europe and Deter Russia," *New York Times*, September 5, 2014, available at http://www.nytimes.com/2014/09/06/world/europe/nato-summit.html.

14. Brooks Tignor, "NATO Works to Flesh out Readiness Action Plan," *Jane's Defence Weekly*, September 17, 2014, p. 5.

15. On the importance of meeting this standard against a credible threat, see John J. Mearsheimer, *Conventional Deterrence* (Cornell University Press, 1983).

16. See the tabulation by Joshua Epstein in "Dynamic Analysis and the Conventional Balance in Europe," *International Security* 12, no. 4 (Spring 1988), p. 156.

17. The ratio of U.S. ground forces to air forces in Europe in the latter period of the cold war was about 4:1. See International Institute for Strategic Studies, *The Military Balance 1982–1983*, pp. 9–10.

18. In Operation Desert Storm in 1991, for example, the United States deployed close to 400,000 soldiers and Marines, out of a total force in the region of some 525,000. See U.S. Army, "War in the Persian Gulf: Operations Desert Shield and Desert Storm August 1990–March 1991," p. 69, available at http://www.history.army.mil/html/books/070/70-117-1/CMH_70-117-1.pdf; U.S.

Marine Corps, "U.S. Marines in the Persian Gulf, 1990–1991," p. 34, available at http://www.au.af.mil/au/awc/awcgate/usmchist/gulf.txt; "Airmen Celebrate 50 Years of Civil Engineering Heritage," Air Education and Training Command, http://www.aetc.af.mil/news/story.asp?id=123426826; and U.S. Navy, "U.S. Navy in Desert Shield/Desert Storm, War Chronology: February 1991," available at http://www.history.navy.mil/wars/dstorm/dsfeb.htm.

19. Joshua M. Epstein, *Conventional Force Reductions: A Dynamic Assessment* (Brookings, 1990), pp. 53–54.

20. Michael E. O'Hanlon, *The Science of War* (Princeton University Press, 2009), pp. 80–85.

21. Trevor N. Dupuy, *Attrition: Forecasting Battle Casualties and Equipment Losses in Modern War* (Fairfax, Va.: HERO Books, 1990), pp. 121–22. Dupuy's models have terms for relative combat effectiveness, sophistication, and mobility that I combine (through multiplication) into the single term for quality.

22. O'Hanlon, *The Science of War*, pp. 72–85.

23. Barry R. Posen, "Measuring the European Conventional Balance: Coping with Complexity in Threat Assessment," *International Security* 9, no. 3 (Winter 1984/1985), reprinted in *Conventional Forces and American Defense Policy*, edited by Steven E. Miller (Princeton University Press, 1986), pp. 99–113.

24. On this methodological approach, see Alain C. Enthoven and K. Wayne Smith, *How Much Is Enough? Shaping the Defense Program, 1961–1969*, rev. ed. (Santa Monica, Calif.: RAND, 2005), p. 70.

25. See, for example, Christopher Bowie, Fred Frostic, Kevin Lewis, John Lund, David Ochmanek, and Philip Propper, *The New Calculus: Analyzing Airpower's Changing Role in Joint Theater Campaigns* (Santa Monica, Calif.: RAND, 1993); and David A. Ochmanek, Edward R. Harshberger, David E. Thaler, and Glenn A. Kent, *To Find, and Not to Yield: How Advances in Information and Firepower Can Transform Theater Warfare* (Santa Monica, Calif.: RAND, 1998).

26. See, for example, Christopher J. Bowie, *The Anti-Access Threat and Theater Air Bases* (Washington: Center for Strategic and Budgetary Assessments, 2002); and Michael J. Lostumbo and others, *Overseas Basing of U.S. Military Forces: An Assessment of Relative Costs and Strategic Benefits* (Santa Monica, Calif.: RAND, 2013).

27. Dupuy, *Attrition*.

28. For more on these various factors, see Dupuy, *Attrition*, pp. 146–52; see also Betts, *Surprise Attack*, pp. 3–8.

29. See Dalibor Pavolka, "What Is NATO and EU Response Force Good for?" (Bratislava, Slovak Republic: Center for European and North Atlantic Affairs, February 2013), available at http://cenaa.org/analysis/what-is-nato-and-eu-response-force-good-for; British Army, "Transforming the British Army—An Update, July 2013" (London, 2013), available at http://www.army.mod.uk/documents/general/Army2020_Report.pdf; and North Atlantic Treaty Organization,

"NATO Response Force" (Brussels, October 2014), available at www.nato.int/cps/en/natolivetopics_49755.htm?selectedLocale=en.

30. Martin Fackler and Mark McDonald, "South Korea Reassesses Its Defenses after Attack," *New York Times*, November 26, 2010, available at http://www.nytimes.com/2010/11/26/world/asia/26korea.html.

31. On North Korea's reactor ambitions, see Kelsey Davenport, "North Korea Makes Progress on Reactor," *Arms Control Today* 42, no. 8 (October 2012): 26–27; on the earlier crisis, see Ashton B. Carter and William J. Perry, *Preventive Defense: A New Security Strategy for America* (Brookings, 1999), pp. 123–42.

32. See, for example, Bruce E. Bechtol Jr., "Maintaining a Rogue Military: North Korea's Military Capabilities and Strategy at the End of the Kim Jong-Il Era," *International Journal of Korean Studies* 16, no. 1 (Spring/Summer 2012): 160–91.

33. General B. B. Bell, "Defending South Korea: Transferring Wartime Operational Command," speech, Heritage Foundation, Washington, D.C., October 7, 2014, available at http://www.heritage.org/events/2014/10/defending-south-korea.

34. Samuel Glasstone, ed., *The Effects of Nuclear Weapons* (U.S. Atomic Energy Commission, 1962), p. 40.

35. Glasstone, *The Effects of Nuclear Weapons*, pp. 174, 246–50, 550.

36. Barry R. Posen, "Measuring the European Conventional Balance: Coping with Complexity in Threat Assessment," *International Security* 9, no. 3 (Winter 1984/1985), reprinted in *Conventional Forces and American Defense Policy*, edited by Stephen E. Miller (Princeton University Press, 1986), p. 108.

37. For a similar view, see James Dobbins, "War with China," *Survival* 54, no. 4 (August-September 2012): 9.

38. Larry M. Wortzel, "PLA 'Joint' Operational Contingencies in South Asia, Central Asia, and Korea," in *Beyond the Strait: PLA Missions Other than Taiwan*, edited by Roy Kamphausen, David Lai, and Andrew Scobell (Carlisle, Pa.: Strategic Studies Institute, U.S. Army War College, 2008), p. 360.

39. See Zbigniew Brzezinski, *Strategic Vision: America and the Crisis of Global Power* (New York: Perseus Books, 2012), p. 85; and Robert Kagan, *The World America Made* (New York: Alfred A. Knopf, 2012), p. 126.

40. See Henry Kissinger, *On China* (New York: Penguin Press, 2011), pp. 80–82; and Aaron L. Friedberg, *A Contest for Supremacy: China, America, and the Struggle for Mastery in Asia* (New York: W. W. Norton, 2011), p. 176.

41. James Steinberg and Michael E. O'Hanlon, *Strategic Reassurance and Resolve: U.S.-China Relations in the Twenty-First Century* (Princeton University Press, 2014), pp. 104–05.

42. Dennis J. Blasko, *The Chinese Army Today: Tradition and Transformation for the 21st Century*, 2nd ed. (London: Routledge, 2012), pp. 116–38.

43. Yong-Sup Han, "The ROK-US Cooperation for Dealing with Political Crises in North Korea," *International Journal of Korean Studies* 16, no. 1 (Spring/Summer 2012): 70–73.

44. Comments by Professor Andrew Erickson of the Naval War College, Henry L. Stimson Center, Washington, D.C., July 30, 2012, used with Erickson's permission.

45. Geoffrey Blainey, *The Causes of War* (New York: Free Press, 1973), pp. 245–49.

46. General David H. Petraeus and Lt. General James F. Amos, *The U.S. Army/Marine Corps Counterinsurgency Field Manual* (University of Chicago Press, 2007), p. 23.

47. James Dobbins, John G. McGinn, Keith Crane, Seth G. Jones, Rollie Lal, Andrew Rathmall, Rachel Swanger, and Angal Timilsina, *America's Role in Nation-Building: From Germany to Iraq* (Santa Monica, Calif.: RAND, 2003), pp. 150–51.

48. The Schlieffen Plan envisioned using close to 90 percent of the German army for an attack to the west; because of China's much greater size, the ratio would likely be significantly smaller in this case, but perhaps still quite large. See John Keegan, *The First World War* (New York: Alfred A. Knopf, 1999), pp. 28–32.

49. See Rachel Schmidt, *Moving U.S. Forces: Options for Strategic Mobility* (Congressional Budget Office, 1997), pp. 48–81; Eric Labs, *The Future of the Navy's Amphibious and Maritime Prepositioning Forces* (Congressional Budget Office, 2004), pp. 1–10; David Arthur, *Options for Strategic Military Transportation Systems* (Congressional Budget Office, 2005), pp. 1–40; and Michael E. O'Hanlon, *The Science of War* (Princeton University Press, 2009), pp. 130–60.

50. Montgomery C. Meigs, *Slide Rules and Submarines: American Scientists and Subsurface Warfare in World War II* (University Press of the Pacific, 2002), pp. 20–23, 53, 83.

51. Captain Wayne P. Hughes Jr., *Fleet Tactics and Coastal Combat*, 2nd ed. (Annapolis, Md.: Naval Institute Press, 2000), pp. 268–79; and Lon O. Nordeen, *Air Warfare in the Missile Age* (Washington: Smithsonian Press, 1985), pp. 201–03.

52. On such scenarios, see Roger Cliff, John F. Fei, Jeff Hagen, Elizabeth Hague, Eric Heginbotham, and John Stillion, *Shaking the Heavens and Splitting the Earth: Chinese Air Force Employment Concepts in the 21st Century* (Santa Monica, Calif.: RAND, 2011); and Christopher J. Bowie, *The Anti-Access Threat and Theater Air Bases* (Washington: Center for Strategic and Budgetary Assessments, 2002).

53. For estimates on China's current capabilities and its modernization plans, see, for example, Blasko, *The Chinese Army Today*, p. 227; and Richard D. Fisher, "Considered Speculation: Future PLA Directions That Should Be Considered," *Republic of China Defense Security Brief* 3, no. 2 (April 2013): 3.

54. China has more force structure than this for amphibious assault or air assault—at least two full divisions for each—but its actual lift capacity appears closer to one division of each type of capability. See International Institute for

Strategic Studies, *The Military Balance 2014* (Oxfordshire, UK: Routledge, 2014), pp. 232–36.

55. See Steinberg and O'Hanlon, *Strategic Reassurance and Resolve,* pp. 139–49.

56. See, for example, Daniel Wasserbly, "Hagel Backs More Precision Strike, Air Defence in Asia," *Jane's Defence Weekly,* October 22, 2014, p. 7; and Bill Sweetman, "Revolutionary Roadmap: The U.S. Air-Centered Strategy Has Top-Level Backing," *Aviation Week and Space Technology,* November 9/10, 2014, pp. 29–30. For an even more emphatic advocacy of this mission, see Jim Thomas, "Why the U.S. Army Needs Missiles," *Foreign Affairs* 92, no. 3 (May/June 2013).

57. Thomas A. Keaney and Eliot A. Cohen, *Gulf War Air Power Survey Summary Report* (Washington: Government Printing Office, 1993), p. 174; and Benjamin S. Lambeth, *NATO's Air War for Kosovo: A Strategic and Operational Assessment* (Santa Monica, Calif.: RAND, 2001), p. 161.

58. Christopher J. Bowie, *The Anti-Access Threat and Theater Air Bases* (Washington: Center for Strategic and Budgetary Assessments, 2002), p. 71.

59. Indeed, the Army considers a tailored brigade to be the right unit for the air and missile defense mission alone, though the size of such a formation may be less than for a standard brigade combat team. See Department of the Army, *Field Manual 3.0: Operations* (Washington, 2008), p. C-12, available at http://fas.org/irp/doddir/army/fm3-0.pdf.

CHAPTER 4

1. See Stephen Philip Cohen, *The Idea of Pakistan* (Brookings, 2004), pp. 97–130.

2. See International Crisis Group, *Unfulfilled Promises: Pakistan's Failure to Tackle Extremism* (Brussels, 2004).

3. David H. Petraeus, James F. Amos, and John A. Nagl, *The U.S. Army/Marine Corps Counterinsurgency Field Manual* (University of Chicago Press, 2007), p. 23.

4. James T. Quinlivan, "Force Requirements in Stability Operations," *Parameters* 25, no. 4 (Winter 1995/1996): 59–69; and James Dobbins, John G. McGinn, Keith Crane, Seth G. Jones, Rollie Lal, Andrew Rathmell, Rachel Swanger, and Anga Timilsina, *America's Role in Nation Building from Germany to Iraq* (Santa Monica, Calif.: RAND, 2003).

5. Michael E. O'Hanlon, *The Science of War* (Princeton University Press, 2009).

6. See, for example, Central Intelligence Agency, *CIA World Factbook: Pakistan* (2014), available at https://www.cia.gov/library/publications/the-world-factbook/geos/pk.html.

7. On this subject, see, for example, the comments by Strobe Talbott and Shivshankar Menon in "India's Role in the World: A Conversation with

Shivshankar Menon" (Brookings Institution, October 7, 2014), available at www.brookings.edu.

8. J. Lelieveld, D. Kunkel, and M.G. Lawrence, "Global Risk of Radioactive Fallout after Major Nuclear Reactor Accidents," *Atmospheric Chemistry and Physics* 12 (2012): 4245, available at http://www.atmos-chem-phys.net/12/4245/2012/acp-12-4245-2012.html.

9. Headquarters, Department of the Army, *Field Manual 3-07: Stability Operations* (University of Michigan Press, 2009), p. 263.

10. See Joshua M. Epstein, *Strategy and Force Planning: The Case of the Persian Gulf* (Brookings, 1987), p. 113.

11. Indeed, the average active person requires about six pounds (three-fourths of a gallon) of water daily just for drinking, so an estimate of five pounds of all supplies combined, including food, is a floor for requirements. When even minimal amounts needed for bathing, cooking, and leakage/waste are factored in, the actual requirements can easily triple. See Federal Emergency Management Agency, "Water" (Washington, 2014), available at http://www.ready.gov/water; and World Health Organization, "How Much Water Is Needed in Emergencies?" (Washington, 2011), available at http://www.who.int/water_sanitation_health/publications/2011/tn9_how_much_water_en.pdf.

12. Inter-Agency Standing Committee, "Response to the Humanitarian Crisis in Haiti" (New York, 2010), pp. 10–15, available at https://www.ifrc.org/docs/IDRL/Haiti/IASC-Haiti_6Mos_Review_USA-2010-005-1.pdf; and Gary Cecchine, Forrest E. Morgan, Michael A. Wermuth, Timothy Jackson, Agnes Gereben Schaefer, and Matthew Stafford, *The U.S. Military Response to the 2010 Haiti Earthquake* (Santa Monica, Calif.: RAND, 2013), pp. 56–57.

13. For a prediction that the conflict could in fact last decades more, see Stephen P. Cohen, *Shooting for a Century: The India-Pakistan Conundrum* (Brookings, 2013).

14. See Bruce Riedel, *Deadly Embrace: Pakistan, America, and the Future of the Global Jihad* (Brookings, 2011).

15. See, for example, ibid., pp. 91–93.

16. It is not clear to what extent Cold Start is a formal doctrine—but Pakistanis are surely aware of the concept. See Jaganath Sankaran, "The Enduring Power of Bad Ideas: 'Cold Start' and Battlefield Nuclear Weapons in South Asia," *Arms Control Today* 44, no. 9 (November 2014): 16–21.

17. Samuel Glasstone, ed., *The Effects of Nuclear Weapons*, rev. ed. (Washington: U.S. Atomic Energy Commission, 1962), p. 40.

18. See Barry R. Posen, *Inadvertent Escalation: Conventional War and Nuclear Risks* (Cornell University Press, 1991); and Bruce G. Blair, *The Logic of Accidental Nuclear War* (Brookings, 1993).

19. For a discussion of this concept, though one focused on a different case, see Martin Indyk, "A Trusteeship for Palestine?," *Foreign Affairs*, May/

June 2003, available at http://www.foreignaffairs.com/articles/58974/martin-indyk/a-trusteeship-for-palestine.

20. See Sumit Ganguly, *Conflict Unending: India-Pakistan Tensions since 1947* (Columbia University Press, 2001).

21. BBC News, "Kashmir Profile," January 31, 2014, available at http://www.bbc.com/news/world-south-asia-11693674.

22. Public Broadcasting Service, "The World's Most Complex Borders: Pakistan/India," July 26, 2005, available at http://www.pbs.org/wnet/wideangle/episodes/border-jumpers/the-worlds-most-complex-borders/pakistanindia/2340/.

23. Center on International Cooperation, *Annual Review of Global Peace Operations, 2013* (Boulder, Colo.: Lynne Rienner, 2013), pp. 48–53.

24. Center on International Cooperation, *Annual Review of Global Peace Operations, 2013*, pp. 114–16.

25. Indeed, Richard Garwin and Georges Charpak once estimated that a billion lives could be lost on Earth from general nuclear war, with untold damage to remaining human infrastructure, economies, and security sure to result too. Richard L. Garwin and Georges Charpak, *Megawatts and Megatons: A Turning Point in the Nuclear Age?* (New York: Alfred A. Knopf, 2001), p. 75.

26. On this dynamic, see "Keith Payne on Nuclear Deterrence," CSPAN, February 17, 2010, transcript available at http://www.c-span.org/video/?292132-4/keith-payne-nuclear-deterrence.

27. See Michael E. O'Hanlon, *The Art of War in the Age of Peace: U.S. Military Posture for the Post-Cold-War World* (Westport, Conn.: Praeger, 1992), p. 68.

28. O'Hanlon, *The Art of War in the Age of Peace*, pp. 66–68; and International Institute for Strategic Studies, *The Military Balance 1992–1993* (London: Brassey's, 1992), pp. 108–10. Lightly armed infantry units receive very low scores by this scale—which is appropriate for the nature of the combined-arms maneuver warfare assumed here, even if not necessarily appropriate for modeling extended urban fighting or combat in mountain ranges or forests.

29. International Institute for Strategic Studies, *The Military Balance 2014* (Oxfordshire, UK: Routledge, 2014), pp. 318–22.

30. On the logistical challenges of operating in northern Iran, see Joshua M. Epstein, *Strategy and Force Planning: The Case of the Persian Gulf* (Brookings, 1987), pp. 47–61.

31. Ben Birnbaum and Amir Tibon, "How John Kerry Built a Peace Process for Israel-Palestine, Then Watched It Burn," *New Statesman*, July 21, 2014, available at http://www.newstatesman.com/politics/2014/07/how-john-kerry-built-peace-process-israel-palestine-then-watched-it-burn.

32. Some argue that Turkey is likely to be a long-term nemesis of the United States and point to the disagreements over Syria policy between Washington and Ankara in recent years, as well as the overall policies of President Erdogan, to make the case. Some, like George Friedman, even forecast an adversarial

relationship over the longer term. However, while Turkey may have certain "Gaullist" tendencies, as scholar Omer Taspinar has noted, and while it is deeply frustrated by Washington's reluctance to do more to unseat President Assad, it does not appear to have core strategic aims fundamentally at odds with those of the United States. See Omer Taspinar, "Turkey's Strategic Vision and Syria," *Washington Quarterly*, Summer 2012, available at http://www.brookings. edu/research/articles/2012/08/turkey-taspinar; and George Friedman, *The Next 100 Years: A Forecast for the 21st Century* (New York: Doubleday/Anchor Books, 2009).

33. Dafna H. Rand and Nicholas A. Heras, "How This Ends: A Blueprint for De-Escalation in Syria" (Washington: Center for a New American Security, November 2014), available at http://www.cnas.org/blueprint-for-de-escalation-in-syria.

34. For a related argument, see comments of Salman Shaikh, "Will It Work? Examining the Coalition's Iraq and Syria Strategy" (Brookings, Washington, October 8, 2014), available at http://www.brookings.edu/events/2014/10/08-iraq-syria-strategy.

35. On the difficulties that one of the world's best militaries has had in attempting to quell unrest in the Levant, see David E. Johnson, *Hard Fighting: Israel in Lebanon and Gaza* (Santa Monica, Calif.: RAND, 2011); and Daniel Byman, *A High Price: The Triumphs and Failures of Israeli Counterterrorism* (Oxford University Press, 2011).

36. For a good treatment of the complexity of this conflict, see Emile Hokayem, *Syria's Uprising and the Fracturing of the Levant* (London: International Institute for Strategic Studies, 2013); Institute for the Study of War Syria Team, "Control of Terrain in Syria" (Washington: Institute for the Study of War, September 11, 2014), available at http://iswsyria.blogspot.com/2014/09/control-of-terrain-in-syria-september.html#!/2014/09/control-of-terrain-in-syria-september.html; and Kenneth M. Pollack, "Building a Better Syrian Opposition Army: How and Why" (Brookings, October 2014), available at http://www.brookings.edu/research/papers/2014/10/building-syrian-opposition-army-pollack.

37. For discussion of some of these kinds of missions, see Dana Priest, *The Mission: Waging War and Keeping Peace with America's Military* (New York: W. W. Norton, 2003), pp. 175–94.

38. See Madeleine K. Albright, William S. Cohen, and the Genocide Prevention Task Force, *Preventing Genocide: A Blueprint for U.S. Policymakers* (Washington: United States Holocaust Museum, 2008).

39. Nick Cumming-Bruce, "Nigeria Is Free of Ebola, Health Agency Affirms," *New York Times*, October 21, 2014, available at http://www.nytimes.com/2014/10/21/world/africa/who-declares-nigeria-free-of-ebola.html?ref=todayspaper&_r=0.

40. "A Nation Divided," *The Economist*, October 25–31, 2014, pp. 39–40.

41. International Crisis Group, "Curbing Violence in Nigeria (II): The Boko Haram Insurgency," Brussels, April 3, 2014, available at http://www.crisisgroup.

org/en/regions/africa/west-africa/nigeria/216-curbing-violence-in-nigeria-ii-the-boko-haram-insurgency.aspx.

42. Brady Dennis, "Ebola Cases Could Cross 20,000 by November, Report Says," *Washington Post,* September 22, 2014, available at http://www.washingtonpost.com/national/health-science/2014/09/22/eff7982e-42c9-11e4-9a15-137aa0153527_story.html.

43. Martin I. Meltzer and others, "Estimating the Future Number of Cases in the Ebola Epidemic—Liberia and Sierra Leone, 2014–2015" (Centers for Disease Control, September 2014), available at http://www.cdc.gov/mmwr/preview/mmwrhtml/su6303a1.htm.

44. Heather Murdock, "As Boko Haram Slaughters Students, Where Is Nigeria's Army?," *Christian Science Monitor,* February 27, 2014, available at http://www.csmonitor.com/World/Security-Watch/2014/0227/As-Boko-Haram-slaughters-students-where-is-Nigeria-s-Army-video; and International Crisis Group, "Curbing Violence in Nigeria (II)."

45. On the causes and consequences of the 2009 coup in Honduras, see Kevin Casas-Zamora, "The Honduran Crisis and the Obama Administration," in *Shifting the Balance: Obama and the Americas,* edited by Abraham F. Lowenthal, Theodore J. Piccone, and Laurence Whitehead (Brookings, 2011), pp. 114–28.

46. See, for example, Vanda Felbab-Brown, "Changing the Game or Dropping the Ball? Mexico's Security and Anti-Crime Strategy under President Enrique Peña Nieto" (Brookings, Latin America Initiative, November 2014), available at http://www.brookings.edu/~/media/research/files/papers/2014/11/mexico-security-anti-crime-nieto-felbabbrown/mexico-security-anti-crime-nieto-v2-felbabbrown.pdf.

47. See, for example, Micah Zenko, *Between Threats and War: U.S. Discrete Military Operations in the Post-Cold War World* (Stanford University Press, 2010), pp. 114–19.

48. Paul R. Pillar, *Terrorism and U.S. Foreign Policy* (Brookings, 2001), pp. 120–23, 136–38.

49. For one assessment of Mexico's hopeful but limited progress to greater stability under President Nieto, see Felbab-Brown, "Changing the Game or Dropping the Ball?"

50. See, for example, Michael E. O'Hanlon, Peter R. Orszag, Ivo H. Daalder, I. M. Destler, David L. Gunter, James M. Lindsay, Robert E. Litan, and James B. Steinberg, *Protecting the American Homeland: One Year On* (Brookings, 2002), pp. 6–8; and Anthony Lake, *Six Nightmares: Real Threats in a Dangerous World and How America Can Meet Them* (Boston, Mass.: Little, Brown, 2000).

51. Office of Technology Assessment, *Proliferation of Weapons of Mass Destruction* (U.S. Congress, 1993).

52. Department of Homeland Security, "This Is CBP" (U.S. Customs and Border Protection, September 20, 2012), available at http://www.cbp.gov/document/forms/september-20-2012-questions-and-answers; and O'Hanlon and others, *Protecting the American Homeland One Year on,* p. 16.

53. Jennifer Steinhauer, "Finances of New York City Staggered by the Emergency," *New York Times,* October 3, 2001, available at http://www.nytimes.com/2001/10/03/nyregion/03BUDG.html; and Steve Bowman, "Hurricane Katrina: DOD Disaster Response" (Washington: Congressional Research Service, September 2005), p. 11, available at http://fas.org/sgp/crs/natsec/RL33095.pdf.

54. On this issue, see, for example, Alain C. Enthoven and K. Wayne Smith, *How Much Is Enough? Shaping the Defense Program, 1961–1969* (Santa Monica, Calif.: RAND, 2005); and Eliot A. Cohen and John Gooch, *Military Misfortunes: The Anatomy of Failure in War* (New York: Free Press, 1990).

55. See Ivo H. Daalder, ed., *Beyond Preemption: Force and Legitimacy in a Changing World* (Brookings, 2007).

CHAPTER 5

1. International Institute for Strategic Studies, *The Military Balance 2015* (Oxfordshire, UK: Routledge, 2015), pp. 52–54.

2. Michael J. Lostumbo and others, *Overseas Basing of U.S. Military Forces: An Assessment of Relative Costs and Strategic Benefits* (Santa Monica, Calif.: RAND, 2013), p. xxv.

3. On the Army, Vietnam, and Vietnam's aftermath, see, for example, Andrew F. Krepinevich Jr., *The Army and Vietnam* (Johns Hopkins University Press, 1986); John A. Nagl, *Knife Fights: A Memoir of Modern War in Theory and Practice* (New York: Penguin Press, 2014), pp. 212–13; and David Fitzgerald, *Learning to Forget: U.S. Army Counterinsurgency Doctrine and Practice from Vietnam to Iraq* (Stanford University Press, 2013). On more recent wars, see Gian Gentile, *Wrong Turn: America's Deadly Embrace of Counterinsurgency* (New York: New Press, 2013).

4. President Barack Obama, introductory remarks to "Sustaining U.S. Global Leadership: Priorities for 21st Century Defense" (Department of Defense, January 2012), available at http://www.defense.gov/news/defense_strategic_guidance.pdf.

5. Brad Knickerbocker, "Gates's Warning: Avoid Land War in Asia, Middle East, and Africa," *Christian Science Monitor,* February 26, 2011, available at http://www.csmonitor.com/USA/Military/2011/0226/Gates-s-warning-Avoid-land-war-in-Asia-Middle-East-and-Africa.

6. See Sydney Freedberg, "VCJCS Winnefeld Tells Army: Forget Long Land Wars," *Breaking Defense,* September 13, 2013, available at http://breakingdefense.com/2013/09/vcjcs-winnefeld-tells-army-to-forget-long-land-wars-congress-get-out-of-our-way.

7. President Barack Obama, "Remarks by the President," Joint Base McGuire-Dix-Lakehurst, N.J., December 15, 2014, available at http://www.whitehouse.gov/the-press-office/2014/12/15/remarks-president-military-and-civilian-personnel-joint-base-mcguire-dix.

8. See, for example, Max Boot, *Invisible Armies: An Epic History of Guerrilla Warfare from Ancient Times to the Present* (New York: Liveright Publishing Co., 2012); see also Russell F. Weigley, *The American Way of War* (Indiana University Press, 1973); and Fred Kaplan, *The Insurgents: David Petraeus and the Plot to Change the American Way of War* (New York: Simon and Schuster, 2013).

9. Conrad C. Crane, "The Lure of Strike," *Parameters* 43, no. 2 (Summer 2013): 1–12.

10. Ivo H. Daalder and Michael E. O'Hanlon, *Winning Ugly: NATO's War to Save Kosovo* (Brookings, 2000), pp. 213–16.

11. See, for example, Thomas P. M. Barnett, *The Pentagon's New Map: War and Peace in the Twenty-First Century* (New York: G. P. Putnam's Sons, 2004).

12. "The Future of Land Power and U.S. Ground Forces" (Brookings, February 24, 2014), available at http://www.brookings.edu/events/2014/02/24-future-of-landpower.

13. "General David H. Petraeus's Retirement Ceremony Remarks," Washington, August 31, 2011, available at http://www.army.mil/article/64706/Gen__David_H__Petraeus__retirement_ceremony_remarks.

14. Carol Kerr, "CSA Discusses Army Operating Concept with Army War College Class of 2015," September 8, 2014, available at www.army.mil/article/133303/CSA_discusses_Army_Operating_Concept_with_Army_War_College_class_of_2015.

15. Thom Shanker, "Win Wars? Today's Generals Must Also Politick and Do P.R.," *New York Times*, August 12, 2010, available at http://www.nytimes.com/2010/08/13/world/13generals.html?pagewanted=all.

16. The First Armored Division from Fort Bliss, Texas, was in Afghanistan, and the First Cavalry Division from Fort Hood, Texas, was in Korea. See http://www.army.mil/article/132943/1st_Cavalry_unit_selected_for_South_Korea_deployment. The First Infantry Division from Fort Riley, Kansas, was in the CENTCOM/Persian Gulf theater. See http://www.army.mil/article/134543/1st_Infantry_Division_HQ_deploying_to_Iraq. The Second Infantry Division was as usual at Camp Casey in South Korea; see https://www.facebook.com/2IDKorea. The Third Infantry Division, from Fort Stewart, Georgia, was in Afghanistan; see http://www.army.mil/article/137188/3ID_HQ_to_deploy_to_Afghanistan_as_drawdown__retrograde_continues. The Fourth Infantry Division, from Fort Carson, Colorado, was not deployed (https://www.facebook.com/MountainWarriorBrigade). The Tenth Mountain Division, from Fort Drum, New York, was in Afghanistan (http://www.drum.army.mil/news/Home.aspx). The Twenty-Fifth Infantry Division, from Schofield Barracks in Hawaii, was headed to Korea in 2015 (http://www.army.mil/article/139140/). The Eighty-Second Airborne Division, from Fort Bragg, North Carolina, was heading out to the CENTCOM/Gulf theater shortly (http://www.armytimes.com/story/military/pentagon/2014/12/01/about-250-fort-bragg-soldiers-deploy-support-iraq-operations/19741789/). The

101st Airborne Division, from Fort Campbell, Kentucky, was in Liberia (http://www.military.com/daily-news/2014/09/30/101st-airborne-troops-headed-to-liberia-in-ebola-fight.html).

17. Quoted in Thomas S. Szayna, Derek Eaton, and Amy Richardson, *Preparing the Army for Stability Operations* (Santa Monica, Calif.: RAND, 2007), p. 10.

18. John A. Nagl, *Learning to Eat Soup with a Knife* (University of Chicago Press, 2002).

19. See, for example, David. C. Gompert, John Gordon IV, Adam Grisson, David R. Frelinger, Seth G. Jones, Martin C. Libicki, Edward O'Connell, Brooke K. Stearns, and Robert E. Hunter, *War by Other Means: Building Complete and Balanced Capabilities for Counterinsurgency* (Santa Monica, Calif.: RAND, 2008); and Robert M. Perito, *Where Is the Lone Ranger: America's Search for a Stability Force*, 2nd ed. (Washington: U.S. Institute of Peace, 2013).

20. General Stanley McChrystal, *My Share of the Task: A Memoir* (New York: Penguin Press, 2013).

21. See, for example, David W. Barno, "The Army's Next Enemy? Peace," *Washington Post*, July 13, 2014, p. B1.

22. See, for example, Bernard Rostker, *I Want You! The Evolution of the All-Volunteer Force* (Santa Monica, Calif.: RAND, 2006); Thomas E. Ricks, *Making the Corps* (New York: Simon and Schuster, 1997); and Bruce Newsome, *Made, Not Born: Why Some Soldiers Are Better Than Others* (Westport, Conn.: Praeger, 2007).

23. For a very thoughtful analysis of this subject, see General Stanley McChrystal, "Securing the American Character," *Politico Magazine*, June 2, 2014, available at http://www.politico.com/magazine/story/2014/06/securing-the-american-character-107318.html#.VGI8pPnF-So.

24. Robert P. Haffa Jr., *Rational Methods, Prudent Choices: Planning U.S. Forces* (National Defense University, 1988), pp. 77–82, 110–26; Alain C. Enthoven and K. Wayne Smith, *How Much Is Enough? Shaping the Defense Program 1961–1969* (Santa Monica, Calif.: RAND, 2005 [1971]), pp. 214–16; John Lewis Gaddis, *Strategies of Containment* (Oxford University Press, 1982), pp. 297, 323.

25. See Gaddis, *Strategies of Containment*.

26. For discussions of the force-sizing debates in this period, see, for example, Frederick W. Kagan, *Finding the Target: The Transformation of American Military Policy* (New York: Encounter Books, 2006), pp. 196–97, 281–86; and Michael E. O'Hanlon, *Defense Policy Choices for the Bush Administration*, 2nd ed. (Brookings, 2002), pp. 9–17, 63–71.

27. William Stueck, "Revisionism and the Korean War," *Journal of Conflict Studies* 22, no. 1 (Spring 2002), available at http://journals.hil.unb.ca/index.php/jcs/article/view/365/576

28. See, for example, Secretary of Defense Les Aspin, *Report on the Bottom-Up Review* (Department of Defense, 1993), pp. 13, 19.

29. General Charles C. Campbell, "ARFORGEN: Maturing the Model, Refining the Process," *Army*, June 2009, pp. 49–54.

30. Major General Mark Graham, "ARFORGEN Overview," U.S. Army, Washington, October 2009, available at http://www.marad.dot.gov/documents/NPRN_WS_2009_Workshop_1_FSLDC_10-1_ARFORGEN_Overview.pdf.

31. Office of the Under Secretary of Defense (Comptroller), "Overview of United States Department of Defense Fiscal Year 2016 Budget Request" (Department of Defense, February 2015), p. A-1, available at www.comptroller.defense.gov/budgetmaterials/budget2016.aspx.

32. See "U.S.-Iraq War: Pros and Cons," Procon.org, September 2010, available at http://usiraq.procon.org/view.resource.php?resourceID=000677.

33. This was a key emphasis of Secretary of Defense Leon Panetta, among others. See the discussion of his June 2012 speech on building partnerships in Richard L. Kugler and Linton Wells II, *Strategic Shift: Appraising Recent Changes in U.S. Defense Plans and Priorities* (National Defense University, 2013), pp. 67–75.

34. Dennis Blair, *Military Engagement: Influencing Armed Forces Worldwide to Support Democratic Transitions*, vol. 1: *Overview and Action Plan* (Brookings, 2013), p. 59.

35. Michael O'Hanlon, "NATO after Crimea: How the Alliance Can Still Deter Russia," Foreignaffairs.com, April 17, 2014, available at http://www.foreignaffairs.com/articles/141227/michael-ohanlon/nato-after-crimea.

36. Michael J. Lostumbo and others, *Overseas Basing of U.S. Military Forces*.

37. John R. Deni, *The Future of American Landpower: Does Forward Presence Still Matter? The Case of the Army in Europe* (Carlisle, Pa.: Strategic Studies Institute, U.S. Army War College, 2012), pp. 10, 34.

38. See, for example, Rosa Brooks, "Portrait of the Army as a Work in Progress," *Foreign Policy*, May/June 2014, pp. 43–51.

39. See "An Interview with General Raymond T. Odierno," *Joint Force Quarterly* 75 (Fall 2014): 9.

40. For a good example of a well-written article by Army officials that nonetheless is short on quantitative specifics, see Kimberly Field, James Learmont, and Jason Charland, "Regionally Aligned Forces: Business *Not* as Usual," *Parameters* 43, no. 3 (Autumn 2013): 55–63.

41. Department of the Army, *I Am the Guard: A History of the Army National Guard, 1636–2000* (Government Printing Office, 2001), pp. 383–88.

42. Martin Binkin, *Who Will Fight the Next War? The Changing Face of the American Military* (Brookings, 1993), pp. 111–40.

43. See Paul Paolozzi, *Closing the Candor Chasm: The Missile Element of Army Professionalism* (Carlisle, Pa.: Strategic Studies Institute, U.S. Army War College, 2013), pp. 16-18.

44. Rostker, *I Want You!*, p. 693.

45. Michael E. O'Hanlon and Jason Campbell, "The Iraq Index" (Brookings, June 2007), available at http://www.brookings.edu/fp/saban/iraq/index20070628.pdf.

46. For a similar view, see Reserve Forces Policy Board, "Final Report to the Secretary of Defense" (Washington, February 2014), p. 14, available at http://www.ngaus.org/sites/default/files/RFPB_Report_RC_Use_Mix_Cost_Savings_Web.pdf.

47. See, for example, John D. Ellis and Laura McKnight Mackenzie, *Operational Reservations: Considerations for a Total Army Force* (Carlisle, Pa.: Strategic Studies Institute, U.S. Army War College, 2014), p. 28.

48. Commission on the National Guard and Reserves, "Transforming the National Guard and Reserves into a 21st Century Operational Force" (Washington, January 2008), p. 81, available at http://www.markswatson.com/CGNR2008.pdf.

49. David W. Barno and Nora Bensahel, "New Challenges for the U.S. Army," in *American Grand Strategy and the Future of U.S. Landpower*, edited by Joseph Da Silva, Hugh Liebert, and Isaiah Wilson III (Carlisle, Pa.: Strategic Studies Institute, U.S. Army War College, 2014), pp. 239–40; and Frances Lussier, John Mayer, and others, *Meeting New National Security Needs: Options for U.S. Military Forces in the 1990s* (Congressional Budget Office, 1990), pp. 14–19.

50. See also Newsome, *Made, Not Born.*

51. For a similar view, see Douglas Macgregor, "Commentary: Building Army Forces for Future War," *Defense News*, October 14, 2013, available at http://www.defensenews.com/article/20141013/DEFFEAT05/310130021/Commentary-Building-Army-Forces-Future-War.

52. See Richard K. Betts, *Military Readiness: Concepts, Choices, Consequences* (Brookings, 1995), pp. 1–143.

53. Michael E. O'Hanlon, *The Science of War* (Princeton University Press, 2009), p. 150.

54. Betts, *Military Readiness*, pp. 227–34.

55. Office of the Under Secretary of Defense for Personnel and Readiness, *Report of the Eleventh Quadrennial Review of Military Compensation* (Department of Defense, 2012), pp. 17–29, available at Militarypay.defense.gov/REPORTS/QRMC/11th_QRMC_Main_Report_Linked.pdf.

56. Carla Tighe Murray, *Evaluating Military Compensation* (Congressional Budget Office, 2007), pp. 13–17, 32.

57. Commission on Military Compensation and Retirement Modernization, *Final Report* (Washington, 2015), available at http://mldc.whs.mil.

58. Office of the Under Secretary of Defense (Comptroller), *National Defense Budget Estimates for FY 2015* (Department of Defense, 2014), pp. 255–56, available at http://comptroller.defense.gov/Portals/45/Documents/defbudget/fy2015/FY15_Green_Book.pdf.

59. For estimates of the same broad magnitude, or perhaps somewhat more ambitious, see Mackenzie Eaglen, "Shrinking Bureaucracy, Overhead, and Infrastructure" (Washington: American Enterprise Institute, March 2013), available at http://www.aei.org/wp-content/uploads/2013/03/-shrinking-bureaucracy-

overhead-and-infrastructure-why-this-defense-drawdown-must-be-different-for-the-pentagon_083503530347.pdf.

60. See, for example, Stephen J. Hadley and William J. Perry, co-chairs, "The QDR in Perspective: Meeting America's National Security Needs in the 21st Century" (Washington: Quadrennial Defense Review Independent Panel, 2010), available at www.usip.org/files/qdr/qdrreport.pdf.

61. Michael E. O'Hanlon, *Healing the Wounded Giant: Maintaining Military Preeminence While Cutting the Defense Budget* (Brookings, 2013), pp. 60–70.

62. See, for example, Thomas G. Mahnken and James R. FitzSimonds, "Revolutionary Ambivalence: Understanding Officer Attitudes towards Transformation," *International Security* 28, no. 2 (Fall 2003): 112–48.

63. See Daniel Byman, "Why Drones Work: The Case for Washington's Weapon of Choice," *Foreign Affairs* 92, no. 4 (July/August 2013): 32–43.

64. P. W. Singer, *Wired for War: The Robotics Revolution and Conflict in the 21st Century* (New York: Penguin Press, 2009), pp. 109–34.

65. Ashton B. Carter, "Running the Pentagon Right: How to Get the Troops What They Need," *Foreign Affairs* 93, no. 1 (January/February 2014): 101–12.

66. Audrey Kurth Cronin, "Why Drones Fail: When Tactics Drive Strategy," *Foreign Affairs* 92, no. 4 (July/August 2013): 44–54.

67. See Singer, *Wired for War*, pp. 428–36.

68. Michael E. O'Hanlon, *Technological Change and the Future of Warfare* (Brookings, 2000), pp. 32–67.

69. On many of the problems with the Future Combat Systems, a program that assumed more radical progress in various technologies than proved feasible, and that was ultimately canceled in large measure, see Frances M. Lussier, *The Army's Future Combat Systems Program and Alternatives* (Congressional Budget Office, 2006).

70. See, for example, Dan Byman and Jeremy Shapiro, "We Shouldn't Stop Terrorists from Tweeting," *Washington Post*, October 9, 2014, available at http://www.washingtonpost.com/opinions/we-shouldnt-stop-terrorists-from-tweeting/2014/10/09/106939b6-4d9f-11e4-8c24-487e92bc997b_story.html.

71. See, for example, Adam Talaber, *Options for Restructuring the Army* (Congressional Budget Office, 2005), pp. 1–12.

APPENDIX A

1. United Nations Department of Economic and Social Affairs/Population Division, "World Population Prospects: The 2012 Revision, Key Findings and Advance Tables" (New York, 2012), available at unfpa.org; and World Bank, *Beyond Economic Growth* (Washington, 2000), p. 16, available at http://www.worldbank.org/depweb/english/beyond/beyondco/beg_03.pdf.

2. United Nations Population Fund, *Motherhood in Childhood* (New York, 2013), pp. 106–11.

3. Martin C. Libicki, Howard J. Shatz, and Julie E. Taylor, *Global Demographic Change and Its Implications for Military Power* (Santa Monica, Calif.: RAND, 2011).

4. Thomas F. Homer-Dixon, "Environmental Scarcities and Violent Conflict: Evidence from Cases," *International Security* 19, no. 1 (Summer 1994): 19.

5. Rear Admiral John Kingwell and others, *Global Strategic Trends— Out to 2045*, 5th ed. (London: Ministry of Defence, 2014), p. xiii, available at https://www.gov.uk/government/uploads/system/uploads/attachment_data/file/348164/20140821_DCDC_GST_5_Web_Secured.pdf.

6. World Bank, "World Bank Development Indicators Databank, Arable Land as Percent of Land Area" (Washington, 2014), available at www.tradingeconomics.com/world/arable-land-percent-of-land-area-wb-data.html.

7. Homer-Dixon, "Environmental Scarcities and Violent Conflict," p. 38.

8. Monika Barthwal-Datta, *Food Security in Asia: Challenges, Policies and Implications* (London: International Institute for Strategic Studies, 2014), pp. 12–18.

9. Ed Pepke, "Today's and Tomorrow's Timber Resources: Can We Sustainably Meet Rising Demand?," paper presented at the Wood Futures Conference, London, November 8, 2007, available at http://www.unece.org/fileadmin/DAM/timber/mis/presentations/PepkeForResMktFuturesPublic081107.pdf; and Working Group III, Intergovernmental Panel on Climate Change, "Mitigation of Climate Change—Technical Summary" (Geneva, Switzerland, 2014), p. 71, available at www.ipcc.ch/report/ar5/wg3.

10. Adam Baske, "Global Fisheries: Management Challenges and a Pacific Snapshot" (New York: Pew Charitable Trusts, November 5, 2013), available at http://www.wilsoncenter.org/sites/default/files/Adam%20Baske%20PPT.pdf.

11. Jared Diamond, *Collapse: How Societies Choose to Fail or Succeed* (New York: Penguin, 2006), pp. 405–07, 480–83.

12. On Africa's resources, see, for example, David E. Brown, *Africa's Booming Oil and Natural Gas Exploration and Production: National Security Implications for the United States and China* (Carlisle, Pa.: Strategic Studies Institute, U.S. Army War College, 2013).

13. Bruce Jones, David Steven, and Emily O'Brien, "Fueling a New Order? The New Geopolitical and Security Consequences of Energy" (Brookings, Project on International Order and Strategy, April 2014), p. 7, available at http://www.brookings.edu/research/papers/2014/04/14-geopolitical-security-energy-jones-steven.

14. Daniel Yergin, *The Quest: Energy, Security, and the Remaking of the Modern World* (New York: Penguin Press, 2011), pp. 239, 260, 715.

15. Daniel McGroarty and Sandra Wirtz, "American Resources Policy Network Report—Reviewing Risk: Critical Metals and National Security" (Washington: American Resources Policy Network, June 6, 2012), available at www.americanresources.org.

16. See Carlos Andres, "World's Top Ten Gold Deposits," Mining.com, August 2013, available at www.mining.com/web/worlds-top-10-gold-deposits.

17. Gemological Institute of America, "Your GIA Ruby and Sapphire Reports" (Carlsbad, Calif., 2007), available at http://www.giathai.net/pdf/GIA_Corundum_7499_050307.pdf.

18. U.S. Geological Survey, "Mineral Commodity Summaries" (Washington, February 2014), pp. 128–29, available at http://minerals.usgs.gov/minerals/pubs/commodity/rare_earths/mcs-2014-raree.pdf; and Under Secretary of Defense for Acquisition, Technology, and Logistics, "Annual Industrial Capabilities Report to Congress" (October 2013), pp. 25–26, available at www.acq.osd.mil/mibp/docs/annual_ind_cap_rpt_to_congress.pdf.

19. U.S. Geological Survey, "Mineral Commodity Summaries," February 2014, pp. 16–17, 26–27.

20. Ibid., pp. 28–29.

21. Ibid., pp. 42–43.

22. Ibid., pp. 46–47.

23. Ibid., pp. 50–51.

24. Ibid., pp. 100–101.

25. Ibid., pp. 110–11.

26. Ibid., pp. 120–21.

27. Ibid., pp. 160–61.

28. Ibid., pp. 168–69.

29. Ibid., pp. 172–73.

30. Ibid., pp. 174–75.

31. Ibid., pp. 186–87.

32. See Kingwell and others, *Global Strategic Trends—Out to 2045*, p. xvi.

33. Homer-Dixon, "Environmental Scarcities and Violent Conflict," p. 7.

34. See NASA, "Tracks and Intensity of All Tropical Storms," in *Historic Tropical Cyclone Tracks* (Washington, 2006), available at earthobservatory.nasa.gov/IOTD/view.php?id=7079.

35. Christopher C. Burt, "The World's Deadliest Tornadoes" (Atlanta, Ga.: The Weather Channel, Atlanta, 2011), available at www.wunderground.com/blog/weatherhistorian/comment.html?entrynum=21.

36. Francis Gassert, Matt Landis, Matt Luck, Paul Reig, and Tien Shiao, "Aqueduct Global Maps 2.0" (World Resources Institute, January 2013), p. 12, available at pdf.wri.org/aqueduct_metadata_global.pdf.

37. Seth M. Siegel, "Israeli Water, Mideast Peace?" *New York Times,* February 16, 2006, available at www.nytimes.com/2014/02/17/opinion/israeli-water-mideast-peace.html?emc=eta1&_r=0.

38. See Global Seismic Hazard Assessment Program, "Global Seismic Hazard Map" (2000), available at http://www.seismo.ethz.ch/static/GSHAP.

39. National Geophysical Data Center, "Interactive Map: Tsunami Events," available at maps.ngdc.noaa.gov/viewers/hazards/?layers=0.

40. Geophysical Fluid Dynamics Laboratory, National Oceanic and Atmospheric Administration, "Global Warming and Hurricanes: An Overview of Current

Research Results" (December 2013), available at www.gfdl.noaa.gov/global-warming-and-hurricanes.

41. Matt Ridley, *The Rational Optimist: How Prosperity Evolves* (New York: Harper Perennial, 2011), pp. 334–37.

42. Christopher Pala, "Warming May Not Swamp Islands," *Science* 345, no. 6196 (August 1, 2014): 496–97.

43. For a thoughtful treatment of this question, see Diamond, *Collapse*, pp. 486–96.

44. Adam Smith, Neal Lott, Tamara Houston, Karsten Shein, and Jake Crouch, "Billion-Dollar U.S. Weather/Climate Disasters, 1980–2013" (Asheville, N.C.: National Climatic Data Center, 2014), available at www.ncdc.noaa.gov/billions.

45. Michael Bloomberg, Henry Paulson, Thomas Steyer, and the Risky Business Project, "Risky Business: The Economic Risks of Climate Change in the United States—A Climate Risk Assessment for the United States" (New York, June 2014), pp. 4, 22, available at riskybusiness.org; see also CAN Military Advisory Board, "National Security and the Accelerating Risks of Climate Change" (Alexandria, Va.: Center for Naval Analyses, May 2014), p. 26, available at www.cna.org/reports/accelerating-risks.

46. Asian Development Bank, *Addressing Climate Change and Migration in Asia and the Pacific* (Manila, Philippines, 2012); Gordon McGranahan, Deborah Balk, and Bridget Anderson, "The Rising Tide: Assessing the Risks of Climate Change and Human Settlements in Low Elevation Coastal Zones," *Environment and Urbanization* 19, no. 1 (April 2007): 17–37; Mukang Han, Jianjun Hou, and Lun Wu, "Potential Impacts of Sea-Level Rise on China's Coastal Environment and Cities: A National Assessment," *Journal of Coastal Research,* Spring 1995, pp. 79–95; and Susmita Dasgupta, Benoit Laplante, Craig Meisner, David Wheeler, and Jianping Yan, "The Impact of Sea Level Rise on Developing Countries: A Comparative Analysis," World Bank Policy Research Working Paper 4136 (Washington, February 2007), available at http://econ.worldbank.org.

47. Bloomberg and others, "Risky Business," p. 5.

48. Government Accountability Office, "Climate Engineering: Technical Status, Future Directions, and Potential Responses" (Washington, July 2011), pp. 30–36, available at www.gao.gov/assets/330/322208.pdf; and Working Group III, Intergovernmental Panel on Climate Change, "Mitigation of Climate Change—Technical Summary," p. 34.

49. Working Group III, Intergovernmental Panel on Climate Change, "Mitigation of Climate Change—Technical Summary," p. 46.

50. See also Office of Technology Assessment, *Proliferation of Weapons of Mass Destruction: Assessing the Risks* (U.S. Congress, 1993).

51. Peter H. Gleick, "Water and Terrorism," *Water Policy* 8 (2006): 481–503; available at http://www2.pacinst.org/reports/water_terrorism.pdf.

52. See, for example, Michael Levi, *On Nuclear Terrorism* (Harvard University Press, 2007), p. 143; and Graham Allison, *Nuclear Terrorism: The Ultimate Preventable Catastrophe* (New York: Times Books, 2004), p. 141.

53. World Nuclear Association Database, "Operational Nuclear Plants by Country" (July 2014), available at http://world-nuclear.org/nucleardata base/rdResults.aspx?id=27569 and http://www.world-nuclear.org/info/Facts-and-Figures/World-Nuclear-Power-Reactors-and-Uranium-Requirements.

54. Matthew Bunn, Martin B. Malin, Nickolas Roth, and William H. Tobey, *Advancing Nuclear Security: Evaluating Progress and Setting New Goals* (Cambridge, Mass.: Belfer Center for Science and International Affairs, Harvard University, 2014), p. 53.

55. World Nuclear Association, "Chernobyl Accident 1986" (London, 2014), available at http://www.world-nuclear.org/info/Safety-and-Security/Safety-of-Plants/Chernobyl-Accident.

56. For a good discussion, see John D. Steinbruner, *Principles of Global Security* (Brookings, 2000), pp. 178–79.

57. For one compilation, from 1996, see Andrew S. Natsios, *U.S. Foreign Policy and the Four Horsemen of the Apocalypse* (Westport, Conn.: Praeger, 1997), p. 8.

58. Otto Kreisher, "Operation Unified Assistance," *Air Force Magazine*, April 2005, available at www.airforcemag.com/MagazineArchive/Pages/2005/April%202005/0405tsunami.aspx; and Department of Defense, "Wall of Water: U.S. Troops Aid Tsunami Victims" (2006), available at www.defense.gov/home/features/2006/2005yearinreview/article2.html.

59. "Kashmir Earthquake of 2005," Britannica.com, 2014, available at www.britannica.com/EBchecked/topic/1483628/Kashmir-earthquake-of-2005.

60. International Federation of Red Cross and Red Crescent Societies, "Final Report, Earthquake: Pakistan" (Geneva, Switzerland, July 2012), available at http://www.ifrc.org/docs/appeals/05/M05EA022FR.pdf.

61. Steve Bowman, Lawrence Kapp, and Amy Belasco, "Hurricane Katrina: DOD Disaster Response" (Washington: Congressional Research Service, September 19, 2005), pp. 6, 11, available at http://fas.org/sgp/crs/natsec/RL33095.pdf.

62. Humanitarian Communication Group, Office for the Coordination of Humanitarian Affairs "Haiti Earthquake Response," (New York, January 2011), available at http://www.un.org/en/peacekeeping/missions/minustah/documents/ocha_haiti_one_year_factsheet.pdf; U.S. Southern Command, "Operation Unified Response: Support to Haiti Earthquake Relief 2010" (March 2010), available at http://www.southcom.mil/newsroom/Pages/Operation-Unified-Response-Support-to-Haiti-Earthquake-Relief-2010.aspx ; and White House Press Secretary, "United States Government Haiti Earthquake Disaster Response" (March 10, 2010), available at www.whitehouse.gov/the-press-office/united-states-government-haiti-earthquake-disaster-response.

63. National Bureau of Asian Research, "Chronology of Operation Tomodachi" (Washington, 2014), available at http://www.nbr.org/research/activity. aspx?id=121; and Kenneth Pletcher and John P. Rafferty, "Japan Earthquake and Tsunami of 2011," Britannica.com, 2014, available at http://www.britannica. com/EBchecked/topic/1761942/Japan-earthquake-and-tsunami-of-2011.

Index